Rereading Empathy

Rereading Empathy

Edited by
Emily Johansen and Alissa G. Karl

BLOOMSBURY ACADEMIC
NEW YORK • LONDON • OXFORD • NEW DELHI • SYDNEY

BLOOMSBURY ACADEMIC
Bloomsbury Publishing Inc
1385 Broadway, New York, NY 10018, USA
50 Bedford Square, London, WC1B 3DP, UK

BLOOMSBURY, BLOOMSBURY ACADEMIC and the Diana logo are trademarks of
Bloomsbury Publishing Plc

First published in the United States of America 2022
This paperback edition published 2023

Cover design by Eleanor Rose
Cover image: *Bare with Me*, Foundation, 5 © Hernease Davis

Bloomsbury Publishing Inc does not have any control over, or responsibility for,
any third-party websites referred to or in this book. All internet addresses given
in this book were correct at the time of going to press. The author and publisher
regret any inconvenience caused if addresses have changed or sites have
ceased to exist, but can accept no responsibility for any such changes.

Library of Congress Cataloging-in-Publication Data
Names: Aase, Emily Johansen, 1981- editor. | Karl, Alissa G., 1976- editor.
Title: Rereading empathy / edited by Emily Johansen Aase and Alissa G. Karl.
Description: New York, NY : Bloomsbury Academic, 2022. | Includes bibliographical
references and index. | Identifiers: LCCN 2021055043 (print) | LCCN 2021055044 (ebook) |
ISBN 9781501376856 (hardback) | ISBN 9781501376894 (paperback) |
ISBN 9781501376863 (epub) | ISBN 9781501376870 (pdf) | ISBN 9781501376887
Subjects: LCSH: Empathy. | Empathy in literature.
Classification: LCC BF575.E55 R47 2022 (print) | LCC BF575.E55 (ebook) |
DDC 152.4/1–dc23/eng/20211129
LC record available at https://lccn.loc.gov/2021055043
LC ebook record available at https://lccn.loc.gov/2021055044

ISBN: HB: 978-1-5013-7685-6
         PB: 978-1-5013-7689-4
       ePDF: 978-1-5013-7687-0
      eBook: 978-1-5013-7686-3

Typeset by Integra Software Services Pvt. Ltd.

To find out more about our authors and books visit www.bloomsbury.com
and sign up for our newsletters.

CONTENTS

CONTRIBUTORS

Emily Johansen, Texas A&M University: Emily Johansen is Associate Professor of English at Texas A&M University, USA. She is the author of *Cosmopolitanism and Place: Spatial Forms in Contemporary Anglophone Literature* (2014), *Beyond Safety: Risk, Cosmopolitanism, and Neoliberal Contemporary Life* (Bloomsbury, 2021) and co-editor, with Alissa G. Karl, of *Neoliberalism and the Novel* (2018). She has published articles in *Ariel*, *Contemporary Literature*, and *Textual Practice*.

Alissa G. Karl, SUNY-Brockport: Alissa G. Karl is Associate Professor of English at SUNY Brockport in New York State, USA. Her work focuses on economics and labor in modern and contemporary Anglophone literature and culture. She is author of *Modernism and the Marketplace: Literary Culture and Consumer Capitalism in Rhys, Woolf, Stein and Nella Larsen* (2009) and co-editor, with Emily Johansen, of *Neoliberalism and the Novel* (2015). Her work has also appeared in major journals and book collections. Currently, she is Vice President for Academics of the largest higher education labor union in the US, United University Professions.

Susan Bruxvoort Lipscomb, Houghton College: Susan Bruxvoort Lipscomb is Professor of English at Houghton College in Houghton, New York, USA.

Kathryn Cai, Mellon/ACLS Public Fellow with PowerSwitch Action: Kathryn Cai's research explores affect, embodiment, and care work in transpacific circuits. She received her PhD in English from the University of California, Los Angeles in 2019.

Ralph Clare, Boise State University: Ralph Clare is Associate Professor of English at Boise State University, USA, specializing in post-45 American literature. He is the author of *Fictions Inc.: The Corporation in Postmodern Fiction, Film, and Popular Culture* (2014) and the editor of the *Cambridge Companion to David Foster Wallace* (2018). His latest book project, *Metaffective Fiction: Structuring Feeling in Contemporary American Literature*, explores the role of emotion and affect in post-postmodern fiction and the neoliberal era in works by David Foster Wallace, Salvador Plascencia, Sheila Heti, Dave Eggers, and Ben Lerner, among others.

Marie-Elisabeth Lei Holm, University of Southern Denmark: Marie-Elisabeth is a postdoctoral researcher at the University of Southern Denmark. Currently, she works on projects that draw out the relevance and potential health benefits of literary reading for elderly people and people with dementia. Her book about literary recognition and social acknowledgment is forthcoming from Routledge.

Tate Shaw, SUNY-Brockport: Tate Shaw is an artist, writer, publisher, and curator living in Rochester, NY. He is the Director of Visual Studies Workshop (vsw.org), a nonprofit organization with a mission to support artists and critics working in still and moving images. Shaw's artist's books are in international collections including the Tate Modern, London, The Museum of Fine Arts, Houston, The School of the Art Institute of Chicago Joan Flasch Artists' Books Collection, Yale Special Collections, and the George Eastman Museum Library, amongst others. He is the author of *Blurred Library: essays on artists' books* (2017), and an Associate Professor of English at SUNY Brockport, USA, where he directs the MFA in Visual Studies program at VSW.

Peter Simonsen, University of Southern Denmark: Peter Simonsen is Professor of European Literature at the Department for the Study of Culture, University of Southern Denmark where he is director of English Studies as well as director of the Centre for the Uses of Literature. He has published monographs on the later poetry of William Wordsworth (2007) and on contemporary fictions about aging in the welfare state (2014) as well as a number of edited volumes on European literature, happiness in Scandinavia, literary theory and criticism, most recently with Emily Hogg, *Precarity in Contemporary Literature and Culture* (Bloomsbury, 2021). His research interests include romanticism, contemporary literature, book history, literary gerontology, precarity, and the social and health dimensions of the practical uses of literature.

Terri Tomsky, University of Alberta: Terri Tomsky is an Associate Professor in the Department of English and Film Studies at the University of Alberta, Canada. Her research examines memory politics and memory economies in postcolonial and post-socialist literatures. She is the co-editor (with Eddy Kent) of *Negative Cosmopolitanism: Culture and Politics of World Citizenship After Globalization* (2017). She has published in the areas of human rights literary studies, life writing, cultural memory and trauma, cosmopolitanism, as well as the Global War on Terror. She is currently completing a book manuscript on Guantánamo and the many forms of cultural activism inspired by the prison's injustices.

Introduction: Why Empathy? Why Now?

Emily Johansen and Alissa G. Karl

In a number of venues across his political career, former US President Barack Obama has used the language of an "empathy deficit" to identify failings in US collective culture. In a 2006 speech, for instance, Obama remarked:

> There's a lot of talk in this country about the federal deficit. But I think we should talk more about our empathy deficit–the ability to put ourselves in someone else's shoes; to see the world through those who are different from us–the child who's hungry, the laid-off steelworker, the immigrant woman cleaning your dorm room.
>
> (Obama 2006)

Obama urges his audiences to rebuild their stores of empathy specifically so that they can encounter economic difference; since his rhetoric presumes that his audience does not share in the economic positions he names (poverty, unemployment, low-wage work), empathy for Obama might hold out the possibility of seeing or experiencing structural conditions in a visceral, personal way. And we infer that enacting empathy in such situations will lead Obama's audience to adopt more equitable economic stances—though this precise link, between empathy and social or political action, goes unnamed. So far, so empathetic. Fast forward to 2018, when Obama's Vice President and later US President, Joe Biden, insisted that he has "no empathy" for millennials who bemoan their seemingly intractable economic precarity. "The younger generation now tells me how tough things are. Give me a break. No, no I have no empathy for it — give me a break," Biden said

(Paiella 2018). Biden's position, which he has repeated many times, is that rather than seeking empathy, young people in difficult straits should, as he said in another interview, "Change it. Change it. Change it. My generation did" (Boboltz 2019). Biden cultivates a tone that is at best dismissive of appeals to empathy and perhaps suggests that they are disingenuous ("give me a break"); he also emphatically severs Obama's implied link between "putting ourselves in someone else's shoes" and the "change" that needs to happen to remedy structural economic inequities. In short, Obama suggests that empathy is one step on the path to structural and economic reforms. Biden holds that empathy impedes them.[1]

Such a divergence in attitudes about empathy from two members of the US centrist liberal establishment raises a number of questions about the circulation of "empathy" today.[2] Most broadly, the fact that both are repeating the language of "empathy" (whether in earnest or sarcastically) signals the prominence of this particular concept in contemporary public discourse: Obama did not say that we should "care" about the plight of others; nor did Biden say that he did not "care" about Millennials' precarity. Indeed, Biden's point that *his* generation (Biden is a "war baby," born in 1942) pursued "change" rather than solicited empathy from others does, in its own backhanded way, locate empathy as a particularly *recent* kind of concern—and distinguishes feelings from actions when it comes to social change. More specifically, we might say that Biden does not presume that feelings in themselves amount to or catalyze outcomes in the way that Obama does. Furthermore, Obama's and Biden's uses of the term make us wonder what is involved in the quantification and distribution of empathetic feeling from one to another. What does it mean to count or amass "empathy" in the manner of a balance sheet? To acquire a "credit," or incur a "deficit," of human affect? What is signified in the deliberate withholding of that affect? Though their postures are in conflict, Obama and Biden both circle around the sense that empathy is an asset to be deployed or denied, spent or hoarded. Uniquely, for Obama, in its very "spending," empathy accumulates. For Biden, to give a "handout" of empathy where it is not warranted is an imprudent expenditure ("give me a break"). In both cases, then, empathy figures as something of a resource, and as we note at later points in this volume, such a notion is not inconsistent with the contemporary emphasis on affective skills in the workplace.[3]

The racial differences between these two speakers would also seem to figure in how they deploy empathy. What does it say about the cultural circulation and uses of empathy today that Obama, an African American man, urges the cultivation of empathy as a tool for social and political deliberation, while a white man, Joe Biden, is comfortable dismissing calls for empathy as juvenile ("the younger generation"), or as forms of weakness? In what ways does this uneven appeal to empathy reference the cultural trope whereby persons of color, minorities, women, and others are responsible for getting others to "see" them and validate their experiences (and also to "see" from the perspective of those who would oppress them), while those in dominant identity positions decide whom they want to see and who they don't?[4] This striking contrast in the deployment of empathy from each half of this prominent political duo points not, we believe, toward "right" and "wrong" appeals to empathy; rather, it signifies the prominence and complex circulation of "empathy" as a cultural and political signifier, and as a capacity or asset, that this volume seeks to explore and understand.[5]

Are we, perhaps, at "peak empathy"? The liberal vacillation detailed above around how much empathy we ought to spend, and where we ought to spend it, is matched by an overall swell in attention to empathy in education, therapeutic, media, and scholarly circles, what Jennifer Wilson (2021) names "the Empathy Industrial Complex."[6] According to philosopher Jesse Prinz (2017), more books have been published with the word "empathy" in their titles since 2010 than in all of the twentieth-century. As Carolyn Pedwell writes, empathy has become "a Euro-American political obsession" (2014: ix). Empathy education is part of the curriculum in many schools. Scholars from the brain sciences to the humanities are investigating what exactly empathy "is," how we can identify and measure it, and how we can enact it more. Popular culture stokes our appetite for empathetic encounters, as reality television offers up-close-and-personal confessions of private hardship and anguish and bosses step into the everyday lives of the workers they employ. The corporate class practices self-described "empathetic leadership." The inception of this very volume occurred when a few of its contributors gathered at the 2017 Society for Literature, Science and the Arts-EU conference in 2017 in Basel, Switzerland, which was devoted to the topic of "Empathies;" here, scholars spanning the fields of literature, communications studies, sociology, philosophy, psychology, and other arts and sciences disciplines joined those in medicine, psychiatry, and other health fields to deliberate on empathy as conceptual phenomenon and clinical and teaching tool.

In the context of this intensified interest, why is it so important right now that we think we can empathize with one another? And why do we think that we ought to? The essays in *Rereading Empathy* examine and historicize the admonition to empathize that is so pervasive in our current social and economic contexts. They question what is involved when "empathy" is deployed and (presumably) enacted in a variety of contexts in order to collectively ask, again: Why empathy? And why now? Our approach to examining empathy is founded upon the conviction that affective concepts emerge from and signify within historical, cultural, and economic conditions. As Pedwell puts it, "emotions are not universal, as dominant liberal and neoliberal narratives of empathy would have it, but rather radically shaped by geo-political relations of history, power and violence" (2014: 14)[7]; we agree with Pedwell that we must approach empathy and other affective notions within the context of the "uneven and contingent" relations of all kinds (2014: 3). Our approach to empathy in this collection is informed by this kind of treatment of the functional aspect of emotions, rather than as objective or organic experiences.

What do we mean by empathy, then, and how is it used by scholars? Empathy generally refers to feeling what another feels.[8] The word "empathy" is a fundamentally twentieth century one—it doesn't appear in English until 1895, according to the *Oxford English Dictionary*, and the first listed usage that correlates to what is usually meant by "empathy" is in 1909. And it is really only in the last half of the twentieth-century that its use grows exponentially. Sympathy, empathy's closest analogue, has a much longer history (dating to the late sixteenth century) but both are still linked inextricably in English with the rise of modern forms of liberal capitalism—and the modern novel. While correlation should not be taken for causation, it is difficult to not see the history of sympathy (and, later, empathy) in relation to the ideological projects of capitalism and the novel, namely in trying to make sense of the place of the newly constituted liberal subject and their relationship to the rest of society. Both sympathy and empathy index modes of relationality; however, where sympathy works through simile ("I feel *like* someone else is feeling"), empathy works through metaphor ("I feel the other's feelings"). This slide between figurative modes suggests a shift in relational transparency that takes place over the twentieth century—and one that is perhaps appropriate to the seemingly totalizing experience of late capitalism.

Yet, if the empathetic turn might parallel the neoliberal turn of the last fifty years, it is also deployed by many liberal scholars as a corrective to the same. Such an appeal to empathy as a corrective to dominant economic relations echoes Adam Smith's similar theorization of sympathy as a brake on *laissez faire* capital. In *A Theory of Moral Sentiments*, for instance, Smith envisions sympathy as the mechanism for managing capitalism's propensity for selfish self-interest. For Smith, sympathy is necessarily limited to one's own sphere, with full sympathy only possible for God:

> The administration of the great system of the universe, however, the care of the universal happiness of all rational and sensible beings, is the business of God and not of man. To man is allotted a much humbler department, but one much more suitable to the weakness of his powers, and to the narrowness of his comprehension; the care of his own happiness, of that of his family, his friends, his country.
>
> ([1759] 2002: 279)

But, as Smith suggests, sympathy ultimately works in a fashion very similar to the market: a rising tide of sympathy raises all boats, for if each subject of capital sympathizes within their own "humbler department," then all subjects will act morally.[9] Sympathy and its attendant morality will, then, ensure that humanity's better impulses temper economic self-interest.

Unsurprisingly, then, as the imperative to prioritize economic self-interest has become seemingly inescapable, there has been a similar turn to consider the way sympathy and empathy might work to mitigate this demand.[10] The precarity generated by late capitalism over the last fifty years has raised new questions about how to counteract the exigency of ever greater and narrower self-interest. Indeed, a widely circulated post attempting to make sense of the mass detentions and family separations happening at the US-Mexico border proclaimed "I don't know how to explain to you that you should care about other people" (Chadwick 2017)—a question that is fundamentally tied to contemporary discourses about empathy. Yet, in the decades preceding the 2016 Brexit referendum and US presidential election, this is the question that has preoccupied many liberal philosophers of ethics, most notably Martha Nussbaum. For Nussbaum, accounting for emotion—and, ultimately, empathy—is central to the project of rejecting anti-liberal and fascist politics: "all political principles, the good as well as the bad, need emotional support to ensure their stability over time, and all decent societies need to guard against division and hierarchy by cultivating appropriate sentiments of sympathy and love" (2013: 2–3). For Nussbaum, literary fiction—and especially canonical works of the nineteenth-century—best "cultivat[es] appropriate sentiments" in readers. This has been, unsurprisingly, a popular claim for English departments in a moment where the number of English majors is in precipitous decline and where the humanities are continually deemed to be in "crisis." Arguments like Nussbaum's are often forwarded as part of the case for the continued importance of a liberal arts education because it presumably, or so the story goes, produces "good" (read: empathetic) citizens. In such claims for the value of the humanities, however, what exactly constitutes good citizenship often remains nebulous and, as the emphasis on canonical texts illustrates, often on maintaining the *status quo*—but one in which we are "nicer" to each other.

Anxieties about the role of the humanities may also be linked to the rise of another major strand of investment in empathy: cognitive approaches to literature and culture. Like the digital humanities, methods that emphasize skills historically associated with STEM fields have become increasingly central to English departments as they try to access increased institutional support and external grant money. Cognitive approaches to empathy often emphasize pre-verbal and somatic modes of affect and tend to contest liberal philosophical accounts of empathy like those popularized by Nussbaum. As Steven Pinker, for instance, suggests,

> the problem with building a better world through empathy ... is that it cannot be counted on to trigger the kind of empathy we want, namely sympathetic concern for others' well-being. Sympathy is endogenous, an effect rather than a cause of how people relate to one another ...

the search for empathy in the human brain has confirmed that vicarious feelings are dimmed or amplified by the rest of the empathizer's beliefs.

(2011: 578)

Indeed, as Pinker here suggests, the bulk of cognitive research on empathy as well as the related "theory of the mind" research (which aims to understand how subjects recognize and interpret the emotional states of others, not necessarily to share them) is focused on the limited effects of empathy. If Nussbaum wants to suggest that empathy produces good citizens, cognitive researchers argue that this isn't likely the case. As Fritz Breithaupt claims, "empathy not only fails to stop … negative acts but in fact motivates and promotes them … malicious acts happen not in spite of empathy, but because of it" (2019: 1).[11] In his best-selling *Against Empathy*, Paul Bloom states that empathy is "a poor moral guide. It grounds foolish judgments and often motivates indifference and cruelty. It can lead to irrational and unfair political decisions, it can corrode certain important relationships … and make us worse at being friends, parents, husbands, and wives" (2016: 2–3).

While both Breithaupt and Bloom make use of deliberately polemical language here, they remain in favor of something not entirely dissimilar to empathy (which Bloom terms "rational compassion"), yet highlight that the consequences of empathy are unpredictable at best. In Suzanne Keen's exploration of the empathetic virtues believed to be taught by novel reading, she draws on the work of cognitive researchers to note that part of the problem of the public discourse on empathy is that it focuses so heavily on responses to suffering, rather than encompassing the broad range of emotions that humans feel: "focusing on empathy with ecstatic, joyful, or sexually aroused emotional states of others can swerve in the direction of hedonism, and any concessions involving novels' titillating or corrupting influences can raise the specter of censorship" (2007: 41). Keen speculates that this is "why advocates of the ethical benefits of novel reading nearly always insist that great literature—Greek tragedies, Shakespeare's plays, canonical novels, and serious literary fiction—best stimulates literary empathy" (2007: 40). If empathy can produce fellow feeling with the tragic situations of suffering others, why wouldn't it also produce fellow feeling with less tragic others? Wouldn't this perhaps suggest that, contra Obama, it isn't that there is an empathy deficit—it's that the bulk of empathy is directed toward billionaires? In other words, perhaps Americans are empathizing, but just not with the people Obama would like them to. As Catherine Liu wonders of Obama himself given the US Government's massive bailout of financial institutions following the 2008 financial crash: "was it possible that Obama empathized more with Jamie Dimon, CEO of JP Morgan Chase, than with ordinary African American families who lost their homes and livelihoods because of the financial crisis" (2021: 53–4)? It's easy, then, to see how empathy can all too easily work in the maintenance of the *status quo*.

What resonates across both strands of empathy theory—whether liberal philosophy or cognitive psychology—is a desire to understand how to produce good citizens, which is also the claim for empathy that Obama makes. However, what similarly abides across both is a vagueness over what exactly a good citizen is or does. In other words, while Nussbaum and the psychologists disagree over whether empathy inspires action or not, they remain invested in the individual as the agent of social change—though what, exactly, it is that good citizens do, apart from empathize with others, is unclear. In her introduction to *Compassion: The Culture and Politics of an Emotion*—a 2004 collection that is a predecessor to this one—Lauren Berlant observes that the cultural conversation around compassion

> carries the weight of ongoing debates about the ethics of privilege—in particular about the state as an economic, military, and moral actor that represents and establishes collective norms of obligation, and about individual and collective obligations to read a scene of distress not as a judgment against the distressed but as a claim on the spectator to become an ameliorative actor.
>
> (1)

While we might suggest that the distinction between "judgment" and "claim" has shifted from either/or to both/and, Berlant highlights an element that is too often missing in much of the existing work on empathy: a consideration of the social values that have made individual empathy such a prominent imagined site of social change—whether from the ostensible left or right of the political spectrum. Berlant and her fellow contributors interrogate the "culture and politics" of compassion in the shadow of both 1980s Reaganism and 1990s "third way" consensus which fully entrenched neoliberalism as common sense, and the immediate aftermath of 9/11 and the early moments of the Iraq and Afghanistan wars.

Rereading Empathy takes up a similar project, also understanding empathy as operating within multiple sociohistorical frames: in the short term, the 2016 Brexit Referendum and US presidential election, and, on a longer arc, the normalization of the regimes of social and economic individuation and amplification of austerity politics over the last fifty years. Situating the call to empathize in its cultural and political context, as the essays in this collection do, allows us to more carefully unpack what empathy is imagined to do in this moment, beyond vague calls for producing "good citizens." While it is certainly important to track the circulation of empathy discourses since 2016, a slightly longer sweep provides us with crucial contexts for the ways in which the concept has been circulating in very recent years. It's striking, for instance, to observe the rise of empathy discourse over the past few decades in concert with the rise of so-called neoliberal economic policies and ideologies of the self. For to emphasize empathy is to train our focus upon supposedly individual feelings. Prinz puts it succinctly when he says that "the jurisdiction of empathy is me and mine" (2018: 16). So it is notable that Obama calls for empathy when he asks his audience to imagine the plight of the hungry child, the unemployed, and the low-wage worker, because each of these three conditions is situated within much larger economic dynamics of wealth inequality and exploitative labor markets. Yet for Obama, the trick to apprehending the conditions that others inhabit is to feel with them individually; his invocation of empathy circumvents a view of whole economic structures and trends at the same time as it seems to draw them to the surface. In short, he calls for empathy, not solidarity, and this is not a surprising move given the patterns of lay reasoning and expert economic orthodoxies which posit the individual as the locus of social form and market activity, and that hold individuals responsible for the conditions that they inhabit. Indeed, Obama handily exposes empathy as one example of the privatization of collective support and care that has been underway for decades.

Obama's incitement to empathy holds each and every member of his audience responsible for the precarious conditions and suffering that they might encounter and with which they ought to empathize. In another way, those individual acts that comprise "responsibility" for the structural plights of others never amount to accountability for them. Individual obligation and feeling thus replace a systemic, collective response to and responsibility for the structural conditions that generate the plights of others; as such, empathy is appropriate to the cultural-economic *status quo* of the past fifty or so years in which, as Margaret Thatcher famously put it, "There is no such thing [as society]! There are individual men and women" (1987). As this regime of individuation has developed across the history of capitalist thought, empathy has emerged as appropriate to its iterations of the past few decades.

In addition, the rise of empathy discourse corresponds to the shift toward new kinds of labor in high-GDP locations. An intensified emphasis on affect attends the growth of service-sector labor of all kinds—creative, tech, communications, care work—over the past few decades; a heightened discourse on empathy in particular is part of the worker's attunement to the requirement for affective and immaterial labor in the workplace, where affects like empathy are generated as part of the job, and in many cases consumed as the products of "customer service." As Elaine Swan puts it in a study of organizational theory, "[i]n the workplace, emotional expressivity is seen as a new workplace resource with intensification of 'soft capitalism' and its demands for emotional and aesthetic labor from a range of types and levels of workers" (2008: 89). Some commentators have termed this current condition "affective capitalism," which Jeffrey Nealon defines as the situation in which "capitalism has become completely territorialized on the production and consumption of affective experience" (2017: 80), and in which life itself becomes a form of work from which surplus value may be extracted.[12]

In both of these contexts, then—that of a political culture that posits the individual as the prime social mover, and that of labor markets that extract surplus value from workers' affect—empathy appears not as a spontaneous or "natural" response to others, but as an orientation toward others that is appropriate to historical conditions. Literary- and cultural-critical approaches to matters of affect, though not necessarily about empathy in particular, contribute to an understanding of empathy in this light. Sianne Ngai's work (2007, 2012) on affect and aesthetics considers both in terms of the economic and labor conditions that attend the production of affective and subjective states; specifically, Ngai exposes contemporary aesthetic modes and so-called "minor" emotions as outcomes of the ambiguous requirements and thwarted agency of life under capital. In a conversant though not identical fashion, Rachel Greenwald Smith has examined approaches to the contemporary American novel in terms of what she identifies as a prioritization of individual affect in the encounter with literature. As Smith has it, "the belief that literature is at its most meaningful when it represents and transmits the emotional specificity of personal experience" (2015: 1), accords with the priorities of the neoliberal era. For Smith, too, affective concepts are part of historical political configurations.

As Berlant states about the *Compassion* volume, desires for greater empathy "are [not] *at root* ethically false, destructive, or sadistic, [but] derive from social training, emerge at historical moments, are shaped by aesthetic conventions, and take place in scenes that are anxious, volatile, surprising, and contradictory" (2004: 7; emphasis in original). Here, we contend much the same for empathy as we consider its centrality in our cultural and political discourses and wonder what it prioritizes, obscures, or excludes. The individual essays do just this as they investigate how empathy operates within economies of race, gender, class, and labor, both presently and in past historical contexts and genres. As importantly, our contributors situate both academic interest in empathy, and broader cultural empathetic imperatives, within contemporary economic and political systems.

The essays begin with an examination of the resonances of nineteenth-century discourses on empathy in contemporary discourses on the same. As the essays move to look at contemporary forms of narrative empathy, they ask about the work that empathy is expected to do and the formal repercussions of this expectation. Across all the essays is an attention to the multitudinous operation of empathy and the way it both finds new ways to accumulate capital and to disrupt or draw attention to the violence of this process. In "Reading George Eliot in the #metoo Era," Susan Bruxvoort Lipscomb reveals the presumptions of much contemporary empathy discourse via a close reading of one of its nineteenth-century variants, and details the ways in which the novel has been used to inculcate sympathetic and empathetic concepts. Through a careful analysis of George Eliot's *Adam Bede* and other novels, as well as Eliot's correspondence, Lipscomb develops an account of Eliot's appeals to what Paul Bloom has recently termed "cognitive empathy," in which subjects are prompted to contemplate the perspectives of others. Cognitive empathy can be distinguished from so-called "emotional empathy," which is predicated upon the idea that we can feel what others feel, and which Lipscomb tracks to contemporary presumptions about what empathy entails. Using this distinction, Lipscomb demonstrates how, for Eliot, empathy is grounded not in the "victim's" vulnerability, but in the common human condition of being a "struggling" and "erring" creature. Following Eliot, Lipscomb ponders whether empathy might be as much about the empathizer's acknowledgement of their own flaws and transgressions—and their solidarity with others on that basis—as it is about feeling into the emotional life of another. Lipscomb's reading of empathy via Eliot adds a helpful complexity to the current discourse of empathy in literary studies and in political commentary by tracking earlier variants of the concept.

In her essay "Putting Empathy to Work: Narrative and the Empathetic Entrepreneur," Emily Johansen considers how the production of an entrepreneurial genre of empathy that demands that trauma is made knowable, shareable, and fixable becomes a necessary stage in personal financial success. Voyeuristic accounts of suffering have long been yoked with capitalist moral philosophy, demonstrating a concern with how the capitalist relates to capital's violence through the development of charitable sympathy. More recently, empathy has come to the forefront in imagining the relationship between the neoliberal subject and this violence. Drawing from research in entrepreneurship studies, an empathetic entrepreneur is increasingly assumed to be more successful than one who downplays emotional linkages with both staff and customers in favor of the untrammeled pursuit of profits. Empathy becomes instrumentalized: it is a job and leadership skill. If empathy has been thought to inspire *moral* action, the discourse on the empathetic entrepreneur illustrates that it is now often assumed to produce *financial* outcomes. Reading Hanya Yanagihara's best-selling 2015 novel, *A Little Life*, and its narrative of both baroque trauma and immense wealth, Johansen argues that it illustrates how, under late capitalism, empathy narratives are deployed to produce empathy (and, subsequently, capital) *in* others, rather than to generate empathy *for* others (and, subsequently, if idealistically, mitigating the extremes of capital). Johansen argues that the desire for narrativized empathy to be a productive and entrepreneurial force is revealed again and again to be impossible in the novel through its attention to the cruelty enacted in the name of transforming trauma into a narrative that generates empathy in others. The novel makes clear the way these demands for individual empathetic narration or fellow feeling are alibis for extractive capitalism's inward turn to accumulate from the self.

Ralph Clare's essay "'You' Can't Feel My Pain: The Limits of Empathy in Claudia Rankine's *Citizen: An American Lyric*" traces the embodied and affective empathy modeled through poetic form in Rankine's book-length poem, which highlights the limits of understanding the other. Clare's reading of Rankine's poetry demonstrates how the assumption of the complete legibility of the other, the premise of popular empathy discourse, actually works to limit anti-racist action. Clare argues that, while the sympathetic white reader may receive a small shock at the potential feeling of being the "you" in a poem in which the speaker experiences racism, Rankine establishes a neutral tone and critical distance via point of view and poetic form that troubles a far too easy "I"dentification for the white reader. Ultimately, Rankine counteracts the possibility of white readers' privilege and ability to appropriate black experiences and suffering. For such "understanding" often leads white progressives—who heed the call of neoliberalism's affective economy by embracing a non-critical empathy—to a disavowal, as Robin DiAngelo argues in *White Fragility* (2018), of their personal stakes in racism and white supremacy, thereby stymying anti-racist action. Instead, Clare suggests, *Citizen* calls for a critical affective empathy—an empathy of feeling with or alongside, not for or instead of—by pointing to the ways in which empathy and the empathetic subject are embedded in social, political, and economic systems of historical-material significance. Not only must the imaginary identification of sharing another's pain be recognized as always coming up short against the otherness of the other, but also empathy must be recognized as being caught up with systemic racism and what the book calls America's "racial imaginary."

Peter Simonsen and Marie-Elisabeth Lei Holm's essay "Limits to Empathy: On the Motif of Failed Empathy in Julian Barnes" considers the operation— or more accurately, the failure—of empathy in selected work by Barnes. Simonsen and Lei Holm demonstrate that Barnes's fiction and its formal and philosophical investment in the operation of high postmodernism have not been typically understood by critics as being in conversation with the post-postmodernist turn to sincerity and empathy. But, as the chapter illustrates, this is to ignore Barnes's complicated engagement in querying the potential for empathetic engagement with others. Indeed, Simonsen and Lei Holm note that this inability by protagonists to empathize with other characters— especially their romantic partners—recurs across Barnes's *oeuvre*. By Simonsen and Holm's account, in Barnes's skeptical fictional universe, enhanced empathetic skills do not attend experience, and characters don't learn from their mistakes even as they have to live with them. The chapter reads this trait across a number of Barnes's texts, *Flaubert's Parrot* (1984) to *The Sense of an Ending* (2011) and *The Only Story* (2018), but focuses on select short stories in *The Lemon Table*. Simonsen and Lei Holm make the case for not only rethinking Barnes's engagement with empathy but for what this might tell us about how postmodernist fiction, long understood as coolly unemotional, engages with the *form* of empathy itself.

Terri Tomsky's essay "Unsettling Empathy: Hassan Blasim, the Iraq War, and the Spectacle of *The Corpse Exhibition*" queries the operation of empathy in human rights discourses, its representation of suffering, and the question of distance between the reader and the subjects of violence. Through a reading of Hassan Blasim's *The Corpse Exhibition*, Tomsky argues that the text's use of a variety of formal techniques and genres asks how violence is mediated and consumed by others and how justice might be imagined. Tomsky explores how Blasim's elaboration of the war's excesses can be read as a strategy to circumvent what Megan Boler calls "passive empathy" and argues that his representation of the war's violence must also be noted alongside Blasim's emphasis on *form* through which experiences of the war are relayed within and beyond Iraq. This attention to form allows Blasim to address *how* suffering and death are mediated for and consumed by others, a point which highlights the risks of empathy, that— to paraphrase Boler—nullify the reader's socio-political responsibilities. Blasim's fictional mediation of a traumatic war presents a fetishization of the war's violence, which does not merely document historical terror; it amplifies and transmutes it into excess, reflecting back assumptions to the reader, and revealing the writer's role as ironic raconteur on the lives of others. Blasim's literary imaginary does not exonerate the reader from modes of responsibility, but instead reveals the impossibility of (literary) closure without accompanying forms of justice, and highlights the discrepancy between (literary) connections and transnational political solidarities.

Alissa G. Karl's "Rachel Cusk's Empathy Work" considers Cusk's recent *Outline* trilogy of novels as an experiment in what it would mean to fully "wage" and commodify empathetic, other affective, and creative labors. Karl interrogates Cusk's construction of a narrative that is organized around the female narrator's acts of listening to others, such that the stories of others comprise the content and episodic structure of each novel, and such that the woman novelist narrator is largely effaced from the narrative itself. Tellingly, then, in Cusk's novels, empathy work precludes the narration of the narrator herself, thus questioning empathy's purportedly "humanizing" functions. Instead, Karl demonstrates how the *Outline* trilogy documents empathy less as a humanistic trait and more as a kind of skilled labor: both as it is commodified in an artwork like the novel, and as a type of "women's work" under contemporary regimes of caring, service, and creative labor. Cusk's intervention on the status of empathy as typically unwaged and feminized is thus twofold: she demonstrates how unwaged and waged affective labors are effectively the same acts, and experiments with their thorough waging through the paid, professionalized labors of her narrator/ protagonist—and ultimately herself, as novelist. Through a reading of Cusk,

Karl contemplates what it would mean to turn a number of presumptions about contemporary empathy on their heads, including the enduring linkage of the novel and empathy and the assumption that affective work could not be fully waged.

Kathryn Cai's "Affective Possibilities Beyond Empathy" charts alternate forms of intersubjective recognition. Cai makes the convincing case that we require a broader range of concepts for understanding how subjects recognize one another, in particular ones that do not rely primarily (as empathy does) on identification. Cai's reading of Ocean Vuong's novel *On Earth We're Briefly Gorgeous* exemplifies how the novel can theorize new affective categories that are appropriate to a wider range of historical subjects—here, migrants and queer subjects—and that are capable, as Cai puts it, of "remak[ing] the world into a place that can accommodate them." Vuong's novel is concerned with the lives of migrants to the United States from Vietnam who, having experienced the extreme violence of war waged by the United States, undertake recognition and relationality in ways that are not captured by empathy. Cai's careful delineation of the nonverbal embodied gestures and acts in the novel posits additional means and modes of recognition that are required if we are to accommodate these subjects and a fuller set of geopolitical histories.

Tate Shaw's "Affective Misplacement and The Image City" also examines the uneven economies of empathy—here, as they involve race, and the institutionalized circulation of images in the realms of photography and photo-bookworks. Shaw's essay begins with a rumination on what is involved in the assumption that white viewers experience "empathy" when viewing video or images of police violence directed at African Americans, reading the too-numerous instances of such in his home of Rochester, New York as a case study. Shaw identifies, however, that many of these presumptions miss the interdependence between what he calls the "empathetic documents" of the images, and the systemic frameworks that surround those documents, and explores a number of ways in which that interdependence is overlooked or unacknowledged. To do this, Shaw examines a prominent image-making project from Magnum Photographers that was undertaken in Rochester, as well as a series of photographic and photo-bookworks projects, including those from the "ruins porn" genre in which photographers collect images from poor, deindustrialized cities. Through a meticulous examination of these projects and their means of production, Shaw demonstrates how the very visual texts and objects that are meant to solicit "empathy" are in fact part of a system of reification that exploits the very subjects with whom viewers ought to empathize. Shaw's essay concludes with a discussion of the work of contemporary black photographer and photobook artist Joshua Rashaad McFadden, whose work Shaw offers as an example of "a photographic practice capable of avoiding empathic reification," but which nonetheless enacts a shared caretaking between viewer, image, and subject.

A rereading of empathy is crucial right now given the prevalence of empathy discourse, and the ways in which it can bind subjects to moral and social imperatives, particularly in the precarious and evolving global conditions from which we write—those of a global pandemic, record unemployment and economic inequality, political extremism and instability, and an unfolding climate catastrophe. We can't help but note that no amount of "feeling with" a patient suffering from Covid-19 will save that patient's life; only public health provisions and adequate health care are capable of doing that. Similarly, "feeling with" the Black people murdered by the police and other agents of the state doesn't end that violence, no matter how many novels white people read. As university professors during this time of disruption, we recognize the incredible strain that our students are under, but we must also acknowledge that no amount of good feeling directed toward them will ameliorate their and their families' (and our, and our families') economic and health insecurities. In this way, the Covid-19 pandemic has not, as some commentators like to say, "changed everything"—rather, it has exposed the stakes of ignoring structural conditions.[13] In this context, we are not—nor are the contributors to this volume—suggesting that we should empathize less; instead, we want to consider carefully why empathy and why now.

Notes

1　Unsurprisingly, both Obama's and Biden's invocations of the uses and limits of empathy are overdetermined by legalistic, national boundaries: these are discourses about empathy with other national citizens. Their notion of empathy is decidedly one that doesn't encompass the global others whose highly exploited labor is central to the operation of the US economy and global hegemony, nor does it include the asylum seekers and undocumented residents, whom both Obama and Biden deported and incarcerated at higher rates than Republican presidents. On the "remaindered lives" necessary for the operation of capital, see Tadiar (2015) and Vora (2015).

2　Obama and Biden are not the only high-ranking US politicians to deploy affective rhetoric. US President Bill Clinton famously told constituents "I feel your pain" in 1992; Kathleen Woodward has claimed that Clinton's emotional display, along with the Republican Party's so-called "compassionate conservatism" is part of a shift in discourses of emotion in the 1990s (2004: 59–61). Alissa G. Karl has discussed elsewhere how it is not just Clinton, but Jimmy Carter before him who established a direct link between personal feelings and aggregate political and economic conditions; Carter did so, Karl argues, when he claimed during the energy crisis in 1979 that Americans must address their "crisis of confidence" if economic conditions were to improve (2020: 282–3). Biden and Obama, then are the latest iterations in a longer genealogy of affective political communication.

3 This also echoes longstanding notions of empathy as capital that must be spent wisely. As Lauren Berlant notes of compassion, "when we are taught, from the time we are taught anything, to measure the scale of pain and attachment, to feel *appropriately* compassionate, we are being trained in stinginess, in not caring, in not knowing what we know about the claim on us to act ... all too human" (2004: 10; emphasis in original). A similar sense of accountancy seems to always go alongside discussions of emotional and affective responses to the suffering of others. It also parallels Eva Illouz's characterization of "emotional capitalism:" "a culture in which emotional and economic discourses and practices mutually shape each, thus producing ... a broad, sweeping movement in which affect is made an essential aspect of economic behavior and in which emotional life ... follow the logic of economic relations and exchange" (5).

4 One example of this and its connection with particularly literary modes of empathy are the endless reading lists that circulate in the wake of racist violence such as the murders of George Floyd and Breonna Taylor or the Atlanta murders (which included the murder of six Asian women). Yet, as Lauren Michelle Jackson (2020) notes, these lists are as much about the appearance of action–and generation of new empathies–as they are actually about doing the reading, suggesting that it is the performed desire to empathize that generates cultural worth, not empathizing itself. See also Saidya Hartman's important work on the racialized dynamics of empathetic voyeurism (1997), as well as Razack (2007) and Wilderson (2013) on the racial limits of empathy.

5 One key venue for both conversations about empathy and concerns about its failures is, of course, the internet and various digital and social media platforms (though a full engagement with digital modes of empathy is beyond the scope of this edited collection). As Megan Boler and Elizabeth Davis note, in "complex ways ... emotion has become one of the central engines driving media and politics in the digital age" (2021: 1)—unsurprising, then, that concerns about empathy (its lack but also its broader circulation) shape so much of how we understand our interactions with digital spaces. Yet, particularly post-2016, the critical and popular discussion has centered around the absence or decline of digital empathy—even while "feeling" has become more central to our digital lives. Carolyn Pedwell suggests that this is to dismiss the potential of digital affect, no matter how contingent: "Black Lives Matter, Occupy, and other broadly leftist networked activisms ... powerfully illustrate how digital technologies can be leveraged to generate affective solidarities that connect a wide range of constituents though varying gestures of witnessing, cooperation, and participation" (2021: 162). Yet, as Lisa Nakamura suggests, VR (virtual reality) technology and its claims for the development of empathy are used by big tech companies like Facebook as "a cultural alibi for a digital media culture that has taken a wrong turn, towards distraction, detachment, and misinformation. Hence its industrial strategy to represent it as inherently more ethical, empathetic, and virtuous than any other media has ever been" (2020: 49). Digital empathy, as well as the uses it is put to in digital platforms, then, is, like all forms of empathy, a deeply ambivalent category—one with political possibility, but also with the potential for maintaining the status quo. For more detailed engagement with digital modes of empathy, see Boler and Davis (2021); Noble (2018); Paasonen, Hillis, and Petit (2015); Pedwell (2021).

6   This renewed scholarly attention is the return of a pendulum swing away from
     earlier scholarly attention which identified the pitfalls and limits of empathy
     as an instigator of political consciousness. Yet, as Frank Wilderson III notes,
     "it rests in the private and quotidian of civil society with all the security and
     permanence of a grammar ... To the extent that it is thought of at all, empathy
     is considered an innate capacity" (183). Though, as Wilderson notes, this is not
     an innate capacity that is believed to extend, in this grammar, to Black people.
     It is empathy's "private and quotidian" operation as unquestioned capacity
     that is the focus of this volume.

7   Indeed, Zoé Samudzi (2019) asks "Does empathy really arise from the
     universal? Is our common humanness heightened or do realizations of the
     ubiquity of sufferings instead overwhelm and nurture a kind of nihilism about
     the inevitability of atrocities?".

8   This is a deliberately basic definition. However, as we will see, while various
     approaches and scholars complicate or expand the definition, feeling the
     (approximate) feelings of another remains the core of what is meant by the
     word. Given that the focus in this collection centers on the cultural politics
     of empathy, we will resist the urge to offer an authoritative definition,
     acknowledging that the slipperiness of the term is, in part, key to its broad
     usage.

9   Indeed, Smith begins *The Theory of Moral Sentiments* by asserting that "How
     selfish soever man may be supposed, there are evidently some principles in his
     nature, which interest him in the fortune of others, and render their happiness
     necessary to him, though he derives nothing from it except the pleasure of
     seeing it" ([1759] 2002: 11)—a statement which seems, on one hand, at odds
     with Chicago School economics that pose economics as the only engine of
     individual action and, on the other hand, an early version of Gary Becker's
     economics of crime and punishment in which morality becomes economized.
     This Smithian market of sympathy remains central to the cultural circulation
     of empathy as we saw in both Obama's and Biden's use of the term.

10   For a thorough historical overview of the intervening centuries, see the first
     two chapters of Suzanne Keen's *Empathy and the Novel* (2007).

11   While not a cognitive scholar, Zoé Samudzi also suggests, in considering the
     calls to empathy that surround cultural memorialization of genocide, the
     ease with which empathy slips into "a kind of nihilism about the inevitability
     of atrocities" (2019). She posits that empathy produces an "odd horseshoe
     that connects two sides of individuals enduring suffering: the humanized
     perpetrator wounded by the infliction of harm and the secondhand witness
     vicariously wounded by the evocation of tragic memory. The most important
     party, the victim, is scrubbed from this affective equation" (2019).

12   For recent analyses of affective and immaterial labor, see also Bernes (2017),
     Hicks (2009), and Weeks (2011).

13   And while the pandemic has seen the explosion in "mutual aid" efforts,
     these have quickly shaded into volunteer-run charitable organizations, rather
     than the engines of community-building that they have been at previous
     historical moments. Similar to the parallel explosions in GoFundMe and other
     crowdsourced fundraisers, these rely heavily on calls to empathy, but by virtue
     of that action being overdetermined by the form of the charitable donation,

these modes of crisis aid end up replicating the operation of the non-profit industrial complex–without even the possibility of paid employment that those industries produce. Another example of this is Samaria Rice's (the mother of Tamir Rice, a child murdered by the Cleveland police) recent anger with the Black Lives Matter Global Network and a variety of celebrity Black philanthropists/ activists (such as Shaun King and Tamika Mallory) about their use of the images of victims of police and state violence in order to "monopolize and capitalize" on these deaths—particularly in the face of the precarity of too many of the families whose loved ones have been killed. Both of these instances illustrate the ways that the language of empathy and social justice can be and is used to generate capital for some, while leaving those who suffer in ever-greater forms of precarity. See Tolentino (2020) and Wilcox (2021).

References

Berlant, L. (2004), "Introduction: Compassion (and Withholding)," in L. Berlant (ed), *Compassion: The Culture and Politics of an Emotion*, 1–13, New York: Routledge.

Bernes, J. (2017), *The Work of Art in the Age of De-Industrialization*, Stanford: Stanford University Press.

Bloom, P. (2016), *Against Empathy: The Case for Rational Compassion*, New York: Ecco Books.

Boboltz, S. (2019), "Joe Biden to Millenials: 'Don't Tell Me How Bad It Is. Change It," *The Huffington Post*, August 3, 2019. Available online: https://www.huffpost.com/entry/joe-biden-millennials-dont-complain-change-it_n_5d45cc9de4b0acb57fcd5486 (accessed February 25, 2020).

Boler, M. and E. Davis. (2021), "Introduction: Propaganda by Other Means," in M. Boler and E. Davis (eds), *Affective Politics of Digital Media: Propaganda by Other Means*, 1–50, New York: Routledge.

Breithaupt, F. (2019), *The Dark Side of Empathy*, Ithaca, NY: Cornell University Press.

Chadwick, K. (2017), "I Don't Know How to Explain to You That You Should Care about Other People," *The Huffington Post*, June 26, 2017. Available online: https://www.huffpost.com/entry/i-dont-know-how-to-explain-to-you-that-you-should_b_59519811e4b0f078efd98440 (accessed May 18, 2020).

Greenwald Smith, R. (2015), *Affect and American Literature in the Age of Neoliberalism*, New York: Cambridge University Press.

Hartman, S. (1997), *Scenes of Subjection*. Oxford, UK: Oxford University Press.

Hicks, H. (2009), *The Culture of Soft Work: Labor, Gender, and Race in Postmodern American Narrative*, New York: Palgrave.

Illouz, E. (2007), *Cold Intimacies: The Making of Emotional Capitalism*, Cambridge, UK: Polity Press.

Jackson, L. M. (2020), "What Is an Anti-Racist Reading List For?," *Vulture*, June 4, 2020. Available online: https://www.vulture.com/2020/06/anti-racist-reading-lists-what-are-they-for.html (accessed March 23, 2021).

Karl, A. G. (2020), "Empathize! Feeling and Labor in the Economic Present," *Criticism*, 62 (2): 271–95.

Keen, S. (2007), *Empathy and the Novel*, Oxford: Oxford University Press.

Liu, C. (2021), *Virtue Hoarders: The Case against the Professional Managerial Class*, Minneapolis: University of Minnesota Press.

Nakamura, L. (2020), "Feeling Good about Feeling Bad: Virtuous Virtual Reality and the Automation of Racial Empathy," *Journal of Visual Culture*, 19 (1): 48–64.

Nealon, J. (2017), "Realisms Redux; or, against Affective Capitalism," in M. Huehls and R. Greenwald Smith (eds), *Neoliberalism and Contemporary Literary Culture*, 70–85, Baltimore: Johns Hopkins University Press.

Ngai, S. (2007), *Ugly Feelings*, Cambridge, MA: Harvard University Press.

Ngai, S. (2012), *Our Aesthetic Categories: Zany, Cute, Interesting*, Cambridge, MA: Harvard University Press.

Noble, S. U. (2018), *Algorithms of Oppression: How Search Engines Reinforce Racism*, New York: New York University Press.

Nussbaum, M. (2013), *Political Emotions: Why Love Matters for Justice*, Cambridge, MA: Harvard University Press.

Obama, B. (2006), "Obama to Graduates: Cultivate Empathy," *Northwestern.edu*, June 19, 2006. Available online: https://www.northwestern.edu/newscenter/stories/2006/06/barack.html (accessed September 10, 2021).

Paasonen, S., K. Hillis and M. Petit (2015), "Introduction: Networks of Transmission: Intensity, Sensation, Value," in K. Hillis, S. Passonen and M. Petit (eds), *Networked Affect*, 1–24, Boston: MIT Press.

Paiella, G. (2018), "Joe Biden Has Some Harsh Words for Millenials," *The Cut*, January 12, 2018. Available online: https://www.thecut.com/2018/01/joe-biden-on-millennials.html (accessed February 25, 2020).

Pedwell, C. (2014), *Affective Relations: The Transnational Politics of Empathy*, Basingstoke: Palgrave.

Pedwell, C. (2021), *Revolutionary Routines: The Habits of Social Transformation*, Montreal: McGill-Queen's University Press.

Pinker, S. (2011), *The Better Angels of Our Nature: Why Violence Has Declined*, New York: Penguin.

Prinz, J. (2017), "On the Genealogy of Empathy," Keynote address to the Society of Literature, Science, and the Arts EU, University of Basel, June 23, 2017.

Prinz, J. (2018), "Empathy and the Moral Self," in Sara Graça Da Silva (ed), *New Interdisciplinary Landscapes in Morality and Emotion*, 12–26, New York: Routledge.

Razack, S. (2007), "Stealing the Pain of Others: Reflections on Canadian Humanitarian Responses," *The Review of Education, Pedagogy, and Cultural Studies*, 29 (4): 375–94.

Samudzi, Z. (2019), "Against (?) Empathy," *Open Space*, September 18, 2019. Available online: https://openspace.sfmoma.org/2019/09/against-empathy/ (accessed March 31, 2021).

Smith, A. ([1759] 2002), *The Theory of Moral Sentiments*, ed. Knud Haakonsson, Cambridge: Cambridge University Press.

Swan, E. (2008), "'You Make Me Feel like a Woman': Therapeutic Cultures and the Contagion of Femininity," *Gender, Work, and Organization*, 15 (1): 88–107.

Tadiar, N. X. M. (2015), "Decolonization, 'Race,' and Remaindered Life under Empire," *Qui Parle*, 23 (2): 135–60.

Thatcher, M. (1987), "Interview with *Woman's Own*," September 1987. Available online: https://www.margaretthatcher.org/document/106689 (accessed September 10, 2021).

Tolentino, J. (2020), "What Mutual Aid Can Do during a Pandemic," *The New Yorker*, May 11, 2020. Available online: https://www.newyorker.com/magazine/2020/05/18/what-mutual-aid-can-do-during-a-pandemic (accessed March 24, 2021).

Vora, K. (2015), *Life Support: Biocapital and the New History of Outsourced Labor*, Minneapolis: University of Minnesota Press.

Weeks, K. (2011), *The Problem with Work: Feminism, Marxism, Antiwork Politics, and Postwork Imaginaries*, Durham, NC: Duke University Press.

Wilcox, R. (2021). [*Twitter*] March 16, 2021. Available Online: https://twitter.com/_Rawilcox/status/1371995843683876865 (accessed March 16, 2021).

Wilderson III, F. B. (2013). "'Raw Life' and the Ruse of Empathy," in P. Lichtenfels and J. Rouse (eds), *Performance, Politics and Activism*, 181–206, New York: Palgrave.

Wilson, J. (2021), "The Empathy Industrial Complex," *BookForum*, March/April/May 2021. Available online: https://www.bookforum.com/print/2801/george-saunders-looks-for-life-lessons-in-russian-literature-24370 (accessed March 23, 2021).

Woodward, K. (2004), "Calculating Compassion," in L. Berlant (ed), *Compassion: The Culture and Politics of an Emotion*, 59–86, New York: Routledge.

1

Reading George Eliot in the #metoo Era

Susan Bruxvoort Lipscomb

Near the end of the *Adam Bede*, Arthur Donnithorne, the heir to the local estate, says to the title character: "Perhaps you've never done anything you've had bitterly to repent of in your life, Adam; if you had, you would be more generous. You would know then that it's worse for me than for you" (Eliot [1859] 2008: 510). Adam forgives Arthur and the scene ends with Adam "feeling that sorrow was more bearable now hatred was gone" (Eliot [1859] 2008: 513). This scene culminates one of the dramatic arcs of the novel, which guides its readers toward this moment of forgiveness and reconciliation. Arthur and Adam have suffered with each other and the readers of *Adam Bede* have felt their suffering. At this moment, Eliot asks her readers to understand Arthur's suffering as greater and Adam's forgiveness as appropriate.

Adam is presented as a far more heroic and admirable character than Arthur and his capacity to forgive Arthur fits his depiction as an ideal figure. Eliot's depiction of this moment of forgiveness and reconciliation, however, may be difficult for some readers to accept. The reader may not be as heroically generous as Adam. The plot of *Adam Bede*, after all, centers on Arthur, a sexual predator who uses his power and privilege to seduce and impregnate a very young woman, Hetty Sorrel, Adam's betrothed. Arthur hides his actions behind his privilege until Hetty abandons her newborn infant, stands trial for infanticide, and is sentenced to death. Arthur only accepts responsibility for his role once he is publicly implicated in her crime.

It's "worse for Arthur" only because he has lost his self-esteem and his reputation in his community.

But Eliot asks her reader to sympathetically feel that it is indeed worse for Arthur, the privileged predator, to live with his guilt than for Adam, the innocent bystander, who has lost the hope of a future with a woman he loves. This plot is part of a carefully designed project to cultivate the empathy of readers. Eliot's project, however, is strikingly at odds with what many assume to be the point of empathetic engagement with literature: to cultivate feeling for those who are particularly oppressed, victimized, or silenced. Eliot's ethics of empathy stand in tension with the current of early twenty-first-century culture that privileges the voices and experiences of victims. Eliot does not ignore the pain of the exploited woman, but she is no less interested in the pain of the exploiter—a man who she sees as particularly broken and in need of empathy.

Eliot's Theory of Empathy

The term "empathy" was not coined until the twentieth century, but Eliot would have used the term "sympathy" for something similar—a feeling of connection and understanding between people.[1] Nearly every scholarly discussion of the role of empathy in George Eliot's fiction cites the following passage from a letter she wrote in 1859 to her friend, Charles Bray:

> I have had heart-cutting experience that *opinions* are a poor cement between human souls: the only effect I ardently long to produce by my writings, is that those who read them should be better able to *imagine* and to *feel* the pains and the joys of those who differ from them in everything but the broad fact of being struggling, erring human creatures.
>
> (Emphasis original. Haight 1954: 111)

Eliot wrote this letter the same year she published *Adam Bede,* her first novel. And the contents of this excerpt appear to fit well with her explicit aims as a novelist: to tell the truth and to depict the full range of human appearances and behaviors. In *Adam Bede,* Eliot both exemplifies and testifies to her aspirations for fiction. In the chapter "In Which the Story Pauses a Little," she lays out a principle of realism, claiming that she is "content to tell my simple story, without trying to make things seem better than they were; dreading nothing but falsity" (Eliot [1859] 2008: 194–5). The realism that she attempts has a further aim beyond avoiding falsity. It is also meant to cultivate empathy with the unlovely. She writes: "Let us love that other beauty too, which lies in no secret of proportion, but in the secret of deep human sympathy" (Eliot [1859] 2008: 196). She connects her choices of how she depicts her characters with an imperative to help her readers love even the unlovely. She links this deep secret of sympathy to the idea that even unattractive men are still loved by their mothers and middle-aged women loved by their husbands and concludes that "human feeling is like the mighty rivers that bless the earth: it does not wait for beauty—it flows with resistless force and brings beauty with it" (Eliot [1859] 2008: 196).

The letter to Bray in which she testifies that "the only effect I ardently long to produce by my writings, is that those who read them should be better able to *imagine* and to *feel* the pains and the joys of [others]" appears to be a reaffirmation of the statements she makes in Chapter 17 of *Adam Bede*. But is Arthur Donnithorne, the pampered son of privilege, really the proper object of empathy? He is physically beautiful and has every advantage that wealth and status can procure. Understanding Eliot's theory of empathy requires definition of its principal subject: a subject surprisingly different from the least-privileged and most-victimized.

The context of the Bray letter illustrates this point. The common interpretation of the letter to Bray, while basically sound, is missing some of the nuance of this moment in Eliot's life and thus a key facet of her theory of empathy. This letter was written in response to a situation in which Eliot was dealing with a particularly difficult person: a person she was struggling to understand empathetically. And it is also significant that Eliot is not calling for empathy on the basis of difference (one should empathize with others so that one can understand perspectives different from one's own) but on the basis of universality: one should empathize with "those who differ from them in everything but the broad fact of being struggling, erring human creatures." It is this "broad fact" that is the key to Eliot's theory of realism and empathy: all people are "struggling, erring human creatures." Eliot does not use the characteristically Romantic assumption of the basic goodness of humanity as the foundation of her theory of empathetic engagement. It is rather a fundamental tenet of Christianity that (perhaps surprisingly) undergirds her ethics: that all have sinned and fallen short. Eliot presents this view in another letter, to John Blackwood, in response to a criticism of her representation of the character of Maggie Tullivar in *The Mill on the Floss*. Eliot writes that "If the ethics of art do not admit the truthful presentation of a character essentially noble but liable to great error—error that is anguish to its own nobleness—*then*, it seems to me, the ethics of art are too narrow, and must be widened to correspond with a widening psychology" (Emphasis original. Haight 1954: 318). "Struggling, erring human creatures," and people "liable to great error" are central to Eliot's fiction and to her theory of the ethical effects of her fiction.

The Struggling, Erring Herbert Spencer

The specific "erring human creature" that prompted Eliot to write the oft-quoted passage about empathy to her friend Bray was none other than the Herbert Spencer, the eminent Victorian sociologist, often credited with developing the idea of "social Darwinism" and who indeed coined the phrase "survival of the fittest." Eliot had known Spencer since 1851; they were frequent companions on excursions around London in their early friendship. They were so much together that rumors began to swirl that they were engaged. Eliot wrote to Bray in 1852 about Spencer: "all the world is setting us down as engaged—a most disagreeable thing if one chose to make oneself uncomfortable ... please to avoid mentioning our names together, and pray burn this note" (as qtd. in Haight 1968: 113). Despite her protests, Eliot did become romantically attached to Spencer and may have wished that the rumors were true. Spencer made it clear, however, that he desired only her intellectual companionship. Eliot pleaded with him to not abandon their friendship: "if you become attached to someone else, then I must die, but until then I could gather courage to work and make life valuable, if only I had you near me" (as qtd in Karl 1995: 146). By 1859, this complicated relationship had simmered into friendship as Eliot had found both intellectual companionship *and* love with George Henry Lewes.

But Spencer was still part of Eliot's larger social circle and, in the wake of the publication of *Adam Bede*, also a source of significant annoyance. At this point in her life, she was living with Lewes as his wife in every sense except the legal. Lewes's journal from March of 1859 recounts a recent visit from Spencer and his deteriorating behavior: "He used to be one of our friends on whom we most relied; but jealousy, too patent and too unequivocal of our success, acting on his own bitterness at nonsuccess, has of late cooled him visibly. He always tells us of the disagreeable things he hears or reads of us and never the agreeable things" (as qtd. in Karl 1995: 311). Lewes's perspective on this visit was that Spencer had behaved badly, "acting on his own bitterness" and jealousy. And just a few days before Eliot wrote to Bray, she heard through another friend, Eugène Bodichon, that Spencer had been gossiping about the authorship of *Adam Bede* (which Eliot had attempted to disguise) and had bragged that "he knew the auth*oress* and had seen her lately" (original emphasis, Haight 1954: 103).

Eliot's well-known lines to Bray are at the end of a letter about how she is feeling about the revelation of her identity as an author. First, she reassures him that she is content to let her identity be known: "Take no trouble about me—and let every one believe—as they will in spite of all your kind efforts—*what they like to believe*" (original emphasis, Haight 1954: 110). Then she turns to a more general statement about how to regard gossip: "I feel so deeply the duty of doubting everything to the disadvantage of another until demonstration comes." Eliot next begs her friend Charles not to think too badly of the people who have gossiped about her—especially, Spencer: "I beg you not to regard the last thing Mr. Lewes told you about Herbert Spencer, as a thing incapable of being so explained as to make it more consistent with our previous conviction concerning his character" (Haight 1954: 111). In this complex double-negative construction, Eliot asks Bray to not judge Spencer solely by his recent behavior but to place that behavior alongside their earlier positive conviction about his character (and its grounds). Lewes was annoyed with Spencer but previously both Eliot and Lewes had admired him. Eliot asks her friend to see Spencer as more than just the recent jealousy he had exhibited. This is the context for her claim that she wants readers to "*imagine* and to *feel* the pains and the joys" of others. As she writes, just above this remark: "If Art does not enlarge men's sympathies, it does nothing morally." In this context, she is asking Bray to imagine and feel the pains and joys of a man who wounded her by his romantic rejection, gossiped about her secret identity, and harshly criticized her out of jealousy. A struggling, erring creature indeed.

The Challenge of Empathy in Eliot's Novels

Eliot has a penchant for creating struggling, erring creatures in her novels. These characters are at the center of plots that instruct readers how they should cultivate their empathy and are thus central to the question of how Eliot thinks about villains and victims. Eliot's cultivation of an empathetic response to these characters is, I will argue, intentional. This goes against two common if generally unstated assumptions about empathy and literature: that readers should not feel empathy toward morally repugnant characters and, if readers do empathize with these characters, then that is not the author's intention. Suzanne Keen makes this assumption in her influential study *Empathy and the Novel* when discussing readers' responses to Eliot's characters. Keen quotes readers who find themselves "empathizing with or identifying with despised characters apparently held up for scorn by authors" (2007: 74). She quotes from readers who identify with Rosamond Vincy and Edward Casaubon from *Middlemarch* and Gwendolyn Harleth from *Daniel Deronda*. The readers say that their empathy has been "secret" and that they find it "a little embarrassing" (Keen 2007: 75) to admit their sense of recognition and fellow feeling with these characters. Keen uses these examples to illustrate "the complex of feelings that can be activated by an empathetic connection with a character, even a risible one" and concludes with the summary claim that "*empathy for a fictional character need not correspond with what the author appears to set up or invite*" (original emphasis, 2007: 75). Keen assumes that Eliot, in creating morally objectionable characters, could not have intended her readers to empathize with them. And Keen also assumes that the author could not herself feel for these morally objectionable characters: "The author need not like the character nor lavish representational attention on the character's state of mind to invoke a reader's empathy." This may be an illuminating remark about other authors. But there is strong evidence that Eliot tries very hard to "like" all her characters and, in the case of these morally corrupt examples from *Middlemarch* and *Daniel Deronda*, she does lavish representational attention on their states of mind as part of an intentional project of cultivating her readers' empathy. It is no accident that readers find themselves secretly identifying with the selfishness of Rosamond, Gwendolyn, and Casaubon.

The character of Arthur Donnithorne in *Adam Bede* is one of Eliot's first attempts to create this response in readers. Twenty-first-century readers, however, may find it particularly difficult to identify with Arthur and, if they feel any sense of fellow feeling for him, might be even less inclined to admit it. Arthur's seduction of Hetty Sorrel has strong resonances to the stories shared by many women as part of the #metoo movement that gained international attention in 2017.[2] Arthur is an entitled young man using his privilege to take sexual advantage of a woman far more vulnerable than himself. Responding only to this summary, one might conclude that *of course* Arthur's life should be wrecked by his actions. Through the lens of the present, the moral of the story is clear. Arthur is the villain. Hetty is the victim. Arthur could be compared to Brock Turner, the Stanford University student on a swimming scholarship who was convicted in 2015 of raping an unconscious woman. The Stanford University swimming star and the heir to the Donnithorne estate share a comparable degree of privilege and their actions have similarly devastating consequences for the women they abuse. The aim of reading a novel with this plot line, for many twenty-first-century readers, would be to cultivate empathy for Hetty and young women like Hetty—to develop the capacity to see the world through Hetty's eyes and feel, with her, her humiliation and degradation. Some advocates for the moral effects of literature argue that readers become better people by learning about the perspectives of victims—like the perspectives of women who are taken advantage of by powerful men. Hetty abandons her baby because she feels desperate and alone. Arthur knew the potential consequences of sleeping with the niece of a tenant farmer on his grandfather's estate. He knew she might get pregnant and then he'd have to support her as a "kept woman." In her naivete, Hetty thought Arthur was planning to marry her, but Arthur knew the possible consequences of their sexual liaison and how it could transform Hetty from a farmer's niece to a fallen woman.

George Eliot's aims, however, are not as simple as asking her readers to feel for Hetty as victim. She does invite her readers to understand what Hetty feels. But she also asks them to feel with and for Arthur. And Eliot also allows her readers to judge Hetty—to feel that she made a terrible and foolish mistake that caused the death of her child. In contrast to her later depictions of women like Rosamond Vincy and Gwendolyn Harleth, Eliot doesn't invite readers to see themselves in Hetty, whom she portrays as unappealingly self-interested and vain. And she doesn't exactly ask them to identify with Arthur. But she asks them to understand both Hetty and Arthur. As I will discuss later, in her framing of her reader's empathetic response, Eliot privileges cognitive empathy over emotional empathy: she invites readers to *think* about how an inexperienced young woman could tragically misunderstand the intentions of a man and how a privileged young man could have a hard time resisting temptation—how he could be coddled by a sense of entitlement into ignoring the nagging voice of reason in his head.

Eliot positions her reader to think about their reactions to these characters at two important moments in the text. With Hetty, Eliot asks readers to understand her motivations. Eliot assumes that we will judge Hetty as foolish and naive and she asks us to see the world through Hetty's eyes: "Bright, admiring glances from a handsome young gentleman, with white hands, a gold chain, occasional regimentals, and wealth and grandeur immeasurable—those were the warm rays that set poor Hetty's heart vibrating" ([1859] 2008: 106). The narrator asks readers to think about the world from Hetty's perspective—how a young dairy maid could be dazzled by a handsome squire.

In the case of Arthur, Eliot asks the reader to imagine how Arthur's position of wealth and privilege sets him up to allow his desire for Hetty to compromise his good judgment. Addressing her readers, she tells them that they know Arthur Donnithorne's type, and that they generally like this type of man:

> You perceive that Arthur Donnithorne was "a good fellow"—all his college friends thought him such: he couldn't bear to see any one uncomfortable; he would have been sorry even in his angriest moods for any harm to happen to his grandfather and his aunt Lydia herself had the benefit of that soft-heartedness which he bore towards the whole sex.
> (Eliot [1859] 2008: 106)

But then Eliot intimates that this type of young man is prone to a certain kind of temptation. He is prone to the temptation to assume that if he ever causes pain to others, he can easily make up for it:

> Whether he would have self-mastery enough to be always as harmless and purely beneficent as his good-nature led him to desire, was a question that no one had yet decided against him; he was but twenty-one, you remember, and we don't inquire too closely into character in the case of a handsome generous young fellow, who will have property enough to support numerous peccadilloes—who, if he should unfortunately break a

man's legs in his rash driving, will be able to pension him handsomely; or
if he should happen to spoil a woman's existence for her, will make it up
to her with expensive bon-bons, packed up and directed by his own hand.

([1859] 2008: 136–7)

So men like Arthur might make some mistakes—they might accidentally
"break a man's legs" or "spoil a woman's existence for her." But men like
Arthur don't worry too much about these kinds of mistakes because they
can always fix them through warm generosity: a handsome pension or
expensive bon-bons. The narrative voice is coolly ironic in this passage.
Having one's legs broken in an era before anesthesia or the welfare state
is a terrible fate. The euphemistic "spoiling" of a woman's existence means
destroying her financial and legal security. Eliot points out the worst that
men like Arthur can do. But then she asks her readers to think about how
society treats men like him:

We use round, general, gentlemanly epithets about a young man of birth
and fortune; and ladies, with that fine intuition which is the distinguishing
attribute of their sex, see at once that he is "nice." The chances are that
he will go through life without scandalizing any one; a seaworthy vessel
that no one would refuse to insure.

(Eliot [1859] 2008: 137)

Eliot's observation that society assumes the best of young men like Arthur
is strikingly similar to a leading claim of #metoo movement activists: that
men of privilege are often not held accountable for their misbehavior. Eliot
implies that Victorian readers should be suspicious of men like Arthur
who have so much latent power over others, but then provides an astute
analysis about why we often do not suspect or judge men like him. Eliot's
presentation of Arthur as a "seaworthy vessel" and a good investment is
bitterly ironic. In the nineteenth century when people could easily lose their
life savings if a ship sank, Eliot and her reader know that even seaworthy
vessels are sometimes overwhelmed by storms. Eliot calls out the kind of
easy insurance given to young men like Arthur and foreshadows that he is
heading for a metaphorical shipwreck.

But even as Eliot explains why men like Arthur can get away with so much
because of biases toward wealth and gentility, she nonetheless paints a detailed
individual portrait of Arthur the man that helps her reader understand how
Arthur comes to act against his own better judgment. Here Eliot's approach
conflicts with a common twenty-first-century approach to thinking about
misbehaving men. She narrates a scene in which Arthur goes to see the local
Rector, Mr. Irwine, to confess that he's been taking too much of an interest
in Hetty and to seek accountability in resisting temptation. But Arthur is too
embarrassed, in the end, to talk about it. Mr. Irwine—who suspects that Arthur

might be mildly infatuated—is like the readers Eliot talked about previously in assuming that Arthur will be protected by his privilege from making too terrible a mistake. Mr. Irwine thinks, "[Arthur's] honest, patronizing pride in the goodwill and respect of everybody about him was a safeguard even against foolish romance, still more against a lower kind of folly" (Eliot [1859] 2008: 189). In this chapter, Eliot sets up the reader to empathize with Arthur, who is too embarrassed to tell his mentor about his relationship with Hetty, but also with Mr. Irwine himself, who wants to think the best of Arthur, so fails to intervene and take Arthur to task even though he suspects that Arthur is behaving inappropriately. She sets up a situation in which readers are led to empathize with a predator and with someone who willfully turns away from intervening in a situation of potential predation. From Eliot's perspective, both Arthur and Mr. Irwine are "struggling, erring creatures" in this scene. They both have a sense of what they should do. Arthur should turn to Mr. Irwine and confess and gain support to help him stay away from Hetty. Mr. Irwine should confront Arthur and sternly warn him. Neither of them makes the right choice. But their struggle and their ultimate wrong decisions are human ones with which the reader can empathize.

Arthur and Mr. Irwine, as "struggling, erring creatures," are nonetheless quite appealing figures. Readers may empathize with them because they imagine themselves to be like these two men: warm-hearted and kind, making a wrong choice out of a too-generous interpretation of the situation. But there are struggling, erring creatures in Eliot's novels who are far less appealing too. As mentioned earlier, in her masterpiece, *Middlemarch*, Eliot creates a character, Edward Casaubon, who is not warm-hearted and kind. He is consistently depicted as both aesthetically and morally repulsive. Yet Eliot nonetheless asks her readers to empathize with him. Casaubon, a middle-aged scholar, marries the young, idealistic Dorothea Brooke with the mistaken belief that she will be able to help him in his great scholarly endeavor. He neglects his wife emotionally and also jealously isolates her from a friendship with his young cousin. He is selfish and even cruel and readers often feel a sense of relief at his demise, relatively early in the novel's plotline; his death frees up his appealing young wife to be wooed by a man who shows her far more understanding and affection. But Eliot never encourages her readers' desire to hate Casaubon. Her narrator even asks them to try to understand him as a man the world expects to be great but who knows in his heart that he is not. She takes her readers aside at one moment in the story to confide in them:

> For my part I am very sorry for him. It is an uneasy lot at best, to be what we call highly taught and yet not to enjoy: to be present at this great spectacle of life and never to be liberated from a small hungry shivering self—never to be fully possessed by the glory we behold, never to have our consciousness rapturously transformed into the vividness of a thought,

the ardor of a passion, the energy of an action, but always to be scholarly and uninspired, ambitious and timid, scrupulous and dim-sighted.

(Eliot [1871] 2008: 263)

Casaubon is more than a selfish and cruel husband who destroys the ideals of his young, ardent wife. He is a "small hungry shivering self." Readers may be pleased when he dies of a sudden stroke halfway through the novel, and it may be easy to remember him primarily as a villain. But Eliot tried to get her readers to pause, for just a couple of sentences, and contemplate his inner life and inner shame. And feel just a little pity for him.

There is certainly anecdotal evidence that Eliot succeeds in this, at least with some readers. Keen quotes a reader who says about Casaubon that "The send of recognition was visceral ... I picture Casaubon, rejecting Eliot's portrayal, as an attractive, enticing figure, tragically misplaced by his community" (as qtd in Keen 2007: 75). This reader makes the same mistake as Keen in assuming that Eliot could not have intended a reader to empathize with a man depicted as so flawed. But the empathetic response was provoked nonetheless. In her memoir, *My Life in Middlemarch*, Rebecca Mead describes how she came to identify with Casaubon in middle age. She describes how, in her twenties, she understood Dorothea's attraction to Casaubon as a person of knowledge but that in her thirties she found it "easier to look down on Casaubon, to regard him as contemptible and repellent" (Mead 2014: 163). In middle age, however, Mead comes to the empathetic response that Eliot intended. Mead reflects that "I realize that it would take a great deal of self-regard on my part not to feel a tender sense of kinship with that sad, proud, desiccated man" (Mead 2014: 164).

The other clear villain in *Middlemarch* is Nicholas Bulstrode. Bulstrode is a pious evangelical banker who has lots of money and power and uses it to get the things he wants: more money and power. In the course of the novel, it becomes clear that Bulstrode had a disreputable past life. He did not honorably earn or inherit the fortune that he brought into the community but ran a business that laundered stolen goods. He allowed his estranged stepdaughter to die in poverty rather than alert her to an inheritance that he wanted to use as capital for his business ventures. He's done illegal and immoral things and yet uses pious religious language to portray himself as a spiritual leader. By the end of the novel, he passively allows the death of the man who might expose his past—an action that cannot prevent his ultimate reckoning as his secrets become public. He, like Arthur Donnithorne, must face humiliation before a community that had previously given him a place of honor. But even Bulstrode gets a moment when readers are invited to empathize with him. Eliot narrates the scene where he must return home to his wife (who was completely ignorant and innocent of his misdeeds) with the understanding that she now knows about his moral failures. Other people have told her what her husband did, but he hasn't confessed to her, yet.

It was eight o'clock in the evening before the door opened and his wife entered. He dared not look up at her. He sat with his eyes bent down, and as she went towards him she thought he looked smaller—he seemed so withered and shrunken. A movement of new compassion and old tenderness went through her like a great wave, and putting one hand on his which rested on the arm of the chair, and the other on his shoulder, she said, solemnly but kindly—

"Look up, Nicholas."

He raised his eyes with a little start and looked at her half amazed for a moment: her pale face, her changed, mourning dress, the trembling about her mouth, all said, "I know;" and her hands and eyes rested gently on him. He burst out crying and they cried together, she sitting at his side. They could not yet speak to each other of the shame which she was bearing with him, or of the acts which had brought it down on them. His confession was silent, and her promise of faithfulness was silent.

(Eliot [1871] 2008: 707–8)

Bulstrode is not exculpated from his crimes. But he is allowed this narrative moment when readers are invited to witness his emotion and be moved by it. Readers are moved by seeing Bulstrode as erring creature, as a person whose life has been shattered by his misdeeds. And while readers may feel that his punishment is wholly appropriate, they get a glimpse of this private moment when his shame is embraced by someone who loves him. This shifts the tone from one of judgment to one of pity. In calling readers to both condemnation and pity rather than simply to condemnation, Eliot challenges contemporary readers who are sometimes inclined to exclude pity as an acceptable response to immoral behavior. Throughout her fiction, Eliot shows that mere judgment is too narrow. Including pity within one's emotional responses is, for Eliot, a move toward the "widening psychology" she calls for in her letter to Bray.

Eliot's Ethical Assumptions

Empathetic engagement with a flawed but repentant soul is an idea deeply resonant with Eliot's Victorian culture, still strongly inflected by Christianity. Although Eliot had ceased to practice Christianity when she was a young woman, her novels and their ethical outlook are nonetheless still colored by this idea of empathy toward a sinner in need of grace. If Eliot could not believe in grace from a divine being offering salvation, her novels offer the grace of empathetic engagement with fellow creatures.

In Eliot's last novel, *Daniel Deronda*, she offers the most explicit discussion of this moral framework. In *Daniel Deronda*, the character of Gwendolyn

Harleth goes through a process of gradual moral transformation as she interacts with the title character. At the outset, Gwendolyn is described as selfish, unable to imagine a perspective beyond her own: "Having always been the pet and pride of the household, waited on by mother, sister, governess, and maids, as if she had been a princess in exile, she naturally found it difficult to think her own pleasure less important than others made it" (Eliot [1876] 1995: 25). By the middle of the novel, however, after she has made a disastrous marriage with an even more self-centered man and experienced tremendous guilt over her passive participation in his drowning, she begins to examine her ethical assumptions. Jealous of Deronda's admiration for a morally unimpeachable woman, she says to him: "I have no sympathy with women who are always doing right. I don't believe in their great sufferings" (Eliot [1876] 1995: 438–9). Deronda agrees that the very righteous person does not inspire as much emotion as the flawed and repentant one:

> "It is true," said Deronda, "that the consciousness of having done wrong is something deeper, more bitter. I suppose we faulty creatures can never feel so much for the irreproachable as for those who are bruised in the struggle with their own faults. It is a very ancient story, that of the lost sheep, but it comes up afresh, every day."
>
> (Eliot [1876] 1995: 439)

Deronda references Jesus's parable of a shepherd who goes out to find one lost sheep and leaves ninety-nine alone to suggest that flawed people are inherently worthier of empathetic engagement than virtuous ones. Eliot's Victorian readers would have known well the text from Luke's Gospel, where Jesus concludes, "I say unto you, that likewise joy shall be in heaven over one sinner that repenteth, more than over ninety and nine just persons, which need no repentance" (Luke 15:7, King James Version). Gwendolyn questions Deronda on this point since he is, in fact, an admirer of the very virtuous Mirah Cohen, whom he will marry (to Gwendolyn's disappointment) by the end of the novel. Deronda concedes that good people are worthy of adoration, but clarifies that "those who would be comparatively uninteresting beforehand may become worthier of sympathy when they do something that awakens in them a keen remorse. Lives are enlarged in different ways. I daresay some would never get their eyes opened if it were not for a violent shock from the consequences of their own actions" (Eliot [1876] 1995: 439). Deronda describes here the process by which a flawed person suffers some terrible consequence of his actions and then becomes worthier of empathy. Gwendolyn's own story of gradual moral awakening doesn't actually fit well with Deronda's description, nor does Edward Casaubon's inner realization of his own inadequacy, known only by narrator and reader. But the invocation of the empathy engendered by the "lost sheep" is a perfect encapsulation of the story of Arthur Donnithorne, who is oblivious to his own flaws until he suffers the violent shock of confronting the fact that Hetty caused the death of their child.

Eliot's Sympathy in Light of Contemporary Perspectives on Empathy

The term "empathy," as mentioned above, didn't come into popular usage (after being coined within the discipline of psychology) until after the Second World War. Hannah Arendt's memorable diagnosis of Adolph Eichmann, the Nazi administrator, was that the decisive flaw in Eichmann's character was "the almost total inability ever to look at anything from the other fellow's point of view" (Arendt 1968: 47–8). Since the 1940s, it has become an unquestioned cultural assumption that understanding others' points of view, understanding what others are feeling, and trying to feel what others feel are essential to ethical behavior. Empathy is an unambiguously positive concept.

Empathy has, however, come under increasing scrutiny in the scholarly community, both by psychologists examining its complex manifestations and by scholars in the humanities questioning the assumption considering the feelings of others necessarily produces more virtuous behavior. The single word "empathy" actually has many different connotations, depending on context. Social psychologist C. Daniel Batson identifies eight different concepts associated with empathy in his essay, "These Things Called Empathy: Eight Related But Distinct Phenomena"—including one that sounds similar to what Arendt found missing in Eichmann: "imagining another's thoughts and feelings." There is an obvious analogy to this kind of empathy in the experience of reading literature: fiction clearly invites readers to imagine what another person, a character, is feeling. But, one might argue, there is a difference between imagining another person's feelings and actually feeling *for* a person. And the links between imagining what another might feel, feeling those emotions oneself, and responding to those emotions with virtuous and non-egotistical behavior, are coming under scrutiny from a number of fronts.

One critic is Paul Bloom, psychologist and author of *Against Empathy: The Case for Rational Compassion*. Bloom's title is provocative rather than descriptive. He's not actually against empathy, but distinguishes between two *kinds* of empathy, one he thinks does not promote ethical behavior and one he thinks does. Bloom labels the empathy of *feeling with and for* another person, "emotional empathy" (2016: 38) and claims that this is not particularly helpful for promoting virtuous behavior. He labels the empathy of *thinking about and trying to understand* someone else's perspective, "cognitive empathy" (Bloom 2016: 36). He argues that this second form of empathy actually prompts people to treat others well.

It seems evident why Bloom would argue that cognitive empathy is a good for promoting virtuous behavior. When people think about why others are behaving as they are, it gives them a greater capacity to act compassionately toward those others. And it might prompt them to act more in others' interest. Returning to Eliot's novels, one can see cognitive empathy in action. If readers understand Hetty as a complex person with multiple motivations, it helps them to feel less horrified and more compassionate about her choice to abandon a newborn infant in the woods. When readers understand that selfish characters like Arthur, Casaubon, and Gwendolyn are more than their actions, they might feel compassion for the plight of their "small, shivering" selves. Cognitive empathy, however, conflicts with a contemporary emphasis on calling-to-account. Understanding why a serial sexual harasser did not stop his behavior, and pitying him as a "small, shivering self" might seem a bridge too far.

While cognitive empathy seems to be, for the most part, a good thing, emotional empathy is more mixed, according to Bloom. He identifies a set of problems with the idea that emotional empathy leads to good behavior. First, it's not true that people need to feel what others are feeling in order to behave well. People do many good things independently of emotional empathy. One does not need to feel what others are feeling in order to participate in virtuous behaviors like picking up litter on the street, citing one's sources, or slamming on the brakes to avoid hitting someone in the road.

Moreover, Bloom points out, people sometimes need a *lack* of feeling to prompt them to do the right thing. One might need to resist the plea of one's student for an extension on a paper—for the student's own good. Or a parent often needs to say no to the pleas of children who want to stay up late or eat more candy or have more screen time. Emotional empathy involves feeling what the child is feeling. But reason tells parents that it would be better for the child to say no. Parents must bear their children's anguish at turning off Netflix or enforcing a bedtime. Too much emotional empathy, as Bloom points out, might also cause a person to feel paralyzed by emotion and stop acting charitably. One can feel so strongly that one withdraws from action. Constantly participating in the pain of others might make one less able to act with compassion because one is overwhelmed. Emotional empathy, in Bloom's analysis, is unnecessary for virtuous behavior and, in some circumstances, it may do more harm than good.

But these features of emotional empathy are not the only problems with the human capacity to feel with and for others. Empathy is also associated with something that Fritz Breithaupt labels "side-taking." In his book *The Dark Sides of Empathy*, Breithaupt identifies a scenario in which "an observer is witness to two parties in conflict and decides to support one" (2017: 99). The witness takes one side in the conflict, begins to identify with the perspective of that side, imagines the situation from that side's perspective, feels the situation from that side's perspective, and thus creates a positive feedback loop. Breithaupt describes the dynamic:

When an observer of a conflict between A and B takes the side of A (be it quickly and intuitively or carefully and deliberately), they will tend to see the situation of the conflict from A's perspective. From this point of view, B appears to be somehow unappealing, wrong, or even hostile since they oppose the chosen side A. B. might be seen as an aggressor who is harming A and the more that the perspective shared by the observer and A distinguishes between the two sides (A and B), the more probably it comes that the observer will also share the pain and feelings of A. In short: the observer experiences the emotional situation of A and develops empathy for A but apathy or antipathy toward B.

(2017: 101)

This feedback loop that increases and hardens one's support for one party in a conflict can lead, as Breithaupt points out, to surprising results. He analyzes this effect as it played out in the political campaign and presidency of Donald Trump, whom Breithaupt labels a "master of empathy" (2017: 103). According to Breithaupt, Trump's depiction of himself as a victim was critical in unifying his supporters behind him: "By presenting himself as a victim, he justifies any outrage, any action: threats about censoring the press, encouraging attacks on demonstrators at his rallies, and the like" and his strong emotional response of anger against his opponents actually works to appeal to and solidify the support of those whose empathy he has gained: "For those who have taken his side, the ugly face of his anger can be directly linked to his being victimized, thus confirming their initial side-taking" (2017: 106). This is an extreme case of how empathy can help solidify support for ideas and actions that one might find, abstractly, objectionable. But a more subtle form of side-taking can happen even in the case of a sympathetic victim.

Taking *Adam Bede* as an example, one can think of the reader as the witness to two parties in conflict: Hetty and Arthur. If a reader takes the side of Hetty and interprets the novel as the story of a vulnerable woman being sexually exploited by a powerful man, then he will join the "side" of sexually exploited women. Using the lens of that "side," he might conclude that men like Arthur deserve whatever they get. But if a reader takes the side of Arthur and interprets this as a story of a man who suffers terribly from the consequences of his poor judgment, then he will join the "side" of men whose careers are ruined by the taint of past mistakes. He may see Hetty as a vain and silly young girl who did a terrible thing in abandoning her baby in the woods instead of seeking the help of the kind people who reached out to assist her. This reader might see Arthur as suffering excessively despite his admission of guilt and significant actions to help Hetty escape the death penalty.

Eliot, however, actively deploys her narrative voice to discourage this kind of "side-taking." Readers are discouraged from siding with either Hetty or Arthur. In the epilogue, the narrator gives a brief glimpse of the fate of each of them. Arthur has just returned home for convalescence after a seven-year absence and, we learn, Hetty has recently died before she could return from her sentence as a transported criminal. Adam's brother, Seth, says: "Adam was greatly moved this morning at the thought of the change he should see in the poor young man, from the sickness he has undergone, as well as the years which have changed us all. And the death of the poor wanderer, when she was coming back to us, has been sorrow upon sorrow" (Eliot [1859] 2008: 588). Hetty is pitiable because although she escapes execution by hanging, she dies before she is able to return to England. Arthur is pitiable as an exile from his home, returning home weakened, having lost his youthful joy. Neither gets the happy ending of Adam, who marries a woman far more suited to make him happy than Hetty was; but they get presented as the appropriate subjects for the reader's emotional empathy.

Empathetic side-taking has been one of the defining features of the #metoo movement; it also bolsters arguments in support of the study of literature. In his essay "Literature and Empathy," Michael Fischer surveys various versions of the "empathy defense" of the study of literature in support of his conclusion that empathy is a "means of releasing the good in each of us" (2017: 434). Fischer discusses a series of possible prompts for empathy as he surveys what contemporary writers have said in defense of empathy; his examples form an interesting sample: an undocumented immigrant brought to the United States as a very young child (449), female adolescents who engage in cutting (2017: 451), people who didn't receive social benefits under President Ronald Reagan's presidency (2017: 452–3), Michael Brown, a Black man killed by a police officer in Ferguson, Missouri (2017: 454), and Elizabeth Eckford, a Black woman who attempted to attend a Little Rock, Arkansas high school in 1957 (2017: 459). The unstated assumption throughout Fischer's essay is that these are the people whose side one should take. In each case there is an assumed and sometimes explicitly named antagonist: those who set immigration policy, those who create stressful conditions for female adolescents, Ronald Reagan, the police officer who shot Michael Brown, and the people who shouted at Elizabeth Eckford. Although Fischer names the problem of the "fracturing of American social and political life into discrete, antagonistic, noncommunicating camps" (2017: 444), his essay amplifies this antagonism through his discussion of examples. Fischer argues that "the internet and unprecedented economic inequality" (2017: 444) are two factors that contribute to this problem of polarization. Fritz Breithaupt, Paul Bloom, and George Eliot might add that it is the very act of concentrating emotional empathy on sympathetic victims that might be contributing to the polarization. Without the feat of cognitive empathy that sees these antagonists as "struggling, erring creatures," those who only feel the pain of others may be left in hopeless rage.

Since the mid-nineteenth century, fiction has been used to prompt readers to understand and to feel empathy for the suffering. Elizabeth Gaskell's *Mary Barton* raised awareness of industrial working conditions in the 1840s; Charles Dickens's novels contain graphic depictions of poverty and instruct his readers how to feel about poor orphans like Oliver Twist or about hypocritical Christian do-gooders like Mrs. Jellyby. Harriet Beecher Stowe's *Uncle Tom's Cabin* is a didactic novel aimed at getting white people to empathetically engage with the plight of the enslaved and join the abolition movement. Didacticism in fiction is nothing new and empathy is its primary tool. Thus, when Eliot started writing fiction in the late 1850s, her readers were very familiar with novels that clearly tell them whom to feel for and whom to condemn. In Chapter 17 of *Adam Bede*, she imagines the voice of a reader telling her to write that kind of novel:

> Let your most faulty characters always be on the wrong side, and your virtuous ones on the right. Then we shall see at a glance whom we are to condemn and whom we are to approve. Then we shall be able to admire, without the slightest disturbance of our prepossessions: we shall hate and despise with that true ruminant relish which belongs to undoubting confidence.
>
> (Eliot [1859] 2008: 194)

But Eliot rejects this advice and tells her imaginary critic that this kind of novel does not prepare one for the moral complexities of life. Didactic novels don't prepare you to know what to do "with your neighbour, Mrs. Green, who was really kind to you in your last illness, but has said several ill-natured things about you since your convalescence" (Eliot [1859] 2008:194). Eliot believes her novels prepare readers for the moral complexity of warm-hearted but Gossipy neighbors while her fiction also nudges them toward more generous interactions with unlovely people: "In this world there are so many of these common coarse people, who have no picturesque sentimental wretchedness! It is so needful we should remember their existence, else we may happen to leave them quite out of our religion and philosophy, and frame lofty theories which only fit a world of extremes" (Eliot [1859] 2008: 196). Readers should be reminded of the existence of the people who are not sympathetic, whose wretchedness is not picturesque. Eliot uses her first-person narrative voice to make this point:

> There are few prophets in the world; few sublimely beautiful women; few heroes. I can't afford to give all my love and reverence to such rarities; I want a great deal of those feelings for my everyday fellow-men, especially for the few in the foreground of the great multitude, whose faces I know, whose hands I touch, for whom I have to make way with kindly courtesy … It is more needful that I should have a fibre of sympathy connecting me with that vulgar citizen who weighs out my sugar in a vilely-assorted cravat and waistcoat, than with the handsomest rascal in red scarf and green feathers.
>
> (Eliot [1859] 2008: 197)

In Chapter 17, Eliot tends toward examples of people who may seem aesthetically repulsive—common coarse people, the vulgar man in the mismatched clothing who serves her in a store. But if we look at her fiction as a whole, we see that she intends us to extend empathy beyond those who seem aesthetically repulsive. She asks us to extend empathy too to those who are morally repulsive.

Throughout her fiction and in her private writings, Eliot calls for an ethic of empathy with those who are struggling. And her writings define those who are struggling and thus deserving of empathy, not by their suffering but by their guilt. She asks Bray to think well of Spencer, who had behaved cruelly and selfishly toward her. And she asks her readers to sympathize with Arthur Donnithorne, the sexual predator, Edward Casaubon, the abusive spouse, Nicholas Bulstrode, the greedy and hypocritical banker, and other characters who are merely as selfish and needy as Gwendolyn Harleth. One might object that these are the very people to whom society too readily grants a generous measure of sympathy. Eliot would not disagree with this claim. As shown by her analysis of the factors that lead her society to think the best of men like Arthur Donnithorne, she is perfectly aware that, on the whole, society is often forgiving of sexual predators, abusive spouses, and greedy bankers. Her project is not to balance the scales of justice by inviting empathy with those to whom empathy is rarely granted. Rather, she hopes to expand our empathetic horizons by depicting these characters as complexly motivated beings who should be judged by the standard that "each of us is more than the worst thing we've ever done" (Stevenson 2015: 17–18). It is this empathy with the "lost sheep" that is characteristic of Eliot's ethic and that grounds her claim that: "If the ethics of art do not admit the truthful presentation of a character essentially noble but liable to great error—error that is anguish to its own nobleness—then, it seems to me, the ethics of art are too narrow, and must be widened to correspond with a widening psychology" (Haight 1954: 318). In the early twenty-first century, psychology has indeed widened to offer a more complex and nuanced understanding of the mechanism of empathy. Empathy can invite readers into both emotional engagement with and cognitive awareness of the feelings of others. Eliot's challenge is as relevant to this moment as to hers: that the ethics of our art widen to match the wideness of our psychology.

Notes

1 I will use the term "empathy" for this psychological phenomenon except when directly quoting Eliot.

2 I am using the label "#metoo movement" as a signifier for a broad cultural phenomenon of women publicly sharing their experiences of sexual harassment and abuse. An analysis of the #metoo movement and its significance and the growing body of scholarly discussion around it is beyond the scope of this essay.

References

Arendt, H. (1968), *Eichmann in Jerusalem: A Report on the Banality of Evil*, New York: Viking.

Batson, D. (2009), "These Things Called Empathy: Eight Related but Distinct Phenomena," in J. Decety and W. Ickes (eds), *The Social Neuroscience of Empathy*, 3–15. Cambridge, MA: MIT Press.

Bloom, P. (2016), *Against Empathy: The Case for Rational Compassion*, New York: HarperCollins.

The Bible. Authorized King James Version.

Briethaupt, F. (2017), *The Dark Sides of Empathy*, trans. A. Hamilton, Ithaca: Cornell University Press.

Eliot, G. ([1859] 2008), *Adam Bede*, New York: Penguin.

Eliot, G. ([1871] 2008), *Middlemarch*, New York: Oxford University Press.

Eliot, G. ([1876] 1995), *Daniel Deronda*, New York: Penguin.

Fischer, M. (2017), "Literature and Empathy," *Philosophy and Literature*, 41 (41), 431–64.

Haight, G. (1954), *The George Eliot Letters*, vol. 3, New Haven: Yale University Press.

Haight, G. (1968), *George Eliot: A Biography*, Oxford: Oxford University Press.

Karl, F. (1995), *George Eliot: Voice of a Century*, New York: W. W. Norton Publishers.

Keen, S. (2007), *Empathy and the Novel*, New York: Oxford University Press.

Mead, R. (2014), *My Life in Middlemarch*, New York: Penguin-Crown.

Stevenson, B. (2015), *Just Mercy: A Story of Justice and Redemption*, New York: Penguin Random House-Spiegel & Grau.

2

Putting Empathy to Work: Narrative and the Empathetic Entrepreneur

Emily Johansen

In a review of Hanya Yanagihara's 2015 novel *A Little Life*, Jane Sutton describes it as an "eyes-wide-open, unwavering record of molesting [that] rewards the reader by gift-wrapping the squalor into the American Dream" (2016: 93). Similarly, in a review in *The Guardian*, Alex Preston describes the book as "*Entourage* directed by Bergman … it's a devastating read that will leave your heart, like the Grinch's, a few sizes larger" (2015). Despite the appearance of that last phrase as a blurb on the paperback edition of the novel, neither is exactly a positive review (Sutton's review is particularly arch in its critique of the novel). But both highlight an element of the novel that I want to interrogate in this chapter: the way trauma is increasingly assumed to be usable as a way of producing wealth through its transformation into empathy-generating narratives.

A Little Life is the story of four men (Malcolm, J. B., Willem, and Jude) who meet as roommates at a fictional Ivy League university. The book has drawn attention for its focus on the relationships between the four friends, rather than on their respective romantic lives (though Willem and Jude, eventually, become romantically involved). In her review of the novel in *The Financial Times*, Maria Crawford calls it "a hymn to serious, lifelong friendship" (2015). Willem, in reflecting on the dynamic between the four men, ponders whether "couplehood [was] truly the only appropriate option? ... Why wasn't friendship as good as a relationship? Why wasn't it even better? [Friendship was] the mutual dedication to a union that could never be codified" (Yanagihara 2015: 256–7). Nonetheless, as the novel progresses, it focuses increasingly on Jude and Willem, and particularly on the baroque trauma of the first fifteen years of Jude's life and its reverberating impact. While the book takes place over, roughly, forty to fifty years, it's all set in a relentlessly present moment, pre-2008 and where 9/11 appears not to have happened (we might imagine it, then, as kind of alternative timeline to the present). It takes place almost exclusively in New York, with other places only entering the narrative briefly as work or leisure trips. And, while only Malcom is born into money, all four men are, by middle age, wealthy and professionally accomplished, principally in "creative" fields (they are architects, artists, actors, and lawyers, respectively). Yet while both Sutton and Preston want to suggest that the wealth of the characters serves to mitigate or ameliorate their various traumas (in a familiar narrative of trauma as the "price" of success), I want to explore the way that the novel is doing something more complicated with the link between wealth and trauma.

I argue that *A Little Life* illustrates that empathy is a narrative technique that produces an economic education, rather than a moral one. Empathy, *A Little Life* suggests, is claimed, in practice, if not quite in explicit rhetoric, to operate as a discursive form to master in order to accumulate capital—both financial and social—rather than a mode of ethical engagement with others. Yet, at the same time, what the novel illustrates through its narratives of extreme trauma, is how empathy discourse actually acts to obscure the violence of this process—even providing an alibi for this violence. Jude's friends want him to transform his violently traumatic past into a narrative that can generate empathy, which will, subsequently, produce a variety of social rewards, financial and otherwise—transforming his suffering and, most importantly, its disclosure into a site of primitive accumulation. At the same time, Jude's resistance to this demand to narrate himself as the object of empathy is shown to be what allows him to accumulate far greater amounts of capital than the rest of his (still wealthy) friends. It is his refusal, in fact, to make his trauma into a palatable narrative—or a narrative at all—and follow the recuperative path prescribed by his friends and caretakers that allows him to be far more predatorially accumulative than any of his other friends. I want to suggest, then, that the novel makes legible the violence that gets hidden behind compensatory visions of empathy. Jude's friends perpetuate liberal fantasies in their desire to imagine accumulation as the reward for the healthy individual; his narrative, instead, makes clear that empathy narratives are a glossy facade for the real work of neoliberalism: constant accumulation of both property and capital.

In Adam Smith's classic formulation, sympathy[1] is supposed to act as a control on *laissez faire* economics' propensity to personal accumulation at the expense of communal good. *A Theory of Moral Sentiments* begins by asserting that "how selfish soever man may be supposed there are evidently some principles in his nature, which interest him in the fortune of others, and render their happiness necessary to him, though he derives nothing from it except the pleasure of seeing it" ([1759] 2002: 3). For Smith, then, our sympathy with others is often at odds with our own benefit—though this sympathy is outside of autonomic control: we feel sympathy involuntarily (illustrating the way that Smithian "sympathy" operates like contemporary "empathy"). Yet, if our sympathies for others exist outside of the market for Smith and subsequent thinkers, they have become yet another arena for market logic under the post-war rise of neoliberalism.[2] While Smith's and the traditional model of sympathy-as-narrative-scene[3] was about the sympathizing subject viewing the suffering other, what *A Little Life* demonstrates is sympathy-as-self-presentation where the subject situates themselves as the suffering other in order to garner cultural capital. Rather than demonstrating and elaborating narrative techniques for generating empathy (and, subsequently, if idealistically, mitigating the extremes of capital) *in* others, the novel demonstrates the way narrative is used for generating empathy *from* others (and, subsequently, capital).

The shifted and shifting function of empathy under neoliberalism and its relationship to the operation of financialization challenge how narrative empathy might be conceptualized as a straightforward good. I follow here from Rachel Greenwald Smith's claim that what distinguishes the neoliberal novel from the liberal version is that in the former, "the individual's economic autonomy is not seen as threatened by affective ties [but that] these ties are invested with an economic imperative" (2015: 40). Greenwald Smith argues that the neoliberal novel posits "attachments to others ... as themselves constitutive of the individual's full realization" (2015: 41), rather than a detailed inner emotional life. The empathetic and affective connections between subjects, then, shape readerly expectation; as she suggests, "for a novel to follow through on its promises ... it has to offer means for this connection: through identification, a sense of alliance, and emotional enrichment" (2015: 42). Greenwald Smith proposes, then, that the neoliberal novel continues to rely on the scene of sympathy that Adam Smith explicates in *A Theory of Moral Sentiments*, though the scene has shifted away from a site of voyeuristic pleasure and individual moral development to one where the individual learns to generate affective ties with others in hopes of generating economic return. The neoliberal novel, in Greenwald Smith's schema, views the moral education of the liberal novel as a "product of exchange" (2015: 42) where "literary investment is understood as most appropriately met with emotional return, based not on the revelation of secret interiors but on the advancement of the reader's self ... readers expect reading to be productive of a specific kind of affective value" (2015: 42). In this sense, *A Little Life* is just one of many examples of "trauma porn" literature where readers can expect to feel "fucking hatefully sad," as Roxane Gay's Goodreads review of the novel holds, or, as Preston's review notes, find the novel "unremitting and ... ghastly, and [as a result, he] had to put the book down several times when [he was] reading it" (2015), yet derive a kind of pleasure from this—both that of a kind of voyeurism but also that of emotional enrichment: as Preston goes on to claim, readers' "hearts grow a few sizes larger" (2015).

Preston and Gay, then, exemplify how the claims made for Yanagihara's novel gesture to its operation as a neoliberal novel where the affective value— the experience of extreme sadness—becomes a site for the development and growth of the self. What they imagine, then, is a commitment to narrative as a site of emotional education that will produce some nebulously defined social good; these reviews (and many others), then, align with a typical assumption about the empathy work done by literary fiction. Like Lauren Berlant notes of compassion, this neoliberal model of narrative empathy implies a "social relation between spectators and sufferers, with the emphasis on the spectator's experience of feeling compassion and its subsequent relation to material practice" and makes "a claim on the spectator to become an ameliorative actor" (2004: 1). The focus in this model of compassion is on the spectator as agential subject, rather than the sufferer. The sufferer exists to suffer and catalyze the spectator's moral development; empathy's projective impulse instrumentalizes the sufferer for the spectator's growth—a process, as Greenwald Smith illustrates, that facilitates the spectator's transformation into a more mature financial actor.

Accounts of empathy focus, almost exclusively, on the spectator who can only *imagine* themselves in a similarly traumatized state. As many critics have observed, empathy is, consequently, a deeply voyeuristic and narcissistic process where the empathizing self projects itself onto and into the suffering body. Empathy, then, for the spectator is a precursive site to accumulation: as I will explain below, empathy becomes a skill that the entrepreneur must develop in order to produce more value for their brand.[4] But is it only the spectator who can use empathy to generate sites of accumulation? *A Little Life*, in its focus on Jude and his interactions with both friends and caregivers, attends to this question of the sufferer as a potentially active agent in the transformation of empathy into entrepreneurial skill. Yet the novel also calls into question the transformation of the spectator that is at the center of discussions of empathetic narrative—both the liberal and the neoliberal versions. The very sublimity of Jude's suffering and its narrative unfolding suggests to readers that "feeling with" Jude is never truly a possibility: just when you think that you "feel with" Jude, new trauma is revealed. Yanagihara consistently forecloses the possibility of full identification; moreover, this readerly desire to understand Jude as an empathizable subject—one whose sadness inspires our sadness—if only he fully confesses all of his trauma aligns readers not, in fact, with Jude but with Jude's friends and caregivers, all of whom want desperately to empathize with Jude and "fix" him, proving the seriousness of their care.[5] Put differently, *A Little Life* suggests the cravenness of this readerly position and view of friendship as a site for entrepreneurial self-development.

I begin by looking at a recurring trope throughout the novel: the concern articulated by Jude's friends and caregivers that they aren't asking the "right" questions that will lead him to disclose the specifics of his experiences, understood by them as necessary for both proper empathy and for "fixing" the effects of trauma. I read this desire to make a coherent narrative of trauma through the work of entrepreneurship studies and its work on the empathetic entrepreneur. This scholarship on empathy as a business skill elucidates the utilitarian operation of self-disclosure that informs Jude's friends' and caregivers' demands of him. These demands, while using the rhetoric of health and care, replicate an entrepreneurial demand to make trauma useful, through narrating the self as one with whom others can empathize. I move on to consider Jude's own resistance to this recuperative notion of care, asserting both his right to his own ongoing vulnerability and to declare himself, in his words, as "normal." Finally, it is Jude's destructive rage in the closing pages of the novel that most actively resists a narrative of necessary personal development and growth and comes close to articulating another path forward for engaging with the traumas of capital and history.

Empathy as Entrepreneurial Skill

A large and growing area of research interest in entrepreneurship studies (a field often based in management and business schools) and organizational psychology is on the relationship between empathy, the entrepreneur, and organizational cultures. Barring minor differences in argument, the claim across much of this work is that an empathetic entrepreneur is more likely to be successful than one who downplays emotional linkages with staff and customers in favor of the untrammeled pursuit of profits.[6] Rania Labaki observes, for instance, about the impetus for this turn to empathy, that "emotions are central to organizational behavior and decision-making" (2013: 265), while Ronald H. Humphrey notes that "there is a growing body of research that suggests that empathy is important to leadership, and it is reasonable to extend this research to include entrepreneurship" (2013: 288). Humphrey goes on to acknowledge that "emotional intelligence has been found to be important to job performance, leadership, and emotional and physical health" and that "cognitive intelligence, emotional intelligence/ competencies, and conscientiousness were the three best predictors of job performance" (2013: 289–90). Similarly, Svetlana Holt et al. note that "a number of conscience-driven leadership approaches have also been introduced in recent years and are characterized by descriptors such as authentic, awakened, benevolent, emotionally-intelligent, moralized, responsible, spiritual—all intended to guide our workforces toward more consciously-attuned performance" (2017: 4)—all descriptors that echo those associated with empathy. The field thus emphasizes an essentially instrumentalized empathy: it is a job and leadership skill, akin to creativity and effective communication. The overlap, then, with understanding entrepreneurship as a creative endeavor, à la Richard Florida, rather than a principally economic one, is clear. Indeed, Florida himself lists "a developed sense of empathy," alongside "the capacity to bring the right people together on a project, persuasion, social perceptiveness [and] the ability to help develop other people [indeed, almost all of these skills are dependent on forms of empathy]" as the "leadership skills that are needed to innovate, mobilize resources, build effective organizations, and launch new firms ... that lead to the very highest paying jobs, and the most robust economies" (2012: 225). The transformation of empathy into skill—and one central to the functioning of the global economy—and away from "moral sentiment," to use Adam Smith's characterization of sympathy, highlights an important development in how empathy is understood and, perhaps more significantly, what it is expected to do. If empathy is typically thought to inspire *moral* action (a claim whose veracity Suzanne Keen, Fritz Breithaupt, and other cognitive scholars challenge), the discourse on the empathetic entrepreneur illustrates that it is now often assumed to produce *financial* action. While this aligns with many similar transformations of the moral or the ethical into the financial under neoliberalism, it is important to note that empathy discourse remains persistently central to much of the popular discourse on both personal trauma and broader questions of social justice, suggesting a lingering and insistent belief that empathizing with those who are not ourselves produces meaningful social change.

What this would all seem to suggest is that empathy can be made profitable, but, more generally, materially useful: one empathizes with one's customers and this provides "an advantage in developing new products and services that most customers want and will buy" (Humphrey 2013: 290). The other side of this, then, is also the expectation that customer emotions are legible and can be transformed into a product or service. In other words, the entrepreneur who can empathize with their customers or staff must also have customers or staff who understand their emotional needs as addressable through specific products or services. A customer who feels too much, not enough, or in a way that resists remediation through financial means is an impossible customer—and, ultimately, probably not a customer at all and thus unnecessary to account for in this interaction. Yet, it is those very people who have felt the most difficult or least generalizable emotions who are frequently characterized as being most in need of empathy.[7] This tension, then, is a reminder that narrative remains constitutively central to the operation of empathy. The entrepreneur constructs a narrative around customer or staff emotional needs that culminates in a transaction; the customer or staff member must present their emotional needs in a narrative form that is recognizable to the entrepreneur, who can then riff off of it in a creative and financial manner. All of this together points to a model in which an emotional need leads to its empathetic recognition, which is followed by a solution to the initial emotional need, however temporarily (because, of course, a thorough fix doesn't lead to future purchases).

Yet while the scholarship on the empathetic entrepreneur, cited above, imagines these encounters as public ones between entrepreneur and customer(s) or entrepreneur and staff member(s), this model of transactional and productive empathy has not remained in commercial arenas but increasingly shapes how we understand our empathetic encounters in many public contexts. One simple example of this is the demand on the part of social media and social justice personalities for financial remuneration (often framed as a "redistribution of wealth") for the emotional labor they perform.[8] This is not to argue that these people (who are predominantly women and nonbinary people of color) shouldn't be compensated for the work that they do. Nor is it to suggest that what they do isn't work. However, it illustrates the prominence of this link between empathy and financial compensation. Again, a neoliberal extension of market criteria for all decisions is replicated, even in encounters that ostensibly seek to disrupt the neoliberal status quo.

In *A Little Life*, Yanagihara interrogates this form of transactional empathy. It can be difficult to identify the operation of this form of empathy when outside of the visible commercial encounter, since doing so seems to call into question some of the feelings most central to how the liberal subject understands their very humanity: their compassion and sympathy.[9] Indeed, Jude's seeming failure to provide a clear or reliable answer to the question central to the empathetic encounter—"how are you feeling?"— and the impossibility of forming a question that will entice him to reveal the necessary information for both full empathetic connection and a subsequent resolution of trauma are central problems of the text. But more than Jude's apparent inability to resolve his own trauma "satisfactorily" (which I will return to in subsequent sections of this chapter), the novel reveals the demand that trauma be narrated in a particular form in order for it to become useful.

Throughout the novel, Jude's friends and principal caregivers express an anxiety that they are not asking the right questions about either his past or his current health to unlock the "problem of Jude." For instance, early in the novel, Willem, Jude's roommate at the time, is asked by Andy, his doctor, whether Jude seems "listless, out of sorts." Willem replies that "'He's seemed fine' ... although the truth was he didn't know. *Had* Jude been eating? *Had* he been sleeping? Should he have noticed? Should he have been paying more attention? 'I mean, he's seemed the same as he always is'" (2015: 80; emphasis in original). And while this question is generally directed inward among the group of friends, Harold, Jude's adopted father, and Andy, it is also occasionally asked of Jude. Andy, after threatening to commit Jude after a particularly intense period of self-harm, asks "have you ever even talked to anyone about what happened when you were a kid … There's something incredibly arrogant about your stubbornness … your utter refusal to listen to anyone about anything that concerns your health or well-being is either a pathological case of self-destructiveness or it's a huge fuck-you to the rest of us" (2015: 157). Andy's frustration with Jude, here expressed as an almost violent concern, highlights the pressure for Jude to both get better in recognizable ways and to articulate his feelings as the pathway to health. Jude's refusal or inability to narrate his past to his doctor and his friends is taken, here by Andy, as a willful refusal of the empathetic dyad in which one half suffers and the other half observes and feels with the first. At the same time, Jude is characterized as a "bad listener," aligning him with the empathetic voyeur, rather than the subject fully in need of empathy. What this would seem to suggest is the expectation that the subject who becomes the object of empathy must be responsive to the person trying to empathize. In other words, they must tailor their narrative and performance to their audience, both to get them to listen and to ensure the correct empathetic response. What Andy inadvertently reveals here is the transactional quality of empathy, but also the sense that there is a "proper" genre in which to express one's experiences and feelings in order to generate empathy, one which ensures the transformation of those experiences and feelings into something usable. And Jude's refusal of this proper form of narration is pathological, selfish, or both. As Andy makes clear, then, that despite its appearances to the contrary, empathy is about the empathizer, not the objectified subject of empathy. In other words, Andy raises the specter of self-interest in his, Willem's, and the other's desire for Jude to make his trauma readily understandable for them; legible empathy is necessary for the ease of the empathizer, not for the person suffering.

Yet, at the same time, Andy's frustration with Jude is shared by the reader, who also doesn't know much about Jude's past yet, and may be finding a similar frustration in their reading experience: why won't Yanagihara just provide an exposition dump that fills in Jude's backstory right at the beginning so we know what we're working with? Andy's frustration is a readerly frustration with a withholding author. But it is also a consumer's frustration with a product that isn't working in the way that one expects. One can easily imagine a reader having a similar response to Andy about the novel's coyness, throwing the book across the room, and then leaving a negative review of the book on Amazon. But, perhaps, this is a moment—for both Andy and the reader—where we might recognize the generic operation of empathy; akin to our frustration in reading a book that we expect to be funny and finding it to be tragic, Andy is prepared to empathize with Jude but needs the disclosure of suffering to align with established genre conventions. This is at odds, then, with so much of how we understand empathy. Empathy, as it is typically understood, operates as an involuntary or autonomic process, one where we feel with someone else automatically. With no conscious control over our empathizing, one either feels it or one doesn't; how then does one learn an autonomic process? Our understandings of empathy, then, often deliberately preclude careful examination or awareness about the conventions that we expect as spectators in order to be able to empathize.

As *A Little Life* makes clear, the empathetic spectator needs the sufferer's pain to be communicated—verbally or otherwise—in a legible way *to the spectator* in order to produce empathy. The spectator's response, then, is understood as autonomic, but the sufferer needs to be aware, to some degree, of the conventions surrounding communicating pain. Andy's aggressive critique of Jude's inability or refusal to articulate his pain, then, illustrates a gap in the communicative process—which, more importantly, means that Andy can't find a way to "cure" Jude's ill-health, undermining *both* Andy's and Jude's entrepreneurial potential in this moment. Andy's rage at Jude's refusal or inability to disclose his suffering inadvertently reveals Andy's ableist desire to "fix" Jude—something which is repeatedly shown to be something that Jude believes is impossible and, thus, a distraction from the relationships he has with Andy and his other friends/caregivers. None of them can transform Jude's past into something usable so long as Jude is unable or unwilling to narrate it. And, as Andy's claim that this makes Jude pathologically self-destructive suggests, a failure to turn one's past trauma into something usable is both unhealthy and outside the entrepreneurial economy; in fact, he effectively renders these terms synonymous. This concern that past trauma be articulated, this demand for making it knowable, empathetically shareable, and therefore something fixable, culminates when Willem, at that point Jude's romantic partner, demands to share and take part in his rituals of self-harm. After a violent and angry explosion of shared cutting of themselves, Willem, now finally having "felt," quite literally, some of Jude's pain, observes "this really hurts ... how can you stand this?" to which Jude replies "you get used to it" (2015: 558). Because, of course, while his cutting rituals are painful and dangerous, they are nowhere near the most substantial pain Jude experiences, both in the present or in his past.

Willem and Andy want Jude to share his pain so that they can empathize with him, fix him, and, then, move past that pain into an accumulative future. Yet, as they and others consistently reveal, they cannot really share even the tip of Jude's traumatic iceberg. So far, so familiar, in terms of trauma theory. But part of the problem, as the novel sees it, is not that trauma can't be shared, but that what Willem and Andy want to do is transform it into something usable and catalyzing, something that follows the pathways of entrepreneurialism. They seek to give Jude's trauma use-value as a way of transforming his narrative of success into a familiar one of triumph over the past. At the same time, while the novel acknowledges that Jude's inability to articulate the violence he was subjected to and his near-constant chronic pain probably isn't a "healthy" decision, it is also a fundamentally understandable one. Moreover, at the end of the novel when he dies by suicide, the instigating trauma isn't the baroquely un-shareable ones of his childhood but Willem's early death in a car accident: something with which many people are all too familiar (i.e. the trauma with which readers can most readily empathize). I will return to the end of the novel in subsequent sections, but, for the moment, it highlights the novel's refusal of trauma as either something to overcome or as something inherently debilitating (after all, Jude is able to be quite successful by most metrics). Willem and Andy are stuck in a recuperative and therapeutic narrative mode that is, ultimately, dependent upon an understanding of empathy as both transactional and entrepreneurial—and which Jude (and *A Little Life*) refuses. In fact, Jude maintains that his sense of his own narrative works in reverse of what Willem and Andy want:

> why [does he] let the first fifteen years of his life so dictate the past twenty-eight. He has been lucky beyond measure; he has an adulthood that people dream about: Why, then, does he insist on revisiting and replaying events that happened so long ago? Why can he not simply take pleasure in his present? Why must he so honor his past? Why does it become more vivid, not less, the further he moves from it?
>
> (2015: 522–3)

They want a narrative that moves forward, toward success, and away from trauma; Jude suggests that this isn't how it works, at least for him. He refuses, then, a vision of trauma healed by an empathetic connection structured around a narrative that culminates, teleologically, in financial success; he insists, instead, on refusing the recuperative and exceptionalizing empathetic mode that Willem and Andy want to enforce.

Empathy and Competing Versions of Liberal Success

Indeed, Jude continually asserts that his past doesn't fit the narrative it is assigned by those who learn it, however obliquely. For instance, when his adoptive father, Harold, offers to give Jude money so that he can continue to work in the public defender's office, rather than go into private litigation, Jude notes that he found himself both frustrated and fascinated by Harold's lack of imagination: in Harold's mind, people had parents who were proud of them, and saved money only for apartments and vacations, and asked for things when they wanted them; he seemed curiously unaware of a universe in which those things might not be givens, in which not everyone shared the same past and future.

(2015: 274)

Harold and Jude hold competing liberal fantasies here: on one hand, the philanthropic benefactor who swoops in to save the deserving poor from hardship and, on the other hand, the self-sufficient individual who pulls themselves up by their bootstraps from destitution to wealth. Indeed, Harold and Jude, while both drawing on tropes of liberalism, are working from the point of view of different contemporary liberal epistemes. Harold's fantasy is that of the Keynesian welfare state, where the benevolent state curbs the excess of capitalist inequalities, while Jude's is that of neoliberal freedom through constant accumulation. Moreover, Jude's need to accumulate is framed as a response to disintegration of the welfare state of Harold's fantasies: Jude wonders, in the face of Harold's "inability or unwillingness to be cynical," "how he could tell [him] that he dreamed not of marriage, or children, but that he would someday have enough money to pay someone to take care of him if he needed it, someone who would be kind to him and allow him privacy and dignity" (2015: 275)? When Jude tells Harold that he needs to accumulate money (referring to his fears about his declining health), Harold cannot begin to understand a life outside of the bounds of the middle-class comforts with which he is familiar: he asks, first, if Jude is in "any kind of trouble" and, when assured that this is not the case, notes that "that's a relief. But Jude, what could you possibly need so much money for, besides an apartment, which Julia and I will help you buy" (2015: 274). For Harold, money exists only to preserve and replicate the liberal family; Jude recognizes that, under financialization, the only security that can be found is through accumulation.[10] Harold, Willem, Andy, and the others operate as though they live in a society governed by the mid-century social contract, while Jude is a child of the 1980s and 1990s.

Both fantasies are equally fantastic, though, as both seek to paper over the true cause of what they seek to correct—and which they are incapable of directly naming: the inequality that is an inherent component of capitalism.[11] Yet, nonetheless, one of these fantasies is more dependent upon empathetic connection. After all, Harold wants to help Jude financially because Jude is his adoptive son (and the stand-in for his own child who died young); he's not making this offer to undeserving strangers. If compassionate philanthropy is often one of the sites where empathy gets put to work, with the non-profit industrial-complex relying heavily on generating empathetic responses in order to garner donations, Harold's rhetoric highlights here how this empathy is dependent on the form of the American nuclear family, implicitly coded white. One either has family who provides for them or philanthropists who stand in as temporary or replacement family. This would also suggest that empathy becomes most transformative when it can be narrated through existing structures of kinship and interdependency. Jude, in refusing this form of narration (both of his own story and of Harold's relation to him), refuses to accede to empathy as the first stage in external investment in the self. Harold wants to tell one story about Jude—the nuclear family romance—but Jude will not go along with this, straightforwardly.[12]

Harold wants to empathize with *and* financially support Jude, but only insofar as Jude's actions and desires map onto middle-class narratives of the happy, successful individual and family. As Jude's frustration with Harold highlights, models of psychological and bodily health and financial accumulation cannot be easily separated. He points to an inchoate awareness of biopolitical operations—yet also reveals a shadow world where the biopolitical does not fully reach (those who do not share this "same past and future"). But it's also significant that Jude doesn't insist on the uniqueness of his own experience here—he is part of an "everyone" who didn't share Harold's middle-class narrative. Later, after Willem convinces him to share the details of his past, Jude states "I think I turned out pretty normal, all things considered or not," to which Willem claims "I think you turned out extraordinary, all things considered or not" (2015: 639). Jude's assertion of his own *un*exceptionality and his desire to locate himself in a broader story of generalized trauma and suffering, is disavowed by Willem's correction that cites his uniqueness. There are many ways in which Jude operates as a reductive personification of US history: his racial origins are unclear, but he is suggested to be, at least partially, Native American, he begins in a Jesuit monastery, then moves throughout the West, and ends up in the financial center of the United States, and the world. Jude's story, then, despite its seemingly idiosyncratic violence, might actually not be as unique as either Willem or readers might want to imagine.[13] Like Andy's and Willem's desire to empathetically translate Jude's pain into a narrative of pathology and healing, Harold and Willem here want to understand Jude's life through a narrative of middle-class exceptionalism. These are all stories that allow Andy, Harold, and Willem (and, implicitly, readers) to "feel alongside" Jude, to simultaneously identify with and recognize his specific unfamiliarity. But these are also stories that "advance the self" in recognizably liberal—and neoliberal—entrepreneurial ways. And, indeed, if Jude's narrative is, as he asserts, unexceptional, that would imply that the ability to empathize with him is *also* unexceptional. As discussed above, Andy and Willem and the rest of Jude's circle are quick to assert that their attempts to empathize with Jude make *them* exceptional; their empathy with a difficult or resistant sufferer illustrates that they are exceptionally skilled spectators in the empathetic dyad. The echo here of Richard Florida's and others who characterize empathy as an essential skill of the neoliberal creative class cannot help but call into question the claims made of this novel as a testament to the ethical possibilities made available only within friendship.

Nonetheless, the narrative infrastructure that Andy, Harold, and Willem offer for Jude also remains indebted to an insistence on narrative as a vehicle for moral instruction: they—and we, as readers—would read Jude's horrific history and be appropriately edified and enriched. Jude is a vehicle, in this mode of narrative, for the moral education of his audience. Yet he is also the subject of *Bildung* in this narrative: his development into proper liberal subjecthood traverses his "education" at the hands of his abusers—and, ultimately and more importantly, at the hands of his friends. Indeed, Jude is explicit in situating himself in this narrative relation to his friends; he observes to a child that he tutors that

> The only trick of friendship, I think, is to find people who are better than you are—not smarter, not cooler, but kinder, and more generous, and more forgiving—and then to appreciate them for what they can teach you, and to try to listen to them when they tell you something about yourself, no matter how bad—or good—it might be, and to trust them, which is the hardest thing of all. But the best, as well.
>
> (2015: 240)

Jude's understanding of friendship as a site of pedagogical exchange (though, notably, one where he is always the student, never the instructor) and also, principally, of moral instruction (kindness, generosity, forgiveness) follows from an understanding of narrative as a site for the conservation of social values.

By contrast, Willem narrates his resentment of Jude's refusal to disclose his past as a failure of friendship:

> he bitterly resented this trick [Jude's ability to conceal his suffering], the year-after-year exhaustion of keeping Jude's secrets and yet never being given anything in return but the meanest smidges of information, of not being allowed the opportunity to even try to help him, to publicly worry about him. This isn't fair, he would think in those moments. This isn't friendship. It's something, but it's not friendship. He felt he had been hustled into a game of complicity, one he never intended to play.
>
> (2015: 260)

Willem's desire for the ability to "publicly worry" about Jude is a telling contrast with Jude's understanding of friendship as a site of individualized personal development. Greenwald Smith, in distinguishing the liberal and the neoliberal novel, claims that "neoliberalism ushers in a shift as to precisely what reading fiction is imagined to offer the individual. Whereas liberal self-improvement was likely to be seen as necessitating processes of self-realization that in turn required separation from structures of attachment, neoliberal self-improvement is more often understood to necessitate strategic alliances with others" (2015: 38). Andy, Harold, and Willem are stuck in between these two modes, in some sense (while Jude remains invested in the liberal model): they articulate their desire for Jude to heal through a "process of self-realization," yet, as Willem makes clear in the quotation above, they're also invested in neoliberal strategic partnerships. Willem reveals—inadvertently—the unspoken reality of demands for empathetic connection: that the person who gains the most social capital in this exchange is often the spectator who empathizes, rather than the sufferer who narrates and represents their suffering. The social capital produced by empathy is, thus, a readerly one: just as Willem turns Jude into a device that reveals Willem's capacity for empathy (his ability help Jude reveals that Willem is the best reader of Jude), so too do readers who point to their reading of books like *A Little Life* as devices for developing and extending their own empathetic capacities.

Refusing Empathetic Exceptionalism

But do all modes of narrating suffering—that ostensibly make that suffering accessible to empathizing others—produce the same neoliberal rewards? After the death of Willem and Malcolm in a car accident, the novel shifts gears in terms of addressing Jude's trauma and its narration. Namely, Jude begins to both articulate rage at what he has been subjected to and demand his right to be the autonomous subject of his life (which, here, is framed as his right to suicide), rather than a pedagogical device for others' empathy. In the face of his overwhelming grief, Jude observes that "he often thought it would be a more effective treatment to make people feel more urgently the necessity of living for others" (2015: 780)—empathy, in other words, is here framed as selflessness, but Jude also understands it as a mode for diminishing, not enhancing, his own agency: "He hadn't understood why they wanted him to stay alive, only that they had, and so he had done it" (2015: 780-1). As he retreats further and further into himself, "he realizes that he has undergone a mutation, that he is no longer even human, and he feels relief … he has been enchanted; his culpability has vanished with his humanity" (2015: 785). When his friends intervene, they work to deny his autonomy by involuntarily committing him, leading him to "becom[e] the monster they always told him he was" (2015: 787). This monstrosity, which he connects to his time as a child in the monastery, is a regression to the past, not liberal advancement; his ability to feel and articulate the loss of Willem and Malcolm isn't a marker, for Jude, of his transformation into an empathizing liberal subject but, instead, a return to his monstrous childhood. Moreover, because his grief is *too* big, his friends and caretakers seemingly cannot begin to empathize with him. Indeed, this is the first moment in the novel—despite all sorts of previous crises (many of which are substantially more exceptional and violent than the relative familiarity of a car accident)—where Jude is involuntarily placed under medical care. Restrained to a hospital bed, Jude observes that this is "the same thing [referring to his childhood] all over again ... but this time it isn't the same. This time he is given no choices ... and so begins his new life, a life in which he has moved past humiliation, past sorrow, past hope" (2015: 787–8). Once released from the hospital and under the carceral care of his friends, Jude notes that "no one seems to care that this isn't what he wants" (2015: 788). What his friends and caretakers would understand as empathetic caretaking (centered principally around suicide prevention) is aligned, by Jude, with the acts of his most-violent abusers because they refuse to accept his rage and grief as productive emotions.

Not only does this last section of the novel call into question, then, the operation of "health" and personal improvement, it also acts as a reminder that audience expectations shape the available forms for presenting suffering and arranging oneself as the subject of empathy. While this is not an unfamiliar claim—empathy is, and has historically been, more readily available for certain kinds of "good" subjects—what I want to emphasize here is Yanagihara's attention to this as a narratological claim, rather than focusing on it solely as a political claim (though the two are inseparable). There is no narrative form for enraged responses to past or ongoing suffering that those in power find acceptable. The only way Jude's rage can be accounted for by his listeners is through, once again, the language of medicine and mental health. Jude's incarceration in hospitals here reveals that, when Willem and Andy were earlier imploring him to just tell them what he was feeling, Jude was correct in his resistance and refusal of their requests, as it returns him to a place where his agency is limited—if not eliminated—by incorporation under the frames of health and medicine and reducing his narrative to one dependent on diagnosis and "healing," exactly the scenario that principally characterized the violence he suffered as a child. If narratives that induce empathy promise to lead to great economic success in this novel, narratives that refuse to accommodate the limited empathy of the audience are shown here to have high stakes. This acts as a compelling reminder of the narrow circumstances under which empathy can be a productive force. When it doesn't follow the pathways of acceptable narrative forms, not only might one not be empathized with, but there might be very real and violent costs in response to a "bad" story, as we see here with Jude's institutionalization.

Readers are, therefore, constantly reminded of the way in which Jude has been successful in exactly the ways neoliberal entrepreneurship would demand. While neoliberalism as an ideology doesn't really care how happy or untraumatized one is, so long as one accumulates, *A Little Life* highlights constantly the practical insufficiency of this notion. Indeed, the title repeats the advice—or, rather, demand—offered by Brother Luke, Jude's kidnapper and pimp, that Jude show "a little life" while being raped by johns. We cannot separate capital, violence, and the need to "feel with others" here. Performance isn't the same thing as empathy, exactly; but Jude is asked to perform empathy here, in a particular way. He needs to reassure the johns that he enjoys their actions, both to help them ignore the violence they enact and to make them repeat customers for Brother Luke. As this moment makes brutally clear, the demand to perform legible emotions for an audience is frequently backed by a threat of violence—and one that often seeks to absolve the empathetic observer of any sense of their own responsibility for the suffering of the subject of empathy. While the novel distinguishes between the empathetic expectations of the johns here and those of Jude's friends, it's hard not to see correspondence between the two. While the "life" that the johns want is performed pleasure, Willem, Andy, and Harold, expect a repeat performance of trauma and, implicitly, gratitude for their friendly ministrations. In both situations, Jude is required to perform the way his audience wants him to in order to generate future investment.

Again, while I don't want to collapse the distinction between the sexual violence Jude experiences and the pressure from friends to grapple with the trauma of his past, it is significant that both depend on making himself a legible subject of empathy. If, as the management theory on empathy would suggest, there is money to be made in learning to empathize with one's customers and crafting unique empathetic encounters that can be solved only by the entrepreneur's products or services, the other side of this scenario is that we assume that there is money to be made in making oneself an object of empathy. There is something perverse and violent about this, particularly when we consider the type and scale of trauma that Jude has lived through, yet the idea that one should turn one's traumatic experience into a resource for future success is one that circulates more widely than perhaps we want to admit. The extremity of *A Little Life*'s trauma narratives serves to highlight the violence that undergirds this expectation that trauma should become a usable skill in order to demonstrate one's entrepreneurial empathy. Yet, at the same time, the novel also makes clear the way these demands for individual empathetic narration or fellow feeling are alibis for extractive capitalism's inward turn to accumulate from the self. Jude is able to be incredibly successful—accumulating vast amounts of money, art, and, perhaps most importantly in the neoliberal metropolis, real estate—while still refusing the demand to behave "properly" within the empathetic dyad. Willem and Jude's other friends want to see success as the reward for the "healthy" liberal self; Jude's refusal is a reminder that, however one defines it, "health" isn't actually something that neoliberal systems are concerned with, so long as unhealthiness produces and maintains new avenues of labor and accumulation. As Jude notes toward the end of the novel, his friends' insistence on "curing" his trauma actually serves to re-traumatize him. The language, then, of empathetic narration as a curative should give us pause in terms of who this curative actually serves. A Little Life shows again and again that empathy as a productive force—or the desire for it to operate in this way—is impossible; even more than that, it works to further oppress in the name of salvation as an alibi for the triumph of logics of accumulation.

Notes

1 While Smith uses the word "sympathy," rather than "empathy," his use actually anticipates contemporary definitions of "empathy" with his emphasis on unconsciously feeling as the suffering other, rather than sympathy's deliberate feeling with the other.

2 While he's not talking about either sympathy or empathy, Gary Becker's attempts to quantify justice in economic equations are a particularly vivid illustration of this overall trend for thinking that turns philosophical categories into economic ones.

3 On sympathy and its visual operation, see Jaffe (2000).

4 Given my argument about the economic operation of empathy, this point about the consumptive project of empathy resonates with Neferti X. M. Tadiar's discussion of the remaindered lives on which capitalism relies (2013 and 2015) and Kalindi Vora's work on outsourcing and vital energy or biocapital as a site of accumulation (2015).

5 Jude's wealth (and that of his friends) is also another way in which Yanagihara forecloses easy identification through empathy—and also highlights the stakes of the empathy narrative form. For while Jude's past is the central thing that cannot be discussed among the friends, neither can they articulate their financial success. It remains consistently and silently in the background, but underpins all their actions.

6 See, for instance, Barsade and O'Neill (2016), Cardon et al. (2012), Diener, Thapa, and Tay (2020), Holt et. al (2017), Humphrey (2013), Kato and Eklund (2011), Labaki (2013), Men and Yue (2019), Miller and LeBreton-Miller (2016), and Shepherd (2004).

7 Moreover, as Suzanne Keen notes, when the case is made for the benefit of developing empathy, it is usually a case for sharing negative emotions such as pain and suffering: "the dominant concern with the effects of negative emotions in empathy studies reflects researchers' beliefs that empathy with pain moves us more surely toward sympathy and altruism than shared joy does" (2007: 41).

8 This request for redistributed wealth was seen most prominently on Rachel Cargle's Instagram feed where she encouraged her followers (now totaling nearly 2 million) to pay her and other Black social justice educators on social media for the information they curate on their feeds. The labor provided in

these encounters is, by no means, exclusively emotional: it often demonstrates and emerges out of research and expertise. However, the slippage between educating their followers and leading their followers to "feel" with them is vast—which is, perhaps, inescapable given that there is frequently no "in person" encounter, limiting the ability to move past the social media infrastructure which makes it easier to have quick emotional responses, positively or negatively, to information.

9   As Leslie Fiedler claims in his mid-century reflection on the American novel, "thanks to the sentimental novel, the artist came quite soon to be thought of not as one who makes things, a man with a talent or a skill, but as one who feels them" ([1960] 2003: 116). The idea of the artist as one who feels, then, is intimately tied to the form of the sentimental novel—which is certainly a key genre in which *A Little Life* operates.

10   It seems telling that in the scene immediately following this conversation between Harold and Jude, Jude is offered a co-op apartment in a building owned by a friend (whose family had acquired a large number of properties which their descendants then inherit as they come of age). Yet Willem has arranged this opportunity for Jude to ensure Jude has a caretaker on the premises, leading Jude to feel "not angry but exposed" because he wants his friends "to think of him as someone reliable and hardy, someone they can come to with their problems, instead of him always having to turn to them" (2015: 282). Again, Willem asserts his desire to manage and control Jude's life through the ableist language of care and empathy, betraying Jude's confidences repeatedly. As Jude observes, it is also a dynamic where Jude is always the sufferer, never the spectator, in the empathy dyad of his friendships. This is only further reinforced when Malcolm, an architect, provides plans for Jude's renovation of the new apartment and, *against Jude's will* (2015: 290–1), designs it with accessibility in mind, again illustrating the way his friends and caregivers use the language of care and empathy but only to obscure their attempts to control how Jude understands himself.

11   This inability to name the violence at the heart of capitalism parallels, in some ways, the central tension between Jude and all other characters: his refusal to allow them full access to the violence he has experienced. Harold, Willem, and Andy want him to confess and put this violence on display, with the goal of correcting it; Jude suggests that the scale of the violence is such that it will not allow the resolution they want. Both the Keynesian and the neoliberal models offered here suggest something equivalent: violence has happened, naming it helps nothing, and produces a stagnant victimhood.

12   Harold is also tied to the fantasy of "meaningful" work as the only good work; Jude, on the other hand, sees work as a means to a (financial) end. This is another way in which the two men act as representatives for dueling liberal narratives about social life. For a succinct discussion of the operation of "meaningful work" as a mode of defending class interests, see Tokumitsu (2014).

13   Given that Yanagihara's first book *The People in the Trees* (2013) similarly uses sexual abuse to interrogate colonial violence, it seems unlikely to be accidental that Jude is linked to the expansion of American imperialism.

References

Barsade, S. and O. A. O'Neill. (2016), "Manage Your Emotional Culture," *Harvard Business Review*, 94 (1): 58–66.

Berlant, L. (2004), "Introduction: Compassion (and Withholding)," in L. Berlant (ed), *Compassion: The Culture and Politics of an Emotion*, 1–13, New York: Routledge.

Breithaupt, F. (2019), *The Dark Side of Empathy*, Ithaca, NY: Cornell University Press.

Cardon, M. S., M. Foo, D. Shepherd and J. Wiklund (2012), "Exploring the Heart: Entrepreneurial Emotion Is a Hot Topic," *Entrepreneurship Theory and Practice*, 36 (1):1–10.

Crawford, M. (2015), "'A Little Life', by Hanya Yanigihara," *The Financial Times*, August 14, 2015. Available online: https://www.ft.com/content/57eef3d0-3f6f-11e5-b98b-87c7270955cf (accessed February 3, 2021).

Diener, E., S. Thapa and L. Tay (2020), "Positive Emotions at Work," *Annual Review of Organizational Psychology and Organizational Behavior*, 7: 451–77.

Fiedler, L. A. ([1960] 2003), *Love and Death in the American Novel*, Chicago, IL: Dalkey Archive Press.

Florida, R. (2012), *The Rise of the Creative Class*, 10th Anniversary ed., New York: Basic Books.

Greenwald Smith, R. (2015), *Affect and American Literature in the Age of Neoliberalism*, New York: Cambridge University Press.

Holt, S., J. Marques, J. Hu and A. Wood (2017), "Cultivating Empathy: New Perspectives on Educating Business Leaders," *The Journal of Values-Based Leadership*, 10 (1): 1–25.

Humphrey, R. H. (2013), "The Benefits of Emotional Intelligence and Empathy to Entrepreneurship," *Entrepreneurship Research Journal*, 3 (3): 287–95.

Jaffe, A. (2000), *Scenes of Sympathy*, Ithaca, NY: Cornell University Press.

Kato, S. and J. Eklund (2011), "Doing Good to Feel Good—A Theory of Entrepreneurial Action based in Hedonic Psychology," *Frontiers of Entrepreneurship Research*, 31 (4): 123–37.

Keen, S. (2007), *Empathy and the Novel*, Oxford: Oxford University Press.

Labaki, R. (2013), "Beyond the Awakening of a 'Sleeping Beauty': Toward Business Models Inclusive of the Emotional Dimension in Entrepreneurship," *Entrepreneurship Research Journal*, 3 (3): 265–76.

Men, L. R. and C. A. Yue (2019), "Creating a Positive Emotional Culture: Effect of Internal Communication and Impact on Employee Supportive Behavior," *Public Relations Review*, 45 (3): 1–12.

Miller, D. and I. LeBreton-Miller. (2017), "Underdog Entrepreneurs: A Model of Challenge-Based Entrepreneurship," *Entrepreneurship Theory and Practice*, 41 (1): 7–17.

Preston, A. (2015), "*A Little Life* by Hanya Yanagihara Review—Relentless Suffering," *The Guardian*, August 18. Available online: https://www.theguardian.com/books/2015/aug/18/a-little-life-hanya-yanagihara-review-man-booker-prize (accessed December 1, 2020).

Smith, A. ([1759] 2002), *The Theory of Moral Sentiments*, ed. Knud Haakonsson, Cambridge: Cambridge University Press.

Shepherd, D. A. (2004), "Educating Entrepreneurship Students and Emotion and Learning from Failure," *Academy of Management Learning and Education*, 3 (3): 274–87.

Sutton, J. (2016) "Stories about Squalor," *Quadrant*, 60 (12): 92–4.

Tadiar, N. X. M. (2015), "Decolonization, 'Race,' and Remaindered Life under Empire," *Qui Parle*, 23 (2): 135–60.

Tokumitsu, M. (2014), "In the Name of Love," *Jacobin*, January 12. Available online: https://www.jacobinmag.com/2014/01/in-the-name-of-love/ (accessed February 8, 2021).

Vora, K. (2015), *Life Support: Biocapital and the New History of Outsourced Labor*, Minneapolis: University of Minnesota Press.

Yanagihara, H. (2013), *The People in the Trees*, New York: Anchor Books.

Yanagihara, H. (2015), *A Little Life*, New York: Anchor Books.

Yanagihara, H. (2022), *To Paradise*, New York: Doubleday.

3

"You" Can't Feel My Pain: The Limits of Empathy in Claudia Rankine's *Citizen: An American Lyric*

Ralph Clare

In Claudia Rankine and Beth Loffreda's introduction to *The Racial Imaginary: Writers on Race in the Life of the Mind*, an edited documentary-collection of essays, letters, poems, images, and art that explores the relationship between race and creativity, the authors assert their desire not to repeat the "common languages" of race and their accompanying tropes, including those of shock, scandal, jadedness, and sentimentalism (2015: 13–16). Such tropes compose a racial imaginary that, when enjoyed by white writers in even "typically heartfelt" ways, often perpetuates rather than challenges historical discourses on race (2015: 15). Further addressing the complexities of the politics of representation, Rankine and Loffreda go on to critique white writers who uncritically claim that they have the "right" to create characters or voices "of color" because they believe that the imagination transcends any worldly limitations. In response, Rankine and Loffreda argue that this concern with "rights" acts as a "decoy" that "points to the whiteness of whiteness—that to write race would be to write 'color,' to write an other" (2015: 15). Writing race, from the "rights" perspective, excludes writing whiteness. The ultimate problem with the rights argument, therefore, is that it "acts as if the imagination is not part of me, is not created by the same web of history and culture that made 'me'" (2015: 15), whereas in truth "our imaginations are creatures as limited as we ourselves are" (2015: 16). What would it mean, Rankine and Loffreda ask, for such writers, "[t]o not simply assume that the most private, interior, emotional spaces of existence [...] are most available for lyric and fictive rendering because they are somehow beyond race" (2015: 18)?

Rankine and Loffreda are therefore wary of white writers who claim innocence if called out on their problematic representations of race and become defensive: "I wanted to imagine you—Isn't that good of me, haven't others said it was good of me to try?" (2015: 20). Such are the pitfalls of a writer's presumed empathy, Rankine and Loffreda suggest, for it is an empathy that privileges the white subject, imagining it as "race-less" and autonomous from the historical-material structures that give rise to it, tacitly assuming that it can transcend its material conditions (including that of race) and achieve a universality in art. Without a recognition of the full scope of the racial imaginary, the problematic "common languages" on race and the forms of racism and white supremacy they directly or indirectly support can thus continue unabated.

Rankine and Loffreda's warning about the ways in which continuing to hold naïve notions of race can thwart empathy or lead it to backfire is instructive not just when considering the act of literary or artistic creation, but also when assuming the empathetic potential of literature itself upon readers: the belief that literature can be a privileged space where we can learn to feel with and understand the other. Nowhere is this truer than in Claudia Rankine's genre-crossing book of poems, *Citizen: An American Lyric* (2014), a text that would seem, through its cataloguing of racism from micro to macroaggressions in both individual and institutional forms, to be aimed at eliciting empathy in its white readers for the plight of Black people living in neoliberal America. After all, *Citizen* is pointedly concerned with historical and present-day racial injustices and their damaging effects, suggesting it is a kind of socially engaged poetry that hopes to foster empathy in its readers and lead to a more just world.

Citizen, moreover, is not merely *about* race and racism. The book complicates things at the level of form as well. Most pointedly, Rankine's compelling employment of the second person point-of-view places the reader in the position of the speaker in many a poem or vignette in which "you" directly experience acts of racism. Time and again, encounters between the speaker, or "you," and white people in the poems break down in what the speaker's interlocutor often considers a "misunderstanding" or is oblivious to, but which the text makes clear is the result of racism and a disavowed history of white supremacy. The implications for the reader appear fairly straightforward: Do you feel what it's like to experience racism? Can you identify? Can you now fully empathize with Black people's suffering and understand the workings of racism better? It is as if Rankine plunges the white reader into a Black subjectivity, as if the white reader can feel and experience racism, as if the white reader can finally "get" or understand how everyday racism subtly works. As if, indeed.

In light of Rankine and Loffreda's contention that the imagination and the self are not neutral and universal concepts, a closer exploration of *Citizen* reveals the same can be said of empathy. In fact, stoking a traditional and uncritical readerly empathy is far from Rankine's aim. For not only do several well-meaning and potentially empathetic interactions between the speaker and others fail miserably, but the speaker's second-person unemotional voice and alienated sense of self serve to interrogate the notion of a universal, autonomous white subject and its presumptions about empathy, race, and "I"dentification. Ultimately, Rankine counteracts the possibility of white readers' privilege and ability to appropriate Black experiences and suffering. For such "understanding" often leads white progressives—who heed the call of neoliberalism's affective economy by embracing a non-critical notion of empathy—to a disavowal, as Robin DiAngelo argues in *White Fragility* (2018), of their personal stakes in racism and white supremacy, thereby stymying anti-racist action and the potential for real change. To be sure, Rankine's text ultimately resists sentimentality, traditional empathy, and forecloses on establishing a comfortable identification for its white readers with the speaker's suffering.

Instead, *Citizen* calls for a critical affective empathy—an empathy of feeling with or alongside, not *for* or *instead of*—by pointing to the ways in which empathy and the empathetic subject are embedded in social, political, and economic systems of historical-material significance. Not only must the imaginary identification of sharing another's pain be recognized as always coming up short against the otherness of the other, but also empathy must be recognized as being caught up with systemic racism and what the book calls America's "racial imaginary." In short, *Citizen* does not appeal to the individual reader to be more emotionally empathetic, potentially excluding oneself from racist practices and systems of oppression and perpetuating common "sentimental" languages on race. Instead, *Citizen* provides a model of an impersonal and relationally based affective empathy that denies any individual subject's claim to sovereignty and autonomy from political and social structures. *Citizen* promotes the notion that feelings and affect themselves traverse both bodies and subjects, bonding or joining them in more communal and collective ways, thereby resisting the urge to justify forms of emotional empathy that remain the private experience of individuals. Such an affective empathy is conscious of the ways in which, as Carolyn Pedwell argues, "empathy is at once imaginative and sensorial, conscious and unwilled, personal and impersonal, cultural and biological, human and non-human; [and] differently produced within shifting networks that materially imbricate the neural, the psychic, the cultural, the social, the political and the economic, among other forces and elements"

(2014: 5). Empathy is thus not some universal quality or action that we can generate more of or activate when we need it, but a culturally relative and contingently mediated behavior. In *Citizen*, affective empathy emerges from the insight that we might gain when we recognize the structural conditions not only of racism and injustice but also, and crucially, of our feelings and empathetic responses to them.

Empathy and Systemic Racism

In its attention to systemic forms of racism, *Citizen* challenges the notion that empathy—no matter the degree of its biological roots—is something natural that exists prior to history, culture, and discourse. As such, empathy is not always "given" or "earned" equally; inequality and discrimination effect both the production and circulation of empathy. Who appears as a subject worthy of empathy is not exactly the result of a neutral or objective process. Rankine, for instance, uncovers a racial component to who gives and receives empathy in the section on Serena Williams, in which Rankine draws an analogy between enforcing the rules of a sport unfairly and living under the stated and unstated "rules" of American society—that is, the workings of systemic racism (2014: 23–36). Williams's anger and rhetorical threat directed at the chair umpire regarding the bad calls made against her in the 2009 US Open (for which she was fined and put on probation in Grand Slam tournaments) led to a media discourse stereotyping her as "crazy," as the "angry Black woman." There was little to no empathy expressed for Williams's heated reaction to the series of egregious calls she experienced during that game and throughout her career to that point, "because her body, trapped in a racial imaginary, trapped in disbelief—code for being black in America—is being governed not by the tennis match she is participating in but by a collapsed relationship that had promised to play by the rules" (2014: 30). Here and elsewhere, *Citizen* reveals that this "racial imaginary" is historical and systemic. Moreover, this racial imaginary not only "colors" white people's perceptions and understanding of Black experience but also their emotional reactions to it—and specifically here, the ability to empathize. In Williams's case, empathy is withheld because she is acting "crazy" or "like a bad sport": when Williams acts in this way, it's appalling and threatening; when John McEnroe does, it's legendary and endearing. Empathy, then, is subject(ed) to a historical racial (and gendered) imaginary.

Citizen thus reveals how systemic racism and empathy are mutually imbricated. The Serena Williams section, as well as the litany of microaggressions represented in *Citizen*, speak directly to Eduardo Bonilla-Silva's claim that systemic racism has resulted in what he calls "racism without racists" (2009: 1–24), in which a majority of white Americans believe that they are not racist and that racism is extinct, thereby perpetuating racist systems in certain ways. If systemic racism allows people to disavow racism personally, we might find a correlative in the possibility of there being "empathy without empathic acts or change." In short, even among those whites who actively empathize with the struggles of people of color, who "listen" to their voices and "validate" their feelings, there is nothing to suggest that this leads to any larger tangible political or social change—what we might call *systemic* empathetic acts. In Bonilla-Silva's "racism without racists" formulation, one can personally deny one is racist while racist structures persist; in the "empathy without change" formulation, one can personally express empathy while racist structures persist. In fact, the two can quite easily overlap: I can personally deny my racism and compensate for it with my empathy for suffering, while simultaneously recognizing systemic racism but advocating nothing to address or change it. But in a neoliberal culture of individual responsibility, my "choice" to empathize is a private and privatized choice and thus neatly avoids consideration of, or can be bracketed from leading to, collective social responsibility and change. And when empathy is only understood as individually or privately bestowed, so to speak, then whether it is sincerely or insincerely intended can make little difference to enacting collective or systemic change.

Empathy, of course, can function in an insincere way as an ideological cover for its very absence. The National Football League, for instance, has cynically advertised its supposed empathy with the struggle for racial justice. After its tacit "blacklisting" of Colin Kaepernick for (his role in leading the) kneeling during the national anthem, which he first did in 2016, the NFL has, in response to the massive, worldwide Black Lives Matter protests in the summer of 2020, apologized—via Commissioner Roger Goodell—for its treatment of Kaepernick. The NFL has subsequently produced a slogan in supposed solidarity with those seeking racial justice: It Takes All of Us. This public relations stunt is one that is meant to signal, in part, the NFL's empathy toward those affected by systemic racial injustice. It even had the gall to use Kaepernick's image in a propaganda-cum-Black-national-anthem video played on the opening day of the 2020 season.[1] Kaepernick, meanwhile, still does not have a job in the NFL, and many Kansas City fans booed those players who chose to kneel that day. Empathy here is a mere public relations scheme for a business—an American institution in its own right—to plausibly deny its own responsibility and part in perpetuating racial injustice. The NFL's decision to "empathize" was clearly driven by concerns over its revenue streams and audience appeal (despite the fact that the disgruntled, booing fans in Kansas City most likely represent a large share of that audience), and probably by the specter of a potential wildcat strike by some NFL players or teams—the kind of strike that was all but welcomed by the NBA during its 2020 season.

Yet, perhaps even more insidiously and in keeping with Bonilla-Silva's formulation of the way in which systemic racism continues "without racists," even when "sincere" empathy is attempted or deployed by white people, the systemic racial imaginary can distort its production and therefore its effects just as easily. Consider, for instance, two of the pieces in *Citizen* that record attempts at connection or communication between the speaker and a white person who is a friend or someone who means to be friendly—in other words, someone who we, and especially the speaker, would imagine is probably empathetic to those suffering racial injustices. In one such encounter, a

> friend says, as you walk toward her, You are late, you nappy-headed ho. What did you say? you ask, though you have heard every word. This person has never before code-switched in this manner. [...] You do not know what she means. You don't know what response she expects from you nor do you care. For all your previous understandings, suddenly incoherence feels violent. You both experience this cut, which she keeps insisting is a joke, a joke stuck in her throat, and like any other injury, you watch it rupture along its suddenly exposed suture.
>
> (2014: 41–2)

The friend's behavior and language—which echo the racial slur radio shock jock Don Imus famously used to describe the Rutgers women's basketball team—suggest a familiarity with and understanding of the speaker. If the friend has empathized here, in some roundabout fashion, it is a radical failure of empathy. The friend has not exactly "mis-empathized." Instead, the act of empathy is undercut by the historical-material racial imaginary. The tacit defense is perhaps *"I thought you would think this was funny because I'm calling attention to this racist action by Don Imus, but I'm not him or racist as my ironic joke, which distances me from its 'real' context, clearly shows."* Yet obviously the friend has little awareness both of the impact of racism in America and of the speaker's lived experience of it. Empathy here misfires, even if it is quite easy to imagine this friend as truly sorry, as empathetic enough to gain understanding and learn from this encounter.

In another scene in which empathy is twisted toward a troubling end, the speaker relates how

> You wait at the bar of the restaurant for a friend, and a man, wanting to make conversation, nursing something, takes out his phone to show you a picture of his wife. You say, bridge that she is, that she is beautiful. She is, he says, beautiful and black, like you.
>
> (2014: 78)

How empathy might be said to work in this encounter is incredibly nuanced, and my reading of it here will be necessarily incomplete. Clearly the man sees himself as attempting to make a connection with the speaker, one ultimately based upon some shared understanding of race. Yet if the man can be said to be expressing empathy here, it too is of a negative variety. Perhaps his comments are meant to suggest to the speaker that he has an empathetic understanding that Blackness has long been denigrated against white standards of beauty (maybe he has read and reflected upon Toni Morrison's *The Bluest Eye* [1970]). Tacitly the man appears to be signaling this empathy primarily by the fact that his wife is Black. He "gets" racism. He, therefore, cannot be racist, and here is the proof. The result is a strange twist on the self-and-collective empowering "Black Is Beautiful" slogan of the Black Arts and Liberation movement that is torn from its social, historical, and political roots and offered up instead as a kind of pronouncement of a fetish object, which blends with the minor undercurrent of sexual forwardness and possible violence. "I feel you" here takes on the possibility of a physical threat as well as a *presumed* understanding based on empathy—a problematic one to say the least.[2]

In both of these occasions, and throughout *Citizen*, empathy simply fails and was all but doomed to from the start. Further, the speaker's ability to speak, her voice, is effectively silenced in a moment of encounter, whether out of shock or the impossibility of replying in any way that will make sense of the matter. Indeed, such silencing becomes one of the primary dangers of assuming the positive value of (one's) empathy. Take, for example, Bill Clinton's famous line "I feel your pain," which, interestingly enough, was not uttered in a truly empathetic spirit but in an attempt to silence criticism.[3] Empathy here—marshalled rhetorically to political ends, of course—suggests a near smothering of the other, a complete cooption and incorporation of another's experiences and feelings. This is empathy for body snatchers who seek to appropriate the voice of the other, which ultimately expropriates the other's agency and subjectivity. In fact, this kind of empathy presumes a free subject who can empathize objectively, yet this subject is generally coded as white and universal.

The individual white subject, then, is somehow considered to be detached or detachable from systemic and structural issues such as racism. Often the subject assumes it can—because of a relation based upon structural inequality—speak or feel for, judge and condescend, and grant or revoke its attention to others—though in every case this means its own subjectivity is always foregrounded. In *White Fragility*, for instance, Robin DiAngelo discusses the way in which "white women's tears" can invalidate experiences of people of color by calling attention to the feelings of the person crying and thus derailing discussions about racism and its impact of people who experience it. As DiAngelo puts it, "[t]ears that are driven by white guilt are self-indulgent. When we are mired in guilt, we are narcissistic and ineffective; guilt functions as an excuse for inaction" (2018: 135). Like Bill Clinton's pronouncement on feeling the other's pain, here a seemingly empathetic act (crying) works to the opposite effect. Moreover, DiAngelo is careful to point out that, while "[m]any of us see emotions as naturally occurring ... emotions are political in [...] key ways" (2018: 132). For instance, "our emotions are shaped by our biases and beliefs, our cultural frameworks" and thus "emotions are not natural; they are the result of the frameworks we are using to make sense of social relations. And of course, social relations are political" (2018: 132).[4] These very "frameworks" or structures are part and parcel of the complex "racial imaginary" that *Citizen* relentlessly interrogates. Serena Williams's cocktail of negative emotions, themselves partly products of historical racism and individually experienced micro-aggressions, were read through an American imaginary that doesn't exactly "distort" empathy—for how could there be some universal "empathy" existing outside of any system, political, social, language-based, or otherwise?—but actually produces empathy, or extinguishes it, that makes it legible in certain ways and in certain contexts.

Whether we consider the many cases of empathy misfiring that *Citizen* parses, or even the flagrant false empathy of the NFL or Bill Clinton, what becomes apparent is that one can claim to empathize (sincerely or duplicitously) with those who suffer racism while still continuing to participate in, and sustain, structural forms of racism. Empathy, *Citizen* demonstrates, is caught up in, and sometimes deployed by, the very systems and institutions it might be imagined as challenging or critiquing. For *Citizen* insists that America's racial imaginary is not some simple illusion that can be waved away or a dream from which one can be easily and forever be "woke." It is constitutive of the very structures that constitute America itself, a system that has (long ago) "collapsed," as the speaker in the Serena Williams section puts it, in its exceptional enforcement of the rules—by enforcing the rules arbitrarily for different people. Empathy and its distribution are likewise affected by inequality and racism.

"I" Feel "You": Empathy and the Other

Literary institutions, traditions, and poetic forms similarly engage in tacit racial imaginaries, and what makes *Citizen*'s critique of empathy so provocative is the ways in which it interrogates language's relationship with race while experimenting with the lyric form and the confessional mode of poetry. Traditionally, the lyric poem is a short form poem that expresses the feelings and thoughts of a single speaker through the first person "I." Rankine, however, subverts the lyric tradition in several ways, via fragmentation, collage, mixed-media (the book contains pieces that are part of larger media-artworks), images (of people, objects, and artworks that are sometimes decontextualized and sometimes suggestively placed next to certain passages), and often by employing prose instead of poetic meter and lineation. Perhaps the most notable subversion is of the lyric "I" itself, which becomes the "you" of the poems. Indeed, Rankine's use of the second person point of view—the "you"—throughout *Citizen* enacts an incredibly unique and visceral experience for the reader, a fully immersive, empathetic reading experience. However, by underscoring the fractured and racialized nature of the lyrical "I" and "you"—that the (lyrical) subject is not universal—Rankine calls into question the reader's ability to empathize from a neutral, sovereign position.

Here are three of the shorter, yet striking, poems using the second person in an immersive fashion. I quote the three, each in its entirety, to give a sense of the cumulative effect that these pieces have in *Citizen* on the whole, as one microaggression leaves a tiny psychological mark that grows daily into a larger individual and collective wound. As one poem puts it, "[e]ach moment is like this—before it can be known, categorized as similar to another thing and dismissed, it has to be experienced, it has to be seen" (2014: 9). Each of these scenes reveals the way that the Black body in America's racial imaginary can be made invisible and hypervisible from one moment to the next:

At the end of a brief phone conversation, you tell the manager you are speaking with that you will come by his office to sign the form. When you arrive and announce yourself, he blurts out, I didn't know you were black!

I didn't mean to say that, he then says.

Aloud, you say.

What? he asks.

You didn't mean to say that aloud.

Your transaction goes swiftly after that. (2014: 44)

Someone in the audience asks the man promoting his new book on humor what makes something funny. His answer is what you expect—context. After a pause he adds that if someone said something, like about someone, and you were with your friends you would probably laugh, but if they said it out in public where black people could hear what was said, you might not, probably would not. Only then do you realize you are among "the others out in public" and not among "friends." (2014: 48)

In line at the drugstore it's finally your turn, and then it's not as he walks in front of you and puts his things on the counter. The cashier says, Sir, she was next. When he turns to you he is truly surprised.

Oh my God, I didn't see you.

You must be in a hurry, you offer.

No, no, no, I really didn't see you. (2014: 77)

At first blush, the second person point of view in each poem suggests the ability of the white reader to feel and understand what experiencing racism in myriad forms might be like, as if Rankine has transformed Langston Hughes's poem "I, Too" into "You, Too." If we are to comfortably assume the "you" is the reader—which, of course, is not a given—then it appears that "we" experience these same moments too. To a certain degree, then, these poems are, as Angela Hume writes, "demanding that the reader relive or imagine what it is like to be on the receiving end of a racist encounter" (2016: 82). Karen Simecek likens Rankine's technique to Charles Olson's notion of projective verse, in which "[t]he shared breath in Rankine's poems enables us to connect to the words on the page as a sharing of some experience with the poetic voice" (2019: 508). Rankine's use of the second person thus "establishes the necessary relation for reciprocity to unfold and so for the emergence of a shared frame of reference" (2019: 510).

Why, however, should we so easily assume that the poem's "shared frame of reference" is truly a transformative space for empathetic understanding when such frameworks so often fail in *Citizen*? For, as we have seen, Rankine is clearly aware of the dangers and limitations of supposed empathetic responses. Even Suzanne Keen's excellent *Empathy and the Novel*, which puts forth an enlightening theory of "narrative empathy" by analyzing several authorial strategies for generating readerly empathy, remains ambivalent about literature's ability to foster empathy. Ultimately, Keen laments that her formalist reading lacks empirical evidence, leading her to conclude that readers "bring empathy to the novel" and not vice versa (2007: 168). In kind, Simecek recognizes that "I am limited by my own perspective and experience and I'm precluded from being able to fully share in that experience" (2019: 512) but insists that these shared experiences could result in a "sense of responsibility [that] may trigger a process of self-reflection that is important to our moral lives" (2019: 516). Much like Keen's cautioning, Simecek's "may" leaves us wondering at the efficacy of empathy in such a model. A formalist critique alone thus leaves an analysis of empathy wanting. Indeed, as Lauren Berlant states, the ability to give or withhold compassion (or in this case empathy) is tied up in an "ethics of privilege" (2004: 1), so that "[c]ompassion turns out not to be so effective or a good itself. It turns out merely to describe a particular kind of social relation" (2004: 9). In *Citizen*, that relationship, as we have seen, is a privileged one that has been situated from the perspective of the universal white subject.

In truth, any reader's comfortable and privileged perspective is precisely what Rankine upsets by not allowing any stable self—whether the speaker's or the reader's—to emerge in the work as a whole. While the above vignettes suggest a single, stable speaker, the rest of the collection troubles the notion of a complete and whole self by multiplying the "I" and "you" in important ways. The second-person technique, even from a formalist standpoint, is thus not simply an empty placeholder for the reader to "fill in." It functions as a way for Rankine to access and subvert the confessional mode of poetry by bringing in personal experience at a distance (she also drew from stories she heard from friends and associates) and making it impossible for the reader to reduce the recounted incidents of racism to merely "personal" encounters. Indeed, Kamran Javadizadeh makes clear that the "collectivity of its sourcing" (2019: 477) means that "no single reader could reliably identify with each 'you'" (2019: 482). Rankine's "you" is *at least* four things: Rankine's and her friends' experiences (already multiple "yous"), the speaker's performative experience, the reader's enforced second person point of view felt as "I;" and finally—perhaps most importantly—a veritable third person "you," as in "this is an everyday experience 'you' have as a citizen/person of color in America." Recall, too, that "citizen" as a pronoun can mean the speaker but also any Black citizen—the individual and the collective—and those whose full citizenship has been or is denied.

Rankine therefore raises several problems with what is a far too easy "I"dentification and a potential appropriation of Black experience by a white reader or any reader for that matter. For instance, any emotional plea for empathy is shut off, as Javadizadeh writes, "by muting the emotional range within the experience of subjectivity claimed by this 'you'" (2019: 482) that Rankine renders "in a voice notable for its emotional flatness" (2019: 482). Time and again, Rankine's speaker simply ends a vignette or poem on an ironic, deadpan note (as evidenced above) or with an unanswerable, rhetorical question: "If you were smiling, what would that tell him about your composure in his imagination?" (2014: 46); "What is wrong with you? The question gets stuck in your dreams" (2014: 54); "Do you remember when you sighed?" (2014: 63). Thus, "the experience of such identification is unlikely to feel epiphanic or cathartic" (Javadizadeh 2019: 482). This is empathy held at a critical distance, one that is suspicious of generating emotions in a subject that capably remains a manager of its private emotions. By withholding any immediate emotional payoff—by offering no real catharsis, since each vignette's questions or responses to situations remain unanswered or unanswerable—empathetic identification is frustrated and not "rewarded," as such, emotionally.

"I"dentification is not only frustrated here, but the reader's sense of self or "I" is similarly disrupted—made fragile by not only the affects and feelings provoked but also by the sudden racialization of the "you" and, therefore, the reader's "I." And it is precisely such a whole and universal "I" and its "I"dentification that *Citizen* challenges by subverting the historical lyric "I" and the confessional mode—traditionally an assumed white subjectivity—and replacing it with the second person.[5] In this sense, Rankine's avoidance of the first person "I" throughout the book is telling. In one poem, the speaker says that the "I" is "[t]he pronoun barely holding the person together" (2014: 71) and that "[s]ometimes 'I' is supposed to hold what is not there until it is. Then *what is* comes apart the closer you are to it" (2014: 71). Taken out of context, such claims might seem to be purely poststructuralist takes on the self that have nothing to do with race—that is, that personhood or subjectivity is a linguistic construction or fiction. But, of course, *Citizen* is not merely playing philosophical games with the "I." The "you," in contrast to the whole self or "I," aptly captures the split-subject—an instance of DuBoisean double-consciousness—or dissociated self that the speaker frequently experiences and meditates upon (in this sense, the "you" is the "I" that has "come apart").

The speaker as "you" and not "I" is made manifest in yet another failed encounter in which a woman calls the speaker by "the name of another woman you work with" and then apologizes in an email "referring to 'our mistake.' Apparently your own invisibility is the real problem causing her confusion" (2014: 43). Here the "you" is connected to a "them," and "they" are all the same. It does not matter if there was no overt racism in the woman's "mistake," that it is not, for instance, a racial slur. As the speaker realizes after listening to Judith Butler speak on racism and language, the aim of racist language is not so much "to denigrate and erase you as a person" but to render a person "hypervisible" because "[l]anguage that feels hurtful is intended to exploit all the ways that you are present" (2014: 49). It follows, then, that *Citizen* could be said to be uninterested in using poetic language to stoke empathy but to enact the ways in which racist language—or simply language itself—can make subjects present (and absent) in material, hurtful ways. For it is forever a racialized "you" (not "I") that is made manifest so often in the poem, made legible by the other, as the above poems make clear—the poems' twists are not mere ironic devices to shock the reader-as-you but moments recording the creation and maintenance of a racialized self. The "you" is ultimately social, historical, and material—not simply a philosophical thought experiment or linguistic play.

If Black selfhood is frequently denied, ignored, and subject to dehumanization by verbal and physical acts of racism, both historically and in the present, then the personal "I" as such is erased and replaced with a racially projected self as imagined by white people. In one such instance, the speaker recounts a friend's idea that Americans have both a "historical self" and a "self self," so that individual interactions of the "self self" break down when the "historical selves, her white self and your black self, or your white self and her black self, arrive with the full force of their American positioning" (2014: 14). The speaker is stunned, and "your attachment seems fragile, tenuous, subject to a transgression of your historical self" (2014: 14). Here the historical "split," which is really a common root, opens up into a chasm, as if it were the speaker's fault(line). Just as troubling is the suggestion that a real, whole "self self" can fully emerge after racism (or history) ends in a post-racial paradise. In fact, it is more precise to maintain the opposite: the reader's self is jolted, split apart, and cannot find a comfortable wholeness in empathizing from a privileged (white, universal) position. The fracturing of the "you," if anything, suggests a fracturing of the reader's ability to safely identify, either closely or from a distance. But the effect of this fragmenting or unmooring of the self is a space or impasse precisely out of which a more critical or affective form of empathy may arise.

Affective Empathy for a Biopolitical Age

Critics have begun to underscore the role of embodiment and materiality in Rankine's poetry, especially via theories of biopolitics or critiques of biopower.[6] It is possible, then, to view *Citizen* as staging or creating biopolitical encounters—affective ones, including those of the speaker in the poems, and the encounter between reader and text—that are not, as we have seen, indicative of an empty poetic formalism or appealing to an emotional empathy based upon identification. Instead, these biopolitical encounters suggest the possibility of what we might call an "affective ethics" in which identification or fellow feeling cannot be achieved wholly or at a safe distance, so to speak. For, as Carolyn Pedwell writes, despite traditional empathy's drawbacks, we must recognize that there can be "possibilities for activating alternative empathies" (2014: 4). *Citizen* provides just such an alternative model through an affective empathy based upon how affect— which traverses material/psychological and individual/collective bodies— can horizontally connect and relate one to another, thereby fundamentally upsetting hierarchical and distanced relationships. Affective empathy thus differs from emotional empathy in that it challenges the notion of empathy as an individual emotional reaction, as if empathy could be so easily privatized for individual, subjective consumption. Instead, the affective facet of empathy suggests its communal and communicative possibilities, those which a traditional notion of empathy would theoretically foster but that, as we have seen, remain problematic.

Affect theory thus informs what I am calling *Citizen*'s affective empathy in particular ways. For instance, one strain of affect theory that includes the work of Hardt and Negri, as well as Brian Massumi, Deleuze and Guattari, and Spinoza makes key distinctions between emotions and affect.[7] In this view, affect is preconscious, transpersonal, and autonomous. Emotion, in contrast, is affect codified or signified, brought into consciousness and subjectively recognized. Affect itself, however, is not signifiable as such, and its existence is suggested in thresholds or in-between spaces—where the body might feel or note something "before" consciousness does. In certain ways, the mind "matters" and the body "knows." As such, distinctions between mind/body, inside/outside, or feeling/knowing may blur or collapse. Affect, then, is a being's very capacity to affect or be affected. And affect, unlike personal emotions, is transpersonal and potentially communal. Affect can traverse bodies, connect and disrupt them. Sara Ahmed, for example, calls this "affective contagion," in which "to be affected by another does not mean that an affect simply passes or 'leaps' from one body to another. The affect becomes an object *only given the contingency of how we are affected.* We might be affected differently by what gets passed around" (2010: 39).

In *Citizen*, affect not only traverses bodies but it materializes—it has material effects too. For instance, while *Citizen* offers a deep look into psychological effects of systemic racism on the self and the formation of subjectivity, it also calls attention to the physical effects and costs of racism on the body, both individual and collective. In one poem, the speaker considers "John Henryism," a medical term accounting for the physiological toll of experiencing racism on a lifelong daily basis (2014: 11). Indeed, the material effects of racism, in addition to the psychological toll, are foregrounded throughout *Citizen*, as the speaker frequently suffers headaches—the head being a symbolic and real space in which stress and pain take on a physical sensation. The psychological/affective and material/physical are therefore not separate spheres affected by racism but overlap and inform one another. *Citizen* therefore insists upon an "embodied double-consciousness" in which pain is not reducible to any one element or physical source—or, indeed, to any single subject.

As Tana Jean Welch posits—in a line just as relevant to *Citizen*—Rankine's *Don't Let Me Be Lonely* (2004) is an "investigative lyric [that] brings materiality to the fore both by encouraging the reader to engage actively with the text" (2015: 127). The text's materiality includes, Welch writes, the force of language, thus "demonstrating how the human and other bodies are shaped by material *and* semiotic forces" (2015: 144). Stressing the materiality of the text here is something quite different from the formalist argument of a shared space for reader-speaker transformation, which suggests an almost one-to-one psychological transfer of emotional empathy from subject to subject via a neutral, dehistoricized language. The material and semiotic "interruptions" become tactile—to the touch, but also in the way the visuals "touch" the eye, collective memory, and affect. This is most notable in the book's incorporation of media images, such as tennis player Caroline Wozniacki's "impression" (with stuffed bra and stuffed back of skirt) of Serena Williams (2014: 37), and various images of artworks, such as the altered "erased lynching" of a famous postcard/image of a lynching (2014: 91), and finally in the numerous blank pages that extend and amplify the troubled silences and impasses of and between the speaker's experiences. Sometimes contextualized and sometimes not, these images disrupt the seemingly smooth (but already troubled) transmission of the speaker's experience to the reader—suddenly, there is a silent speaker, or arranger, behind the book's material composition that calls attention to the book as artifact, as both art and fact, artfully arranged by a speaker/author/Rankine and factually connected to "real life" objects and collective moments/memories.

For Welch, Rankine's investigative lyrical style is a way of "[p]racticing trans-corporeal ethics," which "requires acknowledging how our lives are shaped by others and how we in turn shape others' lives" (2015: 143). A "trans-corporeal" ethics, then, means the fractured subject may begin to see its cracks not as the destruction of what was or is (say, the notion of a universal, white subject) but as a potential to open up to new, or realize already existing, collective connections that suggest the subject was never so autonomous to begin with. In short, the materiality of affect in *Citizen* both challenges the subject's individual autonomy and connects that subjectivity to others—through affects that may spread and be positive or negative[8]—in potentially transformational ways.

In *Citizen*, affect's transpersonality is notable in the book's fragmented, genre-blurring form, in addition to those awkward and broken "in-between" moments when the fragmented speaker (and the pieces that make up *Citizen*) cannot describe and claim personally felt emotions—which are also material feelings that the speaker *physically* feels—instead gesturing to affect itself as something glimpsed within the exposed fissures of the self or the cracked American system. As one piece puts it, "[n]o one should adhere to the facts that contribute to narrative, the facts that create lives. To your mind, feelings are what create a person, something unwilling, something wild vandalizing whatever the skull holds. Those sensations form a someone. The headaches begin then" (2014: 61). Such feelings or affects, stoked by the personally and collectively lived experience of racism, turn out to have material, and thus shareable, dimensions—they may leave the "private" experience of the speaker and enter into the public domain. They are also what lend an impersonal and non-sentimental tone to the book (it is curiously *un*emotional), evidenced in the "divorce" the speaker experiences with her "self." Instead of recording the speaker's personal(ized) emotions and insisting upon readerly empathy, these feelings are set free (but they were always free), are free-floating, are collectively induced by a historical-material, systemic reality in the first place.

Citizen can therefore be said to produce "negative" affects and feelings meant to upset the subject in ways that, indeed, have little to do with empathy. In an essay exploring how *Citizen* speaks "affect to power," thereby countering racialized data and neoliberal surveillance technologies, Katherine D. Johnston argues that "central to the book is thus the effort to simulate the feeling of that accumulative experience [of microaggressions], beyond mere description" (2019: 357) so that "Rankine's lyric accumulates feelings and affects, a response that is powerfully destabilizing" (2019: 358). We can extend Johnston's claims here to make a critical distinction regarding Rankine's use of the second person specifically: that the book does not unify feeling (say, by demanding emotional empathy) but produces an abundance of feelings that may not be locatable as such and are disruptive of power and (powerful) subjectivities. What Johnston notes as the poems' "destabilization"—through revealing the fragility of any subject and subject position, in part by calling attention to free-floating affects—is very different from proposing to instill more empathy into a stable, universal subject. To be "beyond mere description" calls attention to the social, political, and material realm of feelings and affects—as things that cut through, divide, split, and lend illusion to the wholeness of subjects—yet also contain the potential to gather together, to commune, to form communities affectively and socially.

Citizen offers a model for a critical or affective empathy in the poem/script for a video project "Making Room." In this piece, the speaker enters a subway car and notices a woman standing, although there is an empty seat next to a Black man. The speaker intentionally sits in the empty seat and considers what the man must be feeling and thinking—a concerted attempt at empathizing. Though the man does not acknowledge the speaker, the seat, "[f]or him, you imagine, [...] is more like breath than wonder; he has had to think about it so much you wouldn't call it thought" (2014: 131). The speaker continues to wonder that "if the man spoke to you he would say, it's okay, I'm okay, you don't need to sit here" (2014: 132). It is this empty seat, a breath and also a physical and mental space, that provides the space for imaginative identification. Yet "[y]ou don't speak unless you are spoken to and your body speaks to the space you fill and you keep trying to fill it except the space belongs to the body of the man next to you, not to you" (2014: 131). This physical space, a lonely and angry one produced by racism, is nonetheless also respected by the speaker as an autonomous space of an other's self, leading the speaker to consider her own possible misidentification with the man and that her empathetic act might be merely selfish: "You sit to repair whom who? You erase that thought. And it might be too late for that" (2014: 132). However, after a woman begins asking people to move so that she can sit next to her child, "[i]t's then the man next to you turns to you. And as if from inside your own head you agree that if anyone asks you to move, you'll tell them we are traveling as a family" (2014: 133). Here the poem suggests an unspoken solidarity between the two—who are formally united in the second person "you" and become a "we"—on the train, or perhaps the bus, of history that hearkens back to Rosa Parks and the Civil Rights era, though resonates differently in the context of a so-called post-racial society in which one may sit wherever one wants and "giving up one's seat" is no longer a matter of law but of historical custom—that is, the (transit) system's institutionalized racism.

What results is not a poem that attempts to share the man's feelings with the reader to provoke emotional empathy, but a poem that oscillates between identification and misrecognition and suggests, once again, a kind of affective ethics or affective empathy—if we understand affect as traversing and "cutting through" subjects and giving rise to messy feelings and mis-identification—in which the urge to empathize emotionally is intensely felt but ultimately checked out of a fundamental respect for otherness and the others' feelings and a realization that true empathy is impossible. To be sure, there is feeling here—a bare affective response that is unsignifiable and collapses subjective distance and autonomy—but it resists being codified into the simple imperative to feel empathy. The speaker thus insists upon bodily, material presence over spoken words, an affective aligning or alliance with, not a speaking for: "[y]ou put your body there in proximity to, adjacent to, alongside, with" (2014: 131). For there is always an "as if" to identification that takes place, per the poem, "[a]s if from inside your own head"—it is metaphorical like a "family" or "community." One then "takes place" or stands together with, as when a woman whose child is knocked over by a man on the subway demands an apology: "The beautiful thing is that a group of men began to stand behind me like a fleet of bodyguards [...] like newly found uncles and brothers" (2014: 17). When assented to, when the other recognizes the affective call that does not intrude or presume, only then is this metaphor transformed into a true bonding experience where fellow *collective* feeling and may begin.

It is telling that *Citizen's* critical take on empathy is in line with the goals of The Racial Imaginary Institute that Rankine helped to found in 2017 and which she actively curates events for and exhibits with. The community-based organization explores the continuing historical-imaginary construction that is race via artists, writers, activists, and thinkers of all kinds. The Institute's Mission Statement describes itself as "a cultural laboratory in which the racial imaginaries of our time are engaged, read, countered, contextualized and demystified."[9] Its first programming focused upon the issue of whiteness, and questioned "what can be made when we investigate, evade, beset, and call out bloc-whiteness." To be sure, the site's "About" informational section is notable for its rigorous theoretical language and critical orientation. Nowhere in the statement is there an individualist or humanistic appeal to emotion or empathy, to expanding understanding of "the other." The institute is meant to engage difficult questions of race without offering easy answers or platitudes to soothe the empathetic self, not to help "bloc-whiteness" shore itself up but to encourage it to break itself apart.

White readers therefore ought not to put down *Citizen* in a self-congratulatory way, thinking that they have better identified and empathized with Black experience by mere reading alone—and not least because of the continuing struggle for social and racial justice. Each reader ought to notice the long-ago, jerry-rigged construction of white subjectivity to begin with, its propping itself up through othering, and that its supposedly whole self is a prosthetic one, a crutch afforded it by white supremacy. What such readers need to understand is not themselves, but *this* historical self, *this* subjectivity. Heeding a call to be more empathetic would be all too easy and, as *Citizen* details, problematic. *Citizen* demands painful readerly reflection with no easy answers, not instant edification and moral validation. Readers should be disturbed, upset, filled with prickly affects that destabilize, not affirm, identities.

Yet, as we have seen, *Citizen* also suggests a way of standing next to, of allying, of putting one's body and secure sense of self on the line for social and racial justice, of heeding the affective call to explore the "as if" of greater family and community relations, not the "as if" of a presumed empathetic mind-reading. To be sure, *Citizen* emphasizes *relations* over "I"dentifications. Against an empathy that can be biopolitically manipulated by neoliberal political and economic systems, including privatizing empathy by shoring up a presumed universal white subject, an affective ethics or affective empathy recognizes that any imagined identification will always come up short against the otherness of the other, that affect's materiality and transpersonality make it historical, public, and transmissible, and that it is not a matter of feeling for or instead of others but of feeling and mattering alongside them—of putting one's body on the line, so to speak, when it matters most. An affective empathy, in this sense, would be an empathy based upon relationality and affective relations, which are historical-material productions that go beyond reacting to one's mere individual, subjective emotions. In short, Rankine does not appeal to the reader to be more empathetic and human, which could very well continue a racist politics of systemic inclusion and exclusion that hinges on a politics of othering. Instead, *Citizen* provides a model of an affective empathy that must be negotiated psychologically and materially, culturally and politically, individually and systemically in order for a more just and open community to relate to, and collect with, one another.

Notes

1   The video, which contains an entire forty-five-second history lesson on Jim Crow solely during the twentieth (not nineteenth) century, also contains a few images at the end of BLM protests and the names of Emmet Till and Breonna Taylor (apparently George Floyd didn't make the cut) while Alicia Keys sings "Lift Every Voice and Sing." https://www.cnn.com/2020/09/14/us/eric-reid-colin-kaepernick-nfl/index.html.

2   If it is contestable that these are truly empathetic moments (these people aren't trying to "feel" the speaker's emotions, for instance) or adequate examples of empathizing—and that there is a lot more going on emotion-wise and intellectually in each encounter—I would agree but offer a defense via Lisa Zunshine's work on cognitive psychology and novel reading. Zunshine is interested in employing the concept of Theory of Mind to understand how readers come to understand fictional characters and fictional works

themselves through "mind reading." Mind reading is a term "used by cognitive psychologists, interchangeable with 'Theory of Mind,' to describe our ability to explain people's behavior in terms of their thoughts, feelings, beliefs, and desires" (2006: 6). Zunshine, however, is quick to recognize that although Theory of Mind, because it emphasizes cognition and cognitive processes, is not interested in accounting for emotions per se, it is difficult, if not impossible, to separate emotions from cognition (2006: 163–4). The inevitable blending or overlapping of emotion and cognition means that while Theory of Mind is not synonymous with empathy, that it does not exclude empathy, whether empathy is considered purely emotional or intellectual, from contributing to "mind reading." The mind-reading each person engages in with the speaker thus blends cognition and emotion—and, of course, the reader of *Citizen* does so too.

3   Clinton's "I feel your pain" line is generally connected with the presidential candidate debate of October 15, 1992 in response to a question asked by a woman about how the national debt/economic recession had affected each of the candidates (https://www.c-span.org/video/?c4842764/user-clip-clintons-feel-pain-moment). While the questioner chides George H. Bush for not understanding how average people "feel" in dire economic times, she appears to be satisfied with Clinton's charismatic ability to *show* in his answer that he "feels" what Bush cannot—but Clinton never actually says the line. He says the line twice, however, several months *before* the debate in response to an AIDS activist, deemed a "heckler," who questioned whether Clinton would do more than he did as governor of Arkansas to address the AIDS crisis (https://www.nytimes.com/1992/03/28/us/1992-campaign-verbatim-heckler-stirs-clinton-anger-excerpts-exchange.html). What was clearly a tense moment when Clinton twice says "I feel your pain," which was uttered to *silence* someone, has been transferred to a later "good" moment when Clinton's answer had "feeling" and responded to a questioner's perceived "pain" regarding economic hard times. The potential for affective manipulation is striking, since the "feeling" becomes unmoored from its original object and trumps factual reality.

4   While there are critics of *White Fragility*, I do not believe this particular argument by DiAngelo is part of the controversy. Most critics do defer to some of the common sense or "obvious" points of DiAngelo's argument, and their critiques tend to focus on her simplifying of Black and white identities, her inability to truly decenter her (and her target audience's) whiteness, the sense that neither real individual nor political change can occur, and that DiAngelo has drawn from a long tradition of Black studies and thought and has distilled it in a neat self-help form that has proved—as a bestseller and a successful workshop series—highly popular and lucrative in the context of (problematic) institutional attempts (such as anti-bias and sensitivity training) to address issues of race and racism.

In an early review of the book, Justin Gomer and Christopher Petrella argue that while "DiAngelo's assessment of white supremacy [...] is sound" her "seeking out anti-racist pedagogical strategies" in "psychopathology rather than [...] history [...] therefore re-centers whiteness" (2017). DiAngelo, on their view, thus ends up individualizing racism in the psyche at the cost of considering historical-material formations. Lauren Michel Jackson notes the "dearth of contemporary black studies scholarship" in the book and that DiAngelo thus "doesn't really consider black studies a disciplining force in the direction of her work" (2019). As for the aims of the book and the workshops themselves, Jackson argues that "[d]eclaring that whiteness exists—for others or oneself— does not, itself, *do anything*. Saying 'I have privilege' does not do anything besides make the speaker feel good, and feeling good is the anathema to social change" (2019). Danzy Senna asserts that "[i]nterracial worlds friendships, marriages [...] are all but erased" (2021: 93), as are middle and upper middle class Black experiences. Instead, "white people remain the center of the story and Black people are at the margins" (2021: 93). Ultimately the individual-targeted self-help genre leaves "no absolution in view, and no real political action, either. She [DiAngelo] is not interested in police brutality, hate crimes, the criminal-justice system, drug laws, or even [...] the failure of public schools to educate all children" (2021: 93). In a similar vein, Carlos Lozada claims DiAngelo "flattens people of any ancestry into two-dimensional beings fitting predetermined narratives" so that "nothing ever changes, because change would violate its [the book's] premise" (2020). The book should thus be "less about unchangeable conditions than tangible actions, less about workshops and more about life" (2020). And as Kalefa Sanneh puts it, DiAngelo's story "makes white people seem like flawed, complicated characters; by comparison, people of color seem good, wise, and perhaps rather simple" (2019). In the end, while this "narrative may be appealing to its target audience, [...] it doesn't seem to offer much to anyone else" (2019). The fairly conservative John McWhorter, perhaps unsurprisingly, contends the book is "pernicious" and "a racist tract" that "diminishes Black people in the name of dignifying us" (2020).

5 Javadizadeh refers to "the racialized formation of the lyric tradition" and demonstrates that "what underwrites the autobiography of confessional poetry is it construction of whiteness, an identity that assumes its universality even as it anxiously apprehends its sovereignty to be under threat" (2019: 477).

6 In addition to essays by Tana Jean Welch and Katherine D. Johnston, which I reference below, is Angela Hume's essay on *Citizen*'s "biopoetics" via the "wasting" Black body in the poems and in recent American history (Katrina, for instance). Hume, employing both ecocritical and biopolitical critical lenses, delineates the ways in which Black bodies are often exposed and abandoned, through a politics of racism and exceptionality, to harmful and toxic environments that wear them away in a daily war of attrition. As Hume puts it, "[f]or Rankine, whether one can learn to negotiate one's environment becomes a question of life or death; one's biopoetics becomes a matter of survival" (2016: 90). Emphasizing the speaker's constant physical and mental struggles to keep living in and against the structurally racist and toxic environments of America, Hume reiterates Fred Moten's call "to consider exhaustion as a mode or form or way of [Black] life" (2018: 193), and asserts that "[t]he exhaustion of the body and mind in a racist society is a central focus of *Citizen*" (80). For Hume, Rankine ultimately takes on and transforms the lyric form through the speaker's fractured self, so that "[b]y inhabiting an experimental biopoetics—in and through the exhaustion, even failure, of lyric itself—Rankine's poetry illuminates the politics of othering that is constitutive of the present" (2016: 105). Hume

thus highlights, as does Rankine, the materiality of the "wasting" Black body as it is caught up in political, media, economic, and racist structures—against which it struggles nonetheless.

7 See Ticineto Clough (2007), Gregg and Seigworth (2010), and Ahmed (2010).

8 See Ngai (2005).

9 https://theracialimaginary.org/about/

References

Ahmed, S. (2010), *The Promise of Happiness*, Durham, NC: Duke.

Berlant, L. (2004), "Compassion (and Withholding)," in L. Berlant (ed), *Compassion*, 1–14, New York: Routledge.

Bonilla-Silva, E. (2009), *Racism without Racists: Color-Blind Racism and the Persistence of Racial Inequality in America*, New York: Rowman and Littlefield.

DiAngelo, R. (2018), *White Fragility: Why It's So Hard for White People to Talk about Racism*, Boston: Beacon Press.

Gomer, J. and C. Petrella (2017), "White Fragility, Anti-Racist Pedagogy, and the Weight of History," *Black Perspectives*, July 27, 2017. Available online: https://www.aaihs.org/white-fragility-anti-racist-pedagogy-and-the-weight-of-history/

Gregg, M. and Gregory J. Seigworth (eds) (2010), *The Affect Theory Reader*, Durham, NC: Duke.

Hume, A. (2016), "Toward an Antiracist Ecopoetics: Waste and Wasting in the Poetry of Claudia Rankine," *Contemporary Literature* 57 (1): 79–110.

Jackson, L. M. (2019), "What's Missing from *White Fragility*," *Slate*, September 4. Available online: https://slate.com/human-interest/2019/09/white-fragility-robin-diangelo-workshop.html

Javadizadeh, K. (2019), "The Atlantic Ocean Breaking on Our Heads: Claudia Rankine, Robert Lowell, and the Whiteness of the Lyric Subject," *PMLA* 143 (3): 475–90.

Johnston, K. D. (2019), "Profile Epistemologies, Racial Surveillance, and Affective Counterstrategies in Claudia Rankine's *Citizen*," *Twentieth-Century Literature* 65 (4): 343–68.

Keen, S. (2007), *Empathy and the Novel*, Oxford: Oxford University Press.

Lozada, C. (2020), "White Fragility Is Real. But *White Fragility* Is Flawed," *The Washington Post*, June 18. Available online: https://www.washingtonpost.com/outlook/2020/06/18/white-fragility-is-real-whitefragility-is-flawed/

McWhorter, J. (2020), "The Dehumanizing Condescension of *White Fragility*," *The Atlantic*, July 15, 2020. Available online: https://www.theatlantic.com/ideas/archive/2020/07/dehumanizing-condescension-white-fragility/614146/

Moten, F. (2018), *The Universal Machine: Consent Not to Be a Single Being*, Durham, NC: Duke.

Ngai, Sianne (2005), *Ugly Feelings*, Cambridge, MA: Harvard.

Pedwell, C. (2014), *Affective Relations: The Transnational Politics of Empathy*, New York: Palgrave Macmillan.

The Racial Imaginary Institute. Available online: https://theracialimaginary.org/

Rankine, C. (2014), *Citizen: An American Lyric*, Minneapolis, MN: Graywolf Press.

Rankine, C. and B. Loffreda (2015), "Introduction," in C. Rankine, Rankine B. Loffreda, and M. King Cap (eds), *The Racial Imaginary: Writers on Race in the Life of the Mind*, 13–22, Albany, NY: Fence Books.

Sanneh, K. (2019), "The Fight to Redefine Racism," *The New Yorker*, August 12. Available online: https://www.newyorker.com/magazine/2019/08/19/the-fight-to-redefine-racism

Senna, D. (2021), "White Progressives in Pursuit of Racial Virtue: What Two New Books Reveal about the Moral Limits of Anti-Racist Self-Help," *The Atlantic* 328 (2) (September): 90–3.

Simecek, K. (2019), "Cultivating Intimacy: The Use of the Second Person in Lyric Poetry," *Philosophy and Literature* 43 (2): 501–18.

Ticineto Clough, Patricia (ed) (2007), *The Affective Turn: Theorizing the Social*, Durham, NC: Duke.

Welch, T. J. (2015), "*Don't Let Me Be Lonely*: The Trans-Corporeal Ethics of Claudia Rankine's Investigative Poetics," *MELUS* 47 (1): 124–48.

Zunshine, L. (2006), *Why We Read Fiction: Theory of Mind and the Novel*, Columbus, OH: Ohio State.

4

Limits to Empathy: On the Motif of Failed Empathy in Julian Barnes

Peter Simonsen and Marie-Elisabeth Lei Holm

Does Empathy Have Limits?

As any quick and dirty Google nGram search will tell you, "empathy" is on the rise: since around 2000, the graph of an nGram search on the word "empathy" suggests it has been used very frequently. Listening to fans of empathy—Barack Obama, for instance, identifying an "empathy deficit" in 2006 (Karl 2020) and in 2015, in conversation with novelist Marilynne Robinson, presenting the novel as part of the answer (Rylance 2016: 163)— it sometimes sounds as if it holds the key to solving most, if not all, of our problems. It seems as if there are no limits to the good it can do. If only it was possible to truly feel the pain and suffering of any vulnerable, marginalized, and silenced individual or group then they would not be treated with intolerance and injustice by those in power. This "empathy-altruistic" (Keen 2007: vii) argument seems to run through different academic and critical disciplines including literary studies (Booth 1988), human rights research (Hunt 2007), philosophy (Rorty 1989; Nussbaum 1997), medical humanities research (Charon 2001), and it extends to economics as well.

Labor market economist Guy Standing sees the study of realist literature as part of a strategy to counter an empathy deficit in the contemporary world akin to the one Obama identifies. In *A Precariat Charter*, Standing notes that "A number of psychology studies have found that the rich have less empathy and compassion than others. ... As long as [the rich] have no exposure to the insecurities of the precariat, they will have little empathy with it. So they can be easily persuaded to support policies that hit the precariat" (2014: 119–20). Standing goes on to share an anecdote featuring a UK Minister for Welfare Reform claiming that the reason more citizens use food banks is that they are freely accessible. Meanwhile, the economic reality is that more citizens are poor and struggling because of ever harsher austerity legislation–legislation which Standing argues is more easily passed if the poor and unemployed are only understood through stereotypes and clichés about free-riding and inertia.

The 2010 psychology study Guy Standing references by Kraus, Côté and Keltner did three empirical studies of university students and employees. In the first two the researchers found a strong correlation between social class (defined by level of education) and "empathetic accuracy" in judging peoples' emotions as expressed by facial images as well as in one-on-one conversations during a staged interview. They found that members of a lower social class have more empathy by these measures. In the third study, eighty-two student participants were asked to imagine they belonged either to a higher or lower social class and then given an empathetic accuracy test, which had the same results as the two first studies. In other words, empathy in this study was manipulable, not just a matter of genes or mirror neurons, and was explained as the result of having to take more account of one's social class context. The richer and better educated you are (or imagine you are), the less your life depends on your ability to gauge others' emotions, and the less you are in the hands of others: "Lacking resources and control, lower-class individuals tend to focus on the external, social context to understand events in their lives. As a result, they orient to other people to navigate their social environments" (2010: 1721).

These findings might give some credibility to Standing's diagnosis of what he believes is a "[l]oss of social empathy in the neo-liberal dystopia" that is related to an abandonment of a liberal education that would expose students to "the great realist literature of the world." For Standing, such literature "instils empathy ... develop[s] the capacity to understand the complexities of the human condition" (2014: 120) and participates in what he calls the progressives' cause: "to revive empathy, that is also the case for another progressive value, social solidarity" (2014: 121). While our inner progressive idealists might share this diagnosis and line of reasoning, we tend to follow Suzanne Keen's more skeptical premise that it is, to put it mildly, difficult to infer any causality between reading literature, developing empathy, and performing socially beneficial actions in solidarity against the neoliberal dystopia, where you're on your own and can't afford the "luxury" of true compassion. The very study Standing references, for instance, correlates higher education as an indicator of socioeconomic social class with less empathy. Maybe the solution is not to read more difficult novels, after all...

A hesitancy to link literature, education, and increased levels of empathy is a significant theme in one of contemporary Anglophone literature's leading novelists, Julian Barnes. Again and again, Barnes's fiction questions the notion that reading literature allows us to "get" other people and to act on our knowledge of others in a morally enhanced, altruistic manner. On the contrary, Barnes's novels and short stories often give the impression that the more you read, the *less* you understand about what and how others really feel. Whether this, in a paradoxical manner, actually helps us *get* others better is a question we address throughout the chapter and return to in our concluding remarks. Indeed, the prevalent moral and humanistic question of how to treat others with dignity, respect, and solidarity may be best answered if we acknowledge that some people prefer not to give access to their interiority and instead insist on their right to a certain otherness that is unproblematic. Recognizing that there are limits to empathy, and that even if empathy is possible, it is important to maintain that far from everyone wants their inner life invaded, and that many of us would probably not like to be those invaders in the first place, are crucial theoretical prerequisites in the larger context of cultivating and conceptualizing empathy.

In order to expand upon this argument, we investigate the limits and challenges of empathy in Julian Barnes's writing, especially in his signature piece, the postmodern novel par excellence, *Flaubert's Parrot* (1984), but also in a later novel, *The Sense of an Ending* (2011) and the short story "Appetite" (2004). Via interesting if not always reliable narrators, Barnes expresses a certain skepticism about the very possibility and desirability of empathy and, by implication, about the school of thought which sees social solidarity as a beneficial outcome of reading literature. Such an aggrandized claim for literature's agency cannot be made on account of Barnes's work. We argue, however, that it may give us a different and more realistic account of empathy. Because if empathy in Barnes must be understood under the sign of failure it means that we must work harder to compensate for this. Barnes in a sense writes "against empathy" (Bloom 2016) but as such also in favor of a more reasoned compassion not predicated so much on spontaneous sharing of affect as on cooler acts of deliberation and cogitation. Empathy in Barnes must be understood in relation to the conditions of postmodernity: a pervasive skepticism of any emancipatory enlightenment claims and deep doubt about a sense of meaningfulness in human life reflected in a writing style very hesitant and skeptical about its own status, reach, and authority.

Literary Empathy Studies and the Question of Postmodern Empathy in Julian Barnes

Empathy has been called "the grand theme of our time" (De Waal 2009: xi) possibly because it is seen to facilitate and generate altruism. Lynn Hunt, in *Inventing Human Rights,* suggests that the eighteenth-century novel participated in bringing about human rights by enabling middle- and upper-class readers to identify and empathize with common, lower class individuals such as servants, prisoners, or slaves. In this way, according to Hunt, "reading novels created a sense of equality and empathy through passionate involvement in the narrative" (2007: 39). Though he is wary of Hunt's positing of a causal relation between the rise of the novel and the emergence of humanitarianism, Steven Pinker suggests that "Realistic fiction ... may expand readers' circle of empathy by seducing them into thinking and feeling like people very different from themselves" (2011: 175–6). This argument is at the heart of Rick Rylance's *Literature and the Public Good*, which enumerates all the evils contingent on an empathy deficit.[1] Rylance concludes his study by presenting literacy, literature, and a literary education as part of the solution: "[literature] heightens our talents in making and communicating cognitive acts of complexity, understanding, and sophistication. It enhances the capabilities that make us human and enable our societies to function" (2016: 199). The leading streaming service for books in Denmark, Mofibo, which is part of a larger conglomerate, Storytell, says of itself on its website: "Our vision is to make the world more empathic and creative through good stories which can be shared and enjoyed by everyone, everywhere, anytime" (https://mofibo.com/dk/da/om-mofibo). In current liberal humanist discourse, furthermore, empathy is seen as "both the emotional ingredient that binds us together as human subjects and communities and the affective panacea to a wide range of social, political and economic divisions and grievances" (Pedwell 2013: 18).

In what follows we use the concept of empathy as an interpretive platform for the examination of literary fictional texts. We argue it can offer a more profitable and meaningful approach to much that is most central about modern literature insofar as it is engaged in probing questions of identity, self-knowledge, intersubjectivity, and meaning in life. Literature can add meaning, nuance, and substance to commonsensical notions of empathy and let us experience how it works or, as is this chapter's focus, how it sometimes fails to work. As we see it, empathy names the experience of inhabiting not just the perspective but also a part of the lifeworld of another being and thus it's not a matter of cannibalistically taking over or appropriating someone else (what Amy Coplan would call "pseudo-empathy" 2011: 42), but an act of coming to know experiences, thoughts, and emotions of other people, while not necessarily *sharing* their experiences, thoughts, or feelings.

Philosopher Dan Zahavi has done interesting work in the phenomenology of empathy; arguing in the vein of prominent phenomenologists that "basic empathy (...) acquaints you—in the most direct and immediate manner possible—with another's experiential life. Importantly, on this account empathy is not about me having the same mental state as the other, but about me being experientially acquainted with an experience that is not my own" (Zahavi 2021: 104720). Empathy in its most rudimentary form, we might say along similar lines, does not so much entail sharing as a cognitive function through which we take in and make sense of other peoples' interior states. Amy Coplan calls it "genuine empathy" in which "a person represents the other's situation from the other person's point of view and attempts to simulate the target individual's experiences as though she were the target individual" (2011: 54). Following Coplan, talking about empathy has to do with the extent to and the grounds upon which, we can get to know others through a fusion of emotion and cognition. Empathy, on this account, cannot only be approached through a language of mirror neurons and instinctive reactions nor through speculation and cogitation, but calls for rich descriptions of embodied and felt knowledge of self and other. Such descriptions are the stuff of much modern fiction.

As Suzanne Keen in particular has shown (2007), literary empathy studies are particularly suited to specific cultural periods, and to motivate our focus on Julian Barnes and what we take to be his cultivation of a certain postmodern take on literature and empathy (one Keen and others have not explored in depth), we skip over some relatively well-known territory. Studies in the eighteenth-century novel, for instance, find it easy to read Richardson, Sterne, and Fielding together with the moral philosophers such as Adam Smith and David Hume who theorize "sympathy" and "altruism" and "benevolence" through ideas of moral imagination (Hunt 2007). Nineteenth-century Romanticism and Victorianism in general extend this thinking about the importance of cultivating empathetic feelings through art and imagination, something that is often seen to culminate in George Eliot, who seemed to believe that the moral imagination through omniscient narration could facilitate readers' growth of sympathy. As Keen puts it, "Eliot's stated goals lay in the extension of readers' feelings, not necessarily in any particular real-world action to follow" (2007: 54). The Modernist period is also increasingly being scrutinized through the concept of empathy, even as major traits about the aesthetics and literary theory of the period, as Keen has noted, suggest a desire for alienation and disruption, and an emphasis on limited and unreliable perspectives that could counter strong character identification and immersion in illusory worlds where art and life got confused. As Eve Sorum points out in *Modernist Empathy*, "modernist literature encourages us to enter other perspectives even as it also questions the very idea of a self and an other, and, hence, the very possibility of empathy" (2019: 3).

In her more detailed account of this literary historical context for literary empathy studies, Keen leaves the question of *contemporary literature* and empathy more or less moot and does not engage the debate over the implications of postmodernism and literary empathy. Yet, studies in what is now often called "post-postmodern" literature, the "post ironic" or "new sincerity" writing in the wake of David Foster Wallace, Jonathan Franzen, Zadie Smith, George Saunders, Jonathan Safran Foer, Dave Eggers, and others have read these works through the lens of ethics and empathy. As one critic puts it, a large group of contemporary writers seems to find that "the cool, detached irony of postmodernist writing no longer provides a sufficient or appropriate strategy in response to the multifarious socio-economic problems of our neoliberal, neoconservative moment—that is, problems which are supposedly caused or exacerbated by a culture of corporate greed that lacks in solidarity and altruistic behavior" (Basseler 2017: 154). Clearly, postmodern literature, when defined in terms of "cool, detached irony," the "death of the author," the free play of the signifier, and endless deferral of meaning, often figures as the significant "other" of these studies, as the last place to look for empathy inasmuch as the concept seems entangled with an understanding of the self as deep and the human psyche as essentially *accessible* via representation—and representation, in turn, as somehow reliable and sincere. All these notions would be deeply problematic if considered in the light of, for instance, the paranoid vision of Thomas Pynchon's High Postmodernisn in *Gravity's Rainbow* or Samuel Beckett's flat *papier-mâché* characters. In this kind of postmodernist thinking, we are beyond finding it possible to even "question," like the modernists on Sorum's account, the existence of self and other, because they have been exposed as linguistically constructed illusions. This premise is challenged by fiction written after the "death of the author" (and of the liberal subject), so Julian Barnes may seem like an odd choice for a "rereading of empathy." Barnes is a preeminent so-called high postmodern author in Anglophone literature, whose fiction has been described as "display[ing] a self-reflexive, postmodernist skepticism regarding any truth claims, even those which potentially could anchor personal identity" (Holmes 2009: 12).[2] Literary historical categorization aside, and moving on to Barnes, it indeed turns out that searching the MLA database for connections between "Julian Barnes" and "empathy" yields zero results (as of February 19, 2021). In a recent collection of essays on Barnes (Childs 2011: 114) the word is used once, as a synonym for love in analyzing a recent short story, while in Peter Childs's 2011 monograph (based on a simple word search in the pdf) "empathy" appears zero times. Critical interest in Barnes centers on questions of fictionality, history, truth, memory, aging, love, and art as well as "the usual things: death, pain, loneliness"—as Barnes responded when asked in an interview what he most dreaded (Childs also suggests that these concerns inform much of his work [Childs 2011: 4]). In other words, it is not common to investigate Barnes's authorship in light of the increasing interest in questions of narrative empathy. Anne Whitehead, who in general holds, like Barnes, that literary empathy is more problematic than promising, does not include him in her study of contemporary British literature in which she concludes that "contemporary fiction [does not] lead to knowledge or understanding of another; it is more often concerned with the difficulties and deficiencies in our intersubjective encounters, and with their disturbances by the effects of power, and it is fascinated, too, by how, when, and why we fail to care for one another" (2017: 13). This applies not only to the writers Whitehead discusses (Pat Barker, Mark Haddon, Kazuo Ishiguro, Ian McEwan), but also and maybe even more pointedly to Julian Barnes's key works.[3]

There are, no doubt, many good reasons for the neglect of Barnes in literary empathy studies. One of them may simply be that Barnes himself does not talk as readily of empathy as do writers like Foster Wallace or Barnes's contemporary, Ian McEwan, who for instance in response to the September 11, 2001, attacks famously suggested, that if the terrorists had only read novels they would not have carried out these atrocities because they would have empathized with their victims:

> This is the nature of empathy, to think oneself into the minds of others. ... If the hijackers had been able to imagine themselves into the thoughts and feelings of the passengers, they would have been unable to proceed. It is hard to be cruel once you permit yourself to enter the mind of your victim. Imagining what it is like to be someone other than yourself is at the core of our humanity. It is the essence of compassion, and it is the beginning of morality. The hijackers used fanatical certainty, misplaced religious faith, and dehumanising hatred to purge themselves of the human instinct for empathy. Among their crimes was a failure of the imagination.
>
> (McEwan 2001: online)

As Emily Holman notes, "McEwan's piece was about 9/11, but it was also about art. There's the suggestion that the kind of throwing yourself into the mind of another that literature enables may have made a difference, even at a moment of crisis" (2016: 315). In his omnisciently narrated novel *Saturday* (2005), which responds to the context of global terrorism by localizing and personalizing it and partly making it a question of empathy, he even suggested that the experience of Matthew Arnold's Victorian poem, "Dover Beach," caused a criminal, local terrorist-thug to reconnect with his lost humanity—yet it also opens to a reading of how empathy can be used instrumentally as a form of violence. As the novel seems to suggest, there are fine lines between compassionate care for the other and acts of cruelty: when protagonist Henry Perowne through virtuoso brain surgery saves the life of the criminal he himself had (unempathetically) pushed down some stairs to protect his family, he also condemns Baxter to ending his life in prison suffering from the incurable Huntington's Disease.

Another reason why critics may not be interested in empathy and Julian Barnes (and the reason he himself may not be interested in it) is surely the sense of something saccharine associated with the question of literature and empathy that leads to often aggrandized claims on behalf of literary texts. It is tempting for many liberal humanists to suggest that looking into another person by identifying with a literary character or simply delving into works of the imagination by "great writers" our own lives are somehow enriched and enlarged. This is a claim often made on behalf of philosophers like Martha Nussbaum and Richard Rorty, and in a sense they do argue this, but not that it's simple or automatic: it takes a readerly investment and often the intervention of an educational system. But the basic argument is that readers can learn moral lessons from novels' figurations of scenes of identification: "By identification with Mr. Causaubon in *Middlemarch* or with Mrs. Jellyby in *Bleak House*, for example, we may come to notice what we ourselves have been doing" (Rorty 1989: 147). The key word here is "may" which dispels any easy causality and instead calls for active reflection as well as a skeptical "may not." Nussbaum is also hesitant, as here with reference to Ralph Ellison's *Invisible Man*: "Narrative art has the power to make us see the lives of the different with more than the casual tourist's interest—with involvement and sympathetic understanding, with anger at our society's refusals of visibility. ... Understanding, for example, how a history of racial stereotyping can affect self-esteem, achievement, and love enables us to make more informed judgments on issues relating to affirmative action and education" (1997: 88). In Barnes, the dream of empathy being derived from fictional reading that leads to "understanding" and in turn potentially leads to prosocial and more moral behavior is never indulged, or, if it is, coated in thick sarcasm and scathing irony. In Barnes, the mind of the other as well as of the self is opaque, veiled in confusion, misapprehension, denial, and repression. From such a framework, however, it might just be possible to delve into potentially ameliorative life lessons about empathy in Barnes's literary corpus.

Failed Empathy in *Flaubert's Parrot*

In Barnes's international breakthrough novel and signature piece, the metafictional, highly intertextual, and generically hybrid *Flaubert's Parrot* (1984), which Barnes himself in an interview described as "an upside down novel" (Childs 2011: 46), the retired doctor, protagonist, and ageing first-person narrator, Geoffrey Braithwaite, looks back and reflects on his inability to understand his deceased wife's inner life and path to suicide.

This is not his initial and explicit "project" (Barnes 1984: 2) in the narration, however, which seems instead to be to find out the purpose of the stuffed parrot Gustave Flaubert had on his desk as he wrote *Un Coeur Simple* and, by implication, to "chase the writer" (Barnes 1984: 2), as he puts it. So only indirectly and seemingly by accident can the novel be said to be about identification and empathy. It begins with a bizarre moment of failed empathetic identification: Braithwaite feels nothing upon revisiting battlefields in Normandy where he fought during the Second World War, nor does he remember feeling anything back then. That world is closed, he can no longer enter it, and we can understand why the thing Braithwaite identifies with is a ruined stone copy of a copy of a bronze statue of Flaubert: "'Life! Life! To have erections!' I was reading that Flaubertian exclamation the other day. It made me feel like a stone statue with a patched upper thigh" (Barnes 1984: 3). However, seeing the stuffed parrot he thinks inspired the object of his all-consuming interest in retirement (as it also did in his working life), Gustave Flaubert, to write *Un Coeur Simple*, he feels strongly connected to the long-dead writer: "I gazed at the bird, and to my surprise felt ardently in touch with this writer who disdainfully forbade posterity to take any personal interest in him....[H]ere, in this unexceptional green parrot, preserved in a routine yet mysterious fashion, was something which made me feel I had almost known the writer. I was both moved and cheered" (Barnes 1984: 7–8). So begins Geoffrey Braithwaite's quest for Flaubert and the parrot, and the novel functions—accordingly—as his continued attempt to get some firm, reliable knowledge of the author: to enter his mind and emotional life, to get under his skin.

However, the more knowledge Braithwaite amasses about Flaubert, the closer he gets to him through reading texts and material remains, the more the writer disappears. In the first chapter, Braithwaite realizes that there are two parrots who lay claim to being the real one, and in the second chapter we are confronted with three different chronologies of Flaubert's life which, though based in meticulous research and facts, mutually contradict one another. In the end, after much hesitation and many attempts at sidetracking things yet also confronting what the novel is really about (Braithwaite's failed marriage and his wife's consequent suicide), and faced with several different stuffed parrots (symbols of the "writer's voice," spirit, or presence) each of which could be the Loulou of the story, Braithwaite has to admit that he will never know about Flaubert's thoughts and motives—nor will he ever know what drove his wife to suicide or indeed the character of her innermost self. He opens a cupboard and suddenly three more stuffed parrots look at him: "They gazed at me like three quizzical, sharp-eyed, dandruff-ridden, dishonourable old men. They did look—I had to admit—a little cranky. I stared at them for a minute or so, and then dodged away./Perhaps it was one of them" (Barnes 1984: 228–9). Perhaps not, we will never know—all we can do is think about the extent to which it is meaningful to spend one's retirement dreaming of a one-to-one correspondence between life and fiction.

The past and the other are opaque and sealed off or, as Braithwaite puts it early on, the past is like a greased piglet that slips through one's hands (Barnes 1984: 5). In a later metaphor, the past is like a distant shoreline we all view through telescopes but from different perspectives, thus all seeing something different which we believe we have brought into existence (Barnes 1984: 114). In the chapter "Dictionary of Received Ideas" near the end of the novel, in the context of a general recognition of the ultimate unreliability of knowledge of others, we read: "Demand violently: How can we know anybody?" (Barnes 1984: 184). Answer: we can't. We can only speculate, as does Braithwaite in the novel's last chapter:

> Perhaps this was Ellen's weakness: an inability to gaze into the black pit. She could only squint at it, repeatedly. One glance would make her despair, and despair would make her seek distraction. Some outgaze the black pit; others ignore it; those who keep glancing at it become obsessed. She chose the exact dosage: the only occasion when being a doctor's wife seemed to help her.
>
> (Barnes 1984: 217)

Having chattered futilely away about Flaubert for most of the novel, in Chapter 13, "Pure Story," Braithwaite finally gets to what readers might see as the point of his narration, beyond the unraveling of a postmodern *tour de force* showcasing the writer's wit and technical brilliance: his wife died in middle age from an overdose and was kept alive in a coma, and *he* was the one who turned off the ventilator and, in a sense, killed her, leaving himself to mourn and to endlessly ponder the conundrum of who she was, what really moved her in life and why she ended it the way she did. For some reason, inexplicable to Braithwaite, his wife, Ellen (much like the also suicidal Emma Bovary with whom she shares initials) led a mysterious secret life with countless lovers (barely hidden beneath poor lies and deceptions, he knew but never confronted her). To try to understand her existence, he must, as he says, "fictionalize": "We never talked about her secret life. So I have to invent my way to the truth" (Barnes 1984: 197) about why she killed herself. Yet nothing comes of this attempt to use the faculty of which Braithwaite seems quite bereft, the sympathetic imagination. Braithwaite doesn't know and doesn't understand: "both her secret life and her despair [that led to her suicide] lay in the same inner chamber of her heart, inaccessible to me. I could touch the one no more than the other" (Barnes 1984: 198). Here, the idea of empathy meets its limit in the opacity of the loved partner:

> Ellen. My wife: someone I feel I understand less well than a foreign writer dead for a hundred years. Is this an aberration, or is it normal? Books say: she did this because. Life says: she did this. Books are where things

are explained to you; life is where things aren't. I'm not surprised some people prefer books. Books make sense of life. The only problem is that the lives they make sense of are other people's lives, never your own.

(Barnes 1984: 201)

In other words, empathy seems possible in fiction and books, but not in life. At least not in Geoffrey Braithwaite's "life." In this novel, there is no transfer from reading to living the way, for instance, Rorty suggests (and, indeed, a simple reading of *Emma Bovary* posits Emma's reading of cheap romances as the source of her downfall when she really wanted a more dramatic and romantic life inspired by fiction). Despite comprehensive, obsessive knowledge of Flaubert, Geoffrey Braithwaite had no idea who his own wife was. Only in fictionalizing his wife can he feel something, but he cannot share her feeling of despair. Yet, can we trust the claim to ignorance of this unreliable and self-declared "hesitating narrator" (Barnes 1984: 100)? Can this book, despite its message of blocked understanding, be used to help the living?

Keen theorizes that when we know we are reading fiction, we are more eager to empathize and subject ourselves to transformation because we are dealing with something we know not to be ourselves. We are, so to speak, *protected* by fiction, as "paratexts cuing readers to understand a work as fictional unleash their emotional responsiveness" (2007: 98). What, then, of a novel (fiction) which insists that it is searching for the truth (in the form of facts about Flaubert; its motto is a quote from Flaubert on the motive for writing biographies) but via an unreliable narrator who admits that he has to fictionalize in order to get to that truth (a truth he also admits eludes him)? The question may be: even if Geoffrey Braithwaite had felt some kind of spontaneous, visceral sharing of affect, had indeed *felt* he had access to Ellen's deepest interior, could he have alleviated her of her despair? Could empathy have made a difference? What good could it have achieved?

Braithwaite certainly feels complicit in Ellen's despair. Early in the novel he muses, "I thought of writing books myself once. I had the ideas; I even made notes. But I was a doctor, married with children. You can only do one thing well: Flaubert knew that. Being a doctor was what I did well. My wife … died" (Barnes 1984: 3, ellipsis in original). In that hesitation marked by the ellipsis Braithwaite opens the lid to what is really on his mind—which we as readers are of course duped into believing we have access to and find ourselves perhaps sympathetic toward (there is something endearing about Braithwaite, even as we may also feel increasingly frustrated by his lack of insight into himself). Braithwaite lets on that his concern is not Flaubert and what Flaubert "knew," but his wife's death and by implication the meaning of his own life as a widower now that he finds himself gazing into the same abyss she did. Braithwaite acknowledges his lack of access to his wife's interiority and her inability (or refusal?) to give him that access: "Did I try?" to reach out to her, "Of course I tried. But I was not surprised when the mood came upon her" (Barnes 1984: 198). Such "mood" being that of "despair": "Isn't it the natural condition of life after a certain age? I have it now; she had it earlier. After a number of events, what is there left but repetition and diminishment? Who wants to go on living?" (Barnes 1984: 197).

Ellen was about fifty when this "mood" came upon her, Braithwaite fictionalizes/speculates:

> She had had a husband, children, lovers, a job. The children had left home; the husband was always the same. She had friends, and what are called interests; though unlike me she didn't have some rash devotion to a dead foreigner to sustain her. She had traveled enough. She didn't have unfulfilled ambitions (though "ambition", it seems to me, is mostly too strong a word for the impulse that makes people do things). She wasn't religious. Why go on?
>
> (Barnes 1984: 197)

Read as a novel of mid-life crisis and depression, such a question indeed resonates with the reader, yet not all fifty-year-old bored women commit suicide (unlike Emma Bovary, Ellen was not haunted by debt-financed luxury consumption which contributes to the former's suicide), so we are still left wondering about Ellen's motives. We share this wonder with Geoffrey Braithwaite yet unlike him we can perhaps more easily see how his *knowing* inability to see things from her point of view, his enormous sense of restraint, and failure to even fake spontaneity and enthusiasm, maybe allow us some kind of insight into how it must have felt to be in *her* shoes and thus feel *her* despair as we imagine what life with this person must have been like. In one place he characterizes himself as "quite unreasonably literal-minded" (Barnes 1984: 100), as one who actually seems more concerned with establishing the veracity of which stuffed parrot was on Flaubert's desk than confronting his own despair and loneliness or acknowledging his own quite substantial role in Ellen's life and death.

Braithwaite claims he wanted to know "the worst" about Ellen: "I loved Ellen, and I wanted to know the worst. I never provoked her; I was cautious; but I wanted to know the worst. Ellen never returned this caress" (Barnes 1984: 147). In a word, this was a relationship devoid of empathetic will and curiosity: "We never talked about her secret life" (Barnes 1984: 197). Surely a man like that can drive one to suicide when he also leaves you in possession of the right drugs. At one point, Braithwaite tellingly recounts an anecdote about the poet laureate interviewed on television being asked "Does life improve?", a question the laureate answered with: "The only thing I think is very good today is dentistry" (Barnes 1984: 198–9). Braithwaite's version of an answer to the same question would be: "The one thing that is very good in life today is death" (Barnes 1984: 199) by which he seems to mean that we are no longer religiously afraid of death by suicide and have good and ample medications to do so. Writing in retrospect and in denial, Braithwaite on the one hand continually suggests that he was genuinely interested in finding and understanding the truth of his wife's inner life even though he, ironically, clearly is more interested in the truth of a stuffed parrot. And on the other hand, by thus demonstrating his own inability at mind reading he lets us feel that we as readers have privileged access to *his* failed access to the mind of the other. Martha Nussbaum, via Wayne Booth's idea of novels as "friends" we can learn from even if we do not sympathize with the characters or with the values espoused by the "implied author," says that even the failure to understand the other's experience and perspective, for instance a white middle-class reader's inability to identify with and thus fully understand certain aspects of Ellison's *Invisible Man*, "prompts a deeper and more pertinent kind of sympathy" (1997: 95). "This complex interpretative art," she continues, "is what the Stoics required when they asked the world citizen to gain empathetic understanding of people who are different" (1997: 95). While this makes sense and sounds just right (and provides pushback to an often-voiced critique of Nussbaum that she is too optimistic), it still does not resonate with the fictional universe of Barnes's fiction and, *in lieu* of solid empirical evidence, we obviously cannot conclude that it is more than a wish.

"Good" Fiction and its Ends: Appetite for Empathy?

Readers in search of uplifting accounts of the power of reading fiction to create better and more moral citizens—the "good" in good literature—should in other words not prepare to find what they are looking for in Julian Barnes. The experience of realizing too late that you had failed to really understand someone else, that you had failed at empathy and thus to a large extent had wasted your life is a recurrent motif not just in *Flaubert's Parrot* but in much of Barnes's fiction. This occurs perhaps most chillingly in *The Sense of an Ending* in which the hesitant first-person narrator, Tony Webster (who is close in spirit to Geoffrey Braithwaite), who is into his sixties and has given up on most aspects of life, belatedly understands his part in a tragedy from his youth. A friend dies by suicide after an affair with Tony's ex-girlfriend's mother that resulted in an unwanted pregnancy; Tony remarks:

> You get towards the end of life—no, not life itself, but of something else: the end of any likelihood of change in that life. You are allowed one long moment of pause, time enough to ask the question: what else have I done

wrong? … . I thought of what I couldn't know or understand now, of all that couldn't ever be known or understood.

(Barnes 2011: 149)

Part of the novel's irony is how Tony recalls attending literature class at school and being taught that "Real literature was about psychological, emotional and social truth as demonstrated by the actions and reflections of its protagonists; the novel was about character developed over time" (Barnes 2011: 15), a notion of which his own character is a walking contradiction. In Barnes, we typically get the story of the life lived in a quite unadventurous manner told by characters very hesitant to try to get under someone else's skin. Tony captures this earlier in the story where he thinks about how he now, late in life, would contemplate trying to get under the skin of his ex-girlfriend Veronica ("Nowadays I might try to get under Veronica's skin, but I would never try to flay it from her bit by bloody bit" [Barnes 2011: 99]), something his earlier self failed at. Indeed, the common, casual metaphor of getting under someone else's skin that is often used about empathy in a positive way to suggest achieved understanding of the other's perspective is given a macabre spin in this novel. A few pages on, Tony extends the metaphor:

I said I wanted to get under her skin, didn't I? It's an odd expression, and one that always makes me think of [my ex-wife's] way of roasting a chicken. She'd gently loosen the skin from the breast and thighs, then slip butter and herbs underneath. Tarragon, probably. Perhaps some garlic as well, I'm not sure. I've never tried it myself, then or since; my fingers are too clumsy, and I imagine them ripping the skin.

(Barnes 2011: 109)

Indeed, to get under someone's skin can be thought of as a quite violent affair that can be very hurtful for the other if one doesn't know what one is doing and as this image suggests, has something of the postmortem about it. So, rather than give empathy a try and risk hurting someone without knowing, Tony Webster and most of Barnes's ageing male narrators simply abstain from it and try to leave others' skin intact, even if they may have a certain appetite for it. His younger self's fear that "Life wouldn't turn out to be like Literature" (Barnes 2011: 15) but instead be dead boring in the end was well grounded. Like his parents, at best, he "might aspire to the condition of onlookers and bystanders, part of a social backdrop against which real, true, important things could happen" (Barnes 2011: 15).

In "Appetite," a short story from the collection *The Lemon Table* (2004), a retired male dentist develops a cognitive disorder which sounds like Lewy Body dementia but is never given a proper diagnosis. His wife tells the story about what it is like living with a husband who does not recognize her, and who fails completely at empathy even as she is still capable of being empathetic toward him. This story explores how it may feel when your empathy is blocked because the person you empathize with no longer recognizes you or acknowledges your efforts at empathy and instead seems to think you are someone else due to cognitive malfunctioning. The disease means he cannot recognize his wife of many years (his second wife) who reads to him from a book of recipes and sometimes provokes a positive reaction when he recalls a certain gourmet meal. Yet he mostly bickers over the vague or foreign phrasings of the recipes, expresses xenophobia, and loses his sexual inhibitions. These behaviors form the central motif of the story: how to handle someone with a perverse mind who does not want you (who can't even remember you) but instead envisions another woman in your place.

One scene in particular captures this ugly series of misrecognitions and humiliations. It is when the narrator says goodnight to her husband (they have had separate bedrooms for seven years), he replies "Come in with me" and gives her "a look—one of those looks from years before" (Barnes 2004: 164) when they were still intimate. Although she knows he is ill, she imagines that this moment may be spurred by something returning from the past just as when she reads him the recipes—that the appetite for food mirrors an appetite for her: "And the idea that it might be just melted me" (Barnes 2004: 165). She hesitantly takes off her clothes and gets into bed with him; looking back, she recollects: "He said, and I'll remember it until my dying day, he said, in that dry voice of his … 'No, not you'./I thought I'd misheard, and then he said again, 'No, not you, you bitch'" (Barnes 2004: 165). "That was a year or two ago, and there's been worse, but that was the worst, if you know what I mean." The "you" is present throughout the story but never specified. As such it functions for us as readers as a rhetorical ploy to establish intimacy with the first-person narrative voice of this woman who, despite these experiences, uses the word "happy" to name the feeling she gets when her acts of reading to her husband lead to his recognition of a meal, and she feels there is a moment of empathetic connection (Barnes 2004: 162, 173). Employing a "you" to appeal directly to readers not only creates an intimate sphere of communication, but also establishes a clear sense of where to direct one's readerly sympathy: that is, with the caregiving perspective from which we are being directly addressed. It is, however, a sympathy tainted by ambivalence. As readers, we feel sorry for the narrator but, at the same time, cannot help but wonder why on earth she keeps trying to invoke the affection and humanity of a person who clearly has nothing, or only very little, left of either. It is almost physically painful to read how she becomes the target of an endless string of obscenities and profanity from her ailing husband while merely trying to tend to him, and while one's immediate shock and indignation are leveled at the patient, however unfairly, it is hard to not also feel some irritation at *her* for continuing to put up with his crudeness. The narrator's way of addressing readers, one could hence argue, establishes a space in which the difficulty of her efforts to empathize with her husband is mirrored by the reader's struggle to empathize *with her*. Similar to when a friend informs you of a troubled relationship in which she is clearly being wronged but is so head over heels that she will not realize it, the short story makes us want to yell *leave him*, although the root of the problem, tragically, is dementia and not a flawed character, which is what makes her unable to leave. At least not yet. She knows that at some point she will have to get paid care and—while caring for him—silently does the math in a mood of cool, detached cogitation mixed with deep and caring empathetic sympathy:

> I expect I'll find myself doing sums. Like: twenty or thirty years ago he spent two or three days working with all the skill and concentration at his disposal to earn money I'll now spend in an hour or two getting a nurse to wipe his bottom and put up with the jabber of a naughty five-year-old. No, that's not right. A naughty seventy-five-year-old.
>
> (Barnes 2004: 172)

In the language of empathy, we might say that even though the story invokes empathy for the narrator and, by implication, her husband, our efforts to empathize are ultimately restricted by his vulgarity and, in turn, her display of defeatism. In this sense, "Appetite" becomes a testament to the *complexity* and *difficulty* of empathy: that no matter how desolate and sad a given situation might be, regardless of how much it calls on us to empathize, we may still feel other, *uglier* feelings besides empathy, such as annoyance, embarrassment on behalf of others, a sense of knowing better than the characters or, perhaps even a degree of self-satisfaction derived from the fact that our lives are not as bad as the ones we read about. Sianne Ngai refers to these feelings as the "bestiary" equivalent of "rats and possums rather than lions, its categories of feeling generally being, well, weaker and nastier" (2005: 7). In this way, Barnes's writing illuminates the limits and loopholes of empathy and underscores just how easily it can be accompanied or conquered by less desirable affects.

The narrator is both empathetic and concerned with what is left of the humanity of her ill husband, but also in possession of a calculating gaze that allows her to be realistic about her situation vis-à-vis his status. Through its intimate mode of narration and the desperate position of its narrator, the story shows how we are never completely inside the other without also being ourselves even as the experience of being ourselves is one that can be unsettling and teeming with surprises that make us wonder, did I just say or think or feel that?! "Appetite" is a story in which the person in charge ("I've got power of attorney" Barnes 2004: 172) has such split emotions— both total empathy and compassion for this beloved stranger and objective distance from him.

The Gains of Failed Empathy

As noted in the introduction, the aim of this chapter has not been to solidly define empathy or link avid fiction reading with empathetic behavior. Rather, we have been preoccupied with using literature to come to new and more nuanced understandings of how empathy may unfold—or become obstructed—in daily life as imagined through the lens of a distinctly postmodern fictional universe both skeptical of anything innately benevolent in human beings and ironically self-reflexive in its narrative mode. In the particular case of "Appetite," whose narrative situation is extreme even if also a feature of an increasing number of individuals' everyday lives, our analysis has centered on the many potential stumbling blocks that may lie in the way of "successful" empathy and how this can inform more complex accounts of empathy that can extend analyses that, in our minds, too readily either embrace or denounce the concept of empathy as a cornerstone of literary studies. While the question about empathy and its discontents or limits in the short story is related to an outbreak of cognitive disorder that hinders intersubjective communication, in *Flaubert's Parrot* it seems connected to two purely sane minds who are unfortunately, at least according to narrator Geoffrey Braithwaite, ultimately unable to connect because they never try to talk things over and share their secrets. On this note, it is our belief that the role of literary texts is not to underscore *or* reject the centrality of empathy for human interaction but rather, to continue to provide new ways of understanding how empathy progresses, ways in which it connects people or *fails* to do so—because other feelings, such as boredom, self-interest or revulsion, or character traits such as literal-mindedness and lack of curiosity and restraint vis-à-vis an other's inner life experience take precedence. In this sense, descriptions of failed empathy are not problematic or disturbing as much as they are illuminating; by showing us just how *fragile* empathy really is when we test its limit cases, they make us appreciate it even more. Thus, a body of literature many critics would not associate with the question of empathy, Julian Barnes's postmodern metafictions, can in fact be read as both about empathy and as possibly generating stronger empathetic reactions in readers than other forms of more traditional, realistic novelistic depictions of the experience of looking deep into someone else's life to learn what it might be like to not be me. Barnes's cool, ironic, and postmodern attitude and style challenges us to think harder about what it might mean to possess and to empathetically share a rich inner life. Indeed, to return here at the end to our initial discussion of Guy Standing's political and economic argument that the rich are less empathetic and hence more prone to act harshly on those groups they feel less sympathy for, Julian Barnes's "reading lesson" might be that we don't have to claim to look into the heart of people who suffer to do the right things, however hard that is.

Notes

1 For example, "loss of mediation skills; loss of collaboration and intersubjective creativity and innovation; bankrupt communication; depletion of communities and cultural bonding; failures in negotiation of key values and their transmission; hollow relationships; nugatory ethics; negative lives; futility" (2016: 199).

2 Note though that many of his novels do not really fit the category (see Childs and Groes 2011: 2–4).

3 This may also be considered as a generational thing as this group obviously represents an older generation than the "new sincerity" writers, and the group's resistance to embracing a less problematized and skeptical sense of empathy and identificatory modes of reading indeed be squarely related to having more or less come of age as authors during the heyday of high postmodernism in the 1970s and 1980s even if they are not all card-carrying postmodernists (a notoriously problematic term, especially in British literary history). Andrzej Gasiorek provides a concise overview of British postmodernism's difficult history and relation to American criticism as well as native "realism" and split into a radical experimental strain that "use a panoply of metafictional techniques to explore how language and narrative manipulates us" and a more mainstream strain (where Barnes belongs), that "led to a middle ground between social mimesis and linguistic self-consciousness" (2009: 207).

References

Barnes, J. (1984), *Flaubert's Parrot*, London: Picador.

Barnes, J. (2004), *The Lemon Table*, London: Jonathan Cape.

Barnes, J. (2011), *The Sense of an Ending*, London: Jonathan Cape.

Basseler, M. (2017), "Narrative Empathy in George Saunder's Short Fiction," in P. Coleman and S. Gronert Ellerhoff (eds), *George Saunders, American Literature Readings in the 21st Century*, Basingstoke: Palgrave: 153–71.

Bloom, P. (2016), *Against Empathy: The Case for Rational Compassion*, New York: HarperCollins.

Booth, W. (1988), *The Company We Keep: An Ethics of Fiction*, Berkeley: University of California Press.

Charon, R. (2001), "Narrative Medicine: A Model for Empathy, Reflection, Profession, and Trust," *JAMA*, 286 (15): 1897–902.

Childs, P. and S. Groes (eds) (2011), *Julian Barnes: Contemporary Critical Perspectives*, London: Bloomsbury.

Childs, P. (2011), *Julian Barnes*, Manchester: Manchester University Press.

Coplan, A. (2011), "Will the Real Empathy Please Stand Up: A Case for a Narrow Conceptualization," *The Southern Journal of Philosophy*, 49 (s1): 40–65.

De Waal, F. (2009), *The Age of Empathy: Lessons for a Kinder Society*, New York: Crown.

Gasiorek, A. (2009), "Postmodernisms of English Fiction," in R. L. Casiero (ed), *The Cambridge Companion to the Twentieth-Century English Novel*, Cambridge: Cambridge University Press: 192–209.

Holman, E. (2016), "Ian McEwan and the Empathic Imagination: *Atonement* Fifteen Years On," *Literary Imagination* 18 (3): 315–24.

Holmes, F. M. (2009), *Julian Barnes*, Basingstoke: Palgrave.

Hunt, L. (2007), *Inventing Human Rights: A History*, New York: Norton.

Karl, A. G. (2020), "Empathize! Feeling and Labor in the Economic Present," *Criticism*, 62 (2): 271–95.

Keen, S. (2007). *Empathy and the Novel*, Oxford: Oxford University Press.

Kraus, M. W., S. Côté, and D. Keltner (2010), "Social Class, Contextualism, and Empathic Accuracy," *Psychological Science* 21 (11): 1716–23.

McEwan, I. (2001), "Only Love and the Oblivion," *Guardian*, September 15. Online.

McEwan, I. (2005), *Saturday*, London: Jonathan Cape.

Ngai, S. (2005), *Ugly Feelings*, Cambridge, MA: Harvard University Press.

Nussbaum, M. (1997), *Cultivating Humanity: A Classical Defense of Reform in Liberal Education*, Cambridge, MA: Harvard University Press.

Pedwell, C. (2013), "Affect at the Margins," *Space and Society*, 8: 18–26.

Pinker, S. (2011), *The Better Angels of Our Nature: The Decline of Violence in History and Its Causes*, London: Allen Lane.

Rorty, R. (1989), *Contingency, Irony, and Solidarity*, Cambridge, MA: Cambridge University Press.

Rylance, R. (2016), *Literature and the Public Good*, Oxford: Oxford University Press.

Sorum, E. (2019), *Modernist Empathy: Geography, Elegy, and the Uncanny*, Cambridge: Cambridge University Press.

Standing, G. (2014), *A Precariat Charter*, London: Bloomsbury.

Whitehead, A. (2017), *Medicine and Empathy in Contemporary British Fiction: An Intervention in Medical Humanities*, Edinburgh: Edinburgh University Press.

Zahavi, D. and A. V. Fernandez (2021), "Can We Train Basic Empathy? A Phenomenological Proposal," *Nurse Education Today*, 98: 104720.

5

Unsettling Empathy: Hassan Blasim, the Iraq War, and the Spectacle of *The Corpse Exhibition*

Terri Tomsky

This chapter examines the place of empathy in literary representations of the Iraq War. Typically within literary study, empathy is granted a special place as an imaginative activity that enables individuals to connect intimately with distant others, by entering into what has been called "fellow feeling" and so vicariously living through their experiences. In contrast to that imaginative fellowship, war is often comprehended in adversarial terms, structured by seemingly irreconcilable hostilities. Making sense of any conflict is, of course, a challenging endeavor. Elena Baraban, Stephan Jaeger, and Adam Muller, who examine a diversity of stories, perspectives, and experiences about it, remind readers that war is "a multifaceted phenomenon whose complexity resists comprehensive articulation at nearly every turn" (2012: 15). Despite, or perhaps because of, this complexity, a multitude of aesthetic representations, from fine art to films, have nevertheless attempted to communicate the experience of war in its many varieties.[1] As Kate McLoughlin writes in *Authoring War: The Literary Representation of War from the Iliad to Iraq*, literary narratives in particular provide writers with "multitudinous" ways to process the experience of war as well as its aftereffects (2011: 7). They

I want to express my thanks and deep gratitude to Emily Johansen and Alissa G. Karl for their thoughtful feedback, support, and care throughout the review process in a pandemic year.

offer narratological strategies and rhetorical devices (consider, for instance, the role of elisions, interruptions, narrative frame, perspective, tropes, and so on) to approximate the experience of war. For writers, literary narratives create an opportunity to reflect on war on their terms, whether to memorialize the event, to create a record, or warn readers, by expressing the specificities of its horror. As McLoughlin notes, literary representations of war can help impose "discursive order on the chaos of conflict ... [and] render it more comprehensible;" furthermore, she suggests, writing about war can "provide cathartic relief," and even "promote peace" (2011: 7). In other words, while representations of conflict, like the reasons for writing about it, remain heterogeneous, they highlight the continued significance of literary narratives in the search for war's (political, historical, moral, personal) meanings. Given the broad strategies in representing war, many privilege literary narratives as engaging, if not overcoming this problem of complexity. As I will suggest, literary narratives are positioned in this way by readers, the literary marketplace, and even literary theory, because they provide an opportunity for thoughtful reflection and empathetic connections between readers and the subject of the text.

In this chapter, I examine a collection of short stories by expatriate Iraqi writer Hassan Blasim, which challenges our understanding of empathy by scrutinizing the role of writers and readers questing to make sense of war. Blasim's stories illuminate the violence of Iraq's wars in order to bring into view an economy of excess, voyeurism, and spectacle. Rather than guiding the reader into an empathetic relation with his characters and their experience of conflict, Blasim's stories instead unsettle the phenomenon of empathy itself as a desirable goal for readers as they immerse themselves into his representation of war. At some level, I want to suggest, Blasim's stories challenge readers to think critically about their own expectations— about what feelings of empathy will deliver—as they read and consume his literary narratives about a contentious war. This literary strategy of unsettling empathy needs to be understood within the context of a conflict like the Iraq War, which famously poses its own representational challenges in the Western mediascape. The conflict sparked by the US-led 2003 invasion was officially, by the administration of President Obama, said to have ended in 2011, but in fact continues unresolved ten years later. The Iraq War is complex because it is a protracted war, characterized by turmoil and disorder; from the dubious allegations of WMDs used to justify the invasion (alongside the concept of pre-emptive self-defence); the callow application of disaster capitalism as statecraft, the widespread looting, the numerous insurgencies, to the power vacuum and rise of Islamic State (ISIS/ISIL) extremists. The Iraq War is moreover a war without clear boundaries, classified as the Iraq War within a certain temporality, the Iraq Civil War in another, and as the ongoing Global War on Terror in yet another register. It is further complicated by its mediatization in a spectacular society, to use

Guy Debord's phrase ([1967] 2021). While Debord's concept of the society of the spectacle must be updated to account for today's contemporary mediascape, which, as Douglas Kellner observes, is a contested terrain made up of corporate journalism, political agents, individuals, state broadcasters, and NGO institutions (2010: 117), the war's representation in the media overwhelmingly focused on spectacular warfare and a heroic narrative that favored the US-led coalition troops. Such a focus, as Lilie Chouliaraki has shown, came out of the US government's attempt to control media representation, seen in their censorship of the war and regulation of journalists, who were embedded within military units (see Chouliaraki 2010, 2012). In its discursive dimensions, the Iraq War is a site of contested information, criticized by scholars who view it as an imperial war, in the mold of past colonial conflicts. This interpretation not only provokes a crisis in terms of the war's legitimacy, and the corollary belief in the US's uncontested dominance, but further complicates—indeed impugns—the reasons for the US occupation to begin with. For some scholars (Encarnación 2005: 52), this belief has been borne out by the abuse of Iraqis at Abu Ghraib prison as well as the fact that Iraq's oil reserves were prioritized for protection over and sometime against its civilians and its cultural heritage.

Such factors illuminate the challenges for the average citizen to grasp either the magnitude or the minutiae of the Iraq War and its ongoing legacy. In the face of such complexity, literary representations become valuable mediating tools. With their ability to move between the granularity of individual experience to the generationally significant outline of what cultural theorist Raymond Williams once called "structures of feeling" ([1961] 2001) literary representations not only convey a conflict's complexities, its injustices and traumas, but they also help elicit greater insight and empathy. When I say empathy, I have Jesse Prinz's definition in mind: empathy is a "fellow-feeling," "an emotion we share with another" (2011: 230). Literary representations of the Iraq War can construct those emotional connections for readers, enabling them to take up the perspective of others, perspectives which may be occluded or short circuited by media coverage of the war. The possibility of such connections, if not comprehension, seems to be an important goal for Western readers, given their concern over their countries' role in the war. I am thinking of the determining role of the US and allied nations in both the drive for war as well as the circumstances that led to the war's destabilizing effects; but additionally, we could also consider the coordinated mass demonstrations, with millions of people protesting the war in at least eighteen countries. Unfortunately, literary narratives addressing the Iraq War, as Roger Luckhurst observes, are surprisingly few within either the US or Iraqi contexts, leading him to claim: "No defining literary texts have emerged from the overlapping contexts of the [US led] invasion, the Iraqi civil war, or the occupation" (2012: 713).[2] While Luckhurst may be correct, there are nonetheless some very well-known literary texts about

the war, such as Kevin Powers' award-winning *Yellow Birds* (2012), a novel
about three American soldiers fighting in the war, or Brian K. Vaughan and
Niko Henrichon's graphic novel, *Pride of Baghdad* (2006), a story about the
four lions who escaped from the Baghdad zoo after it is bombed during the
US occupation. Both texts offer imaginative inroads for empathy, drawing
readers into the horror, trauma, and pathos the characters feel in witnessing
or participating in combat. While such narratives enable connections
(whether with humans or anthropomorphized animals), they do so at the
expense of Iraqi suffering since both texts evacuate or marginalize the
experience of Iraqis. We might see these attempts at cultivating empathy as
ex post facto efforts at sense-making that are nevertheless contained by the
political horizon in which they circulate. As such, their political potential
is both constrained and problematic, curative for—and reflective of—their
community, while ignoring others outside of it.

In this chapter, I turn to Hassan Blasim's 2014 short story collection, *The
Corpse Exhibition and Other Stories of Iraq*,[3] because it mediates the war
in ways that explicitly counter this kind of limited empathy. I suggest his
literary representations of a complex war offer a useful site to investigate
the narratological techniques that relay the brutality of conflict as well as
construct the writer's relationship to his imagined readers. But whereas
literature about war (for example Wilfred Owen's First World War poems or
Irène Némirovsky's novel about the Second World War) more typically seeks
to draw readers in to witness collective suffering and to mobilize sympathy
for those undergoing the shock of conflict, Blasim's stories sidestep any
kind of humanitarian narrative about suffering and pain. His stories
are characterized by their jarring portraits of violence and the *failure* of
empathy. This is not to say that all of Blasim's stories and his characters are
unsympathetic or unlikeable, but rather, that Blasim constructs his stories
in ways that undercut empathy as a desirable activity by highlighting the
deep divides between his characters and his readers. Blasim's stories are
uncomfortable to read because they refuse "to make us see the lives of the
different with more than a casual tourist's interest—with involvement and
sympathetic understanding" to use Martha Nussbaum's words referring
to a different context in her essay, which extols (and is named) "The
Narrative Imagination" (1997: 88). I posit that Blasim's stories seem to
suggest exactly the opposite of what Nussbaum claims: that readers *are*
casual tourists and that, consequently, his stories open up a different sort of
conversation about the role of literature in relation to the representation of
war and its atrocities. Blasim's stories frame Iraq as a place of unrelenting
violence, in which ordinary people attempt to live and carry out their jobs
in often impossible circumstances. But his representations do not celebrate
this resilience. Instead, in his portraits of ordinary people, Blasim frequently
reveals how Iraq's violence often upstages these characters. What does
Blasim's refusal of empathy (or, more specifically, his refusal to invite readers

into empathizing with the suffering of his characters) signify in relation to Iraq's war and its horrific forms of injustice? Reliable estimates from groups like the British-based NGO, Iraq Body Count (IBC) suggest that the war (2003–11) was responsible for some 208,000 Iraqi deaths (a much more conservative figure than earlier estimates by *The Lancet*), and that it has displaced millions more.[4] I argue that Blasim's difficult stories unsettle empathy in order to implicate the reader as a consumer of inconceivable violence and of other people's pain. In this strategy, Blasim directs attention to the stage-management of empathy in a literary marketplace of feelings, calling on the reader to consider their own positionality vis-à-vis texts that trade in portraits of distant conflict and suffering. Such a stance, I suggest, provokes readers to think more self-reflexively about empathy as a poor substitute for critical analysis and historical accountability.

Imagining Iraq

Blasim's aesthetic critique of empathy comes from his awareness of how Iraq has long been interpellated by Western readers and institutions, which express prejudice through what Edward W. Said called their "geopolitical awareness" about the world, and about the Islamic Middle East in particular ([1978] 1994: 21). As one of the few Iraqi writers whose work has been translated into English and distributed by international publishers, Blasim's stories have traveled far, and they have subsequently transfixed readers.[5] His writing has been celebrated in the United States, the UK, and across Europe, where it has won prizes (Flood 2014); his stories have been praised especially for their surrealism as well as for ostensibly revealing "an inside" view of a war-torn Iraq (Kipen 2014).[6] Blasim thus appears to provide one of the few "authentic" counterpoints to a war whose representation in the West has been structured by the hegemonic interests of Western powers.[7] For the many opposed to the war, or who were suspicious of the objectivity of a Western media that frequently "embedded" reporters with military forces, a writer like Blasim potentially appears as a valuable counterpoint. It is hard not to ask cynical questions about this popularity since it seems that Western readers are fascinated by stories about the countries they are bombing or invading. When Penguin Random House published *The Corpse Exhibition,* they marketed the text as "the first major literary work about the Iraq war from an Iraqi perspective," with the publisher's blurb on the back cover describing Blasim as an "explosive new voice" emerging "from the rubble of Iraq ... to show us his war-torn country from the inside."[8] This marketing ploy, which uses the tragedy of the war to sell copy, extends further to the peritext; the printed text shows a somber black cover and each of the fourteen stories begin with a fully blacked-out page with the story's title in white font, communicating to the reader a funereal affect as well as a visual reminder of the gravity of the book's subject. Blasim's depiction of Iraq as a place of extreme atrocities has led reviewers to describe his work as "dark fantasy" (Flood 2014: paragraph 3) and as a "dark dystopian vision" (Fifer 2017: paragraph 3). Others, like Max Rodenbeck, the Cairo-based correspondent for *The Economist*, read him as a realist (rather than a fantasist) dystopian, arguing that: "In another country such a story might be thought fantastical. In Iraq it could well be true; fiction here seems merely to be more concise than fact" (2014: n.p.). This is obviously a problematic assertion, the same kind of assertion that often accompanied the publication of Orientalist tales at the height of the British Empire. It is also a patent exaggeration, given some of the outlandish and fantastical events that occur in Blasim's stories.

In a 2013 interview with the British political magazine, *New Statesman*, Blasim was asked how war and instability shaped his perception of Iraq, which—for the interviewer—appears in the stories as an "unfathomable" place (Maughan 2013). Blasim responds to the interviewer's desire for a "fathomable" or comprehensible place by citing a few lines from a story he wrote: "We have put dinosaur bones and cracked stone water jars in museums, but we haven't put hatred or fear in a glass case for people to look at and take pictures" (Maughan 2013). Blasim's museum analogy is assuredly ironic, reflecting back to the journalist the desire of others to observe human emotions as though they were rare artifacts on display for the comfortable contemplation of the reader or viewer. His analogy moreover implicitly connects to the title of his story collection, *The Corpse Exhibition and Other Stories of Iraq*. Blasim's title reminds us, to some extent, of the position of both spectator and reader. I return to the significance of the title in more detail below, but it is worth considering how an exhibition and its implied spectator illuminate certain positionalities. To return to Blasim's museum analogy, the spectator envisages Iraq and its people in certain ways. Whether the spectator's gaze is objectifying, pitying, or even appreciative, it is clear that the spectator is not neutral but is instead situated in a complex hierarchical relationship, which is consolidated by social structures of unequal power and colonial history. The museum analogy is particularly resonant given Blasim's subject matter, since one of the terrible outcomes of the US-led invasion, was the looting of many Iraqi museums for Western collectors. As political scientist Eric Davies notes, the plunder of Iraq's antiquities has long been a colonial pastime, since the excavation movement of the early nineteenth century. Davies writes:

> thousands of items found their way into European and later American museums as well as into the private collections of wealthy collectors of art. ... It was almost as if foreigners saw the country's Arab and Muslim inhabitants as interlopers who might threaten what they considered their legitimate efforts to appropriate knowledge and representations of the

"cradle of (Western) civilization." The Iraqis often feel "invisible" in the eyes of the Westerner, who, in preferring the necropolises and monuments of ancient Mesopotamia to all other aspects of the country's heritage, would just as soon have seen the land devoid of its modern inhabitants.

(1994: 92)

Davies's astute observation reminds readers not only of the (neo)imperial arc of colonial exploitation and theft, but also of the extent to which Iraq often is cast as a symbol of something meaningful to the West, whether ancient (Western) civilization or its vast resources of Oil (and wealth). In this signification, the Iraqi people, their communities, and material realities are obliterated. Feminist postcolonial scholars have noted a similar signification following the wars in Iraq and Afghanistan in the public's rush for stories about oppressed and veiled women from the very countries they were occupying. Popular memoirs like *Zoya's Story: An Afghan Woman's Struggle for Freedom* (2002) and *My Forbidden Face: Growing Up Under the Taliban: A Young Woman's Story* (2001), for instance, appealed to Western liberal readers through their exotic titles, which situate the veil as a signifier of otherness and oppression, as well as impending female liberation. As Gillian Whitlock (2006) and Daphne Grace (2004) note, many of these stories were instrumentalized in problematic ways to shore up the righteousness of Western interventions. What these disparate examples relay is a tension between the West's temporary interests, what we might see as limited forms of empathy or sympathy, extended to these devastated communities and the erasure to which they are often subjected. It is notable that Blasim's museum analogy is depopulated of actual Iraqis, in its emphasis on their now objectified and preserved trophies of "hatred" and "fear." Blasim's analogical reasoning has powerful ethical implications for the readers of his fiction. Like the international black market for Mesopotamian cultural artifacts, Blasim is aware that his representations of hate and fear become available for enjoyment, theft, or appropriation by a certain kind of reader. This certain kind of reader is evoked in Blasim's writing and, perhaps even helps explain Blasim's anti-humanitarian style of representation, which reminds us of the way stories of atrocity circulate and are valued. Like the museum artifacts of reified "hatred" and "fear," those stories speak to the divide Blasim sees between (Western) readers and their perception of those they consider distant strangers or, as Richard Rorty puts it, "people very unlike us" (2002: 77).

To be clear, empathy has been championed by scholars precisely as a way to engage with those distant strangers; but, as a concept, empathy has been understood broadly and diversely. Unlike sympathy, which is often linked to feelings of care, or a moral obligation toward another, empathy is understood in terms of an enduring identification with someone else's feelings. It involves a strong sense of someone else's subjective experience, what Amy Coplan calls "affective matching" (2011: 6).[9] Empathy is generally cast in positive terms as an act of "moral imagination" (Frank 2016: 152) or "fellow feeling," which can facilitate good moral conduct, such as altruism.[10] Yet, a growing number of scholars are having mixed feelings about empathy; Paul Bloom, Megan Boler, Fritz Breithaupt, E. Ann Kaplan, Sherene Khadar, Jesse Prinz, among others, have challenged the idea that it may necessarily lead to altruism or action. From false empathy to fantasy empathy, "empty empathy" to "passive empathy," the varieties of what might be called bad or negative empathy are being theorized and debated.[11] These terms refer to fleeting or fragile forms of empathy where empathy *is* mobilized via an identification with another person's suffering, but is structured either through the affect of hopelessness, or through temporary, pleasurable affect—neither of which leads to any political responsiveness or positive social action. Suzanne Keen, in her 2007 study, *Empathy and the Novel*, also casts a skeptical look at empathy, arguing that the cultivation of empathy through literature only works because fiction is delimited: as a "safe zone," literature allows readers to feel empathy "without experiencing ... a demand on real-world action" (2007: 4). Keen suggests that claims about literature's capacity to produce caring are merely tactics that seek to elevate the status of literature, rather than invoke justice (2007: 20–1).

Fiction has been elevated to this position, perhaps, because alternative modes of representation have failed to generate empathy, instead producing limited forms of concern about others or deactivating it altogether, by normalizing complacency in relation to oppressive situations taking place elsewhere. For instance, to return to the context of Iraq, many readers in the West view the terror perpetrated during the Iraq War as shocking. But media coverage of that conflict—on television, in print, and in photojournalism—has not always helped individuals to connect empathetically with victims in Iraq. Coverage of the violence has been extensive, but also distorted for reasons that are part of a news cycle, dependent on spectacle and factual entertainment. The public knows about ISIS/ISIL, through a litany of spectacular atrocities made available through the news or podcasts, like the *New York Times* controversial longform podcast *Caliphate* (2018), which in December 2020, added an editorial note on its website to flag falsehoods and discrepancies within its central testimony of a supposed ISIS member.[12] Rarely are Western viewers made aware of the living conditions of people residing in neighborhoods taken over by ISIL, who are then subjected to bombings by US and allied forces. Such accounts *seem* well positioned to mobilize what has been called "distress empathy," where readers and viewers relate to humanizing narratives about the lives of ordinary people who face ongoing traumas. Yet, scholars have questioned whether empathy is actually enabled via these mediated stories. E. Ann Kaplan, for example, has cautioned that empathy is flattened in what she calls a "trauma culture" facilitated by a mediascape that focuses only on war and terrorism. Kaplan outlines the dangers of what she calls "empty empathy" as individuals consume daily, media-induced spectacles of horror, but are "numb[ed] by the succession of catastrophes displayed before the viewer" (2011: 257, 265). In the context of Iraq, this kind of media coverage makes Iraq's violence appear even more distant: the iconography of violence simply confirms Iraq's status as Other. Indeed, this Othering interrelates to a *scaling down* of empathy, as historian Steven E. Aschheim suggests in his analysis of the role of place in what he calls the *"post-facto political geography of empathy"* (2016: 25, original emphasis). For Aschheim, places that are "geographically and morally relatively detached from our cultivated 'Western' epicenter" (25)—his examples include Rwanda, Cambodia, Bosnia, and Sudan—shape a far less empathetic response from Westerners. In a similar vein, albeit in the context of the mass media, economists Thomas Eisensee and David Stromberg (2007: 694) concluded how biases in the U.S. media meant that coverage of natural disasters in Africa and the Pacific were often "crowded out" by a focus on smaller disasters in Europe (with forty times fewer deaths), and that, additionally, the size of news coverage correlates directly to the level of received relief. While Aschheim here conceives of the social formation of empathy shaped in relation to "our mental maps" (2016: 25), Eisensee and Stromberg's research indicates something more pervasive. Aschheim's notion of "mental maps," like those allegedly "morally" distant places, gestures toward the cultural production of a place as Other since it is often the *perception* of those geographies "as either primitive or civilizationally [sic] alien" that closes down empathy (26). Thus while Aschheim's analysis highlights the importance of familiarity of place in relation to the mobilizing of empathy, his theory also brings to mind Edward W. Said's critical idea of imaginative geography, where places are discursively constructed as Other, invested with certain ideologies and emotions. Such Orientalist renderings consolidate the Manichean opposition between places considered familiar and humane against those assumed not to be: why else would Bosnia—a largely Muslim space positioned in a predominantly Christian Europe—be on Aschheim's list?

Reading Blasim

Given the explicitly Othered violence of the Iraq War, as well as the banality of spectacular media representations, what do Blasim's stories add to our understanding of how empathy operates? On the one hand, they reproduce the structure of those media representations, with Iraqi society experiencing a succession of catastrophes throughout the fourteen stories. On the other hand, the level of idiomatic detail the stories provide about local neighborhoods and communities seems to promise a foundation for a humanitarian empathetic connection between the Western reader and the Iraqi subject. That promise is repeatedly thwarted, though, by the constancy of extreme violence. In other words, the succession of catastrophes is not part of the background, an obstacle that might be overcome, interpreted, mediated, or comprehended through a focused attention on the individual and the granular. Rather, the extreme violence is foregrounded and featured as much as any individual character. Moreover, there is no single, or singular set, of outrages to attach with; nor is there any consistent attachment or fellow feeling for another fully fleshed human life. This much is demonstrated in Blasim's story, "A Thousand and One Knives," a story about local teenagers growing up in Baghdad's middle-class neighborhood, Karada, who have a strange talent for making knives disappear and reappear, what the characters call "the disappearing knife trick" (2014: 108). While the title of the story alludes to this trick, it further suggests a contemporary, if ironic take on the "The Thousand and One Nights," where the romance of these Arabian fables has transmuted into violence.[13] Even the main character realizes this: "I soon came to the idea that the knives were just a metaphor for all the terror, the killing, and the brutality in the country" (111).

In Blasim's story, the narrator functions as a "bridge character" (Keen 2007: 34), a point of connection as he introduces readers to his way of life, his group of friends, and his growing love for his future wife, Souad. But even he—and, by extension, Blasim—recognize the difficulty of empathy in a catastrophic war that continues day after day, "in the relentless daily cycle of bloody violence" (2014: 116). The narrator describes how Iraq's "wars and the violence were like a photocopier churning out copies, and we all wore the same face, a face shaped by pain and torment" (123). Blasim's simile of the photocopier and its technological reproduction of "copies" of "violence" and "pain" registers the scale of the disaster and suffering in Iraq, but it does so in a way that recalls the material production of news copy. In his description of wearing the "same torment" as everybody else, the narrator recognizes how the war's collective suffering itself has been flattened (123). Rather than a face expressing an individual experience of pain, Blasim's image evokes victims of mass suffering as a saturation of sameness. Here, the description relays how empathy is thwarted in relation to widespread violence and pain. As a feeling that connects one with others, empathy is typically channeled toward *individuals*, rather than collectives. When suffering is scaled up, in terms of transcending individuals, or becoming de-individualized as the comparison with "copies" suggests, Blasim reveals the limits of empathy. The amplification of suffering at a collective level, especially through the mass media, creates what Susan Moeller (1999) famously called "compassion fatigue," an empathy deficit as viewers and readers are left desensitized by prolonged and overwhelming coverage of crises. In describing suffering as "copies" of "pain," Blasim offers a provocation to the reader, who may well view all Iraqis in this distancing way through the mediated accounts of distant wars in the international news.[14] Against this, Blasim nevertheless opens an all too brief window into individualized suffering. For instance, Blasim introduces a woman, Umm Ibtisam, with five daughters whose husband is killed by a bomb and who is stricken with "grief for her husband [that] broke her heart and disrupted her sleep" (120). In a recurring nightmare, she sees "an enormous man slaughtering her husband with a knife" (120). While this narrative illustrates the lingering terror of post-traumatic shock, the narrative frame of the story also stands as a counterpoint to the portrayal of indifference and mass suffering. The narrator's personal storytelling celebrates the love between himself and his wife, Souad, evoking its implicit namesake, *A One Thousand and One Arabian Nights* where notably, Scheherazade's stories build up empathy (and responsibility) in her husband, leading to his declaration of love for her. In his depiction of pervasive suffering, Blasim raises the question whether it is possible for the outsider to be empathetically attached to characters in such circumstances, who themselves understand the de-individualizing and dehumanizing effects of extensive suffering. But, simultaneously, in his reference to the *Arabian Nights*, Blasim knowingly gestures to the power of storytelling itself and the way that stories both suspend reality and lead back to it.

In another of his stories, Blasim offers a contrast to the idea of mechanical reproduction in relation to the "Thousand and One Nights" of violence and suffering. The first story of Blasim's collection,[15] which is also the book's titular story, "The Corpse Exhibition" sets up an awareness of violence as, simultaneously, both spectacle and artwork. An "exhibition" after all relates to a visual display that anticipates a spectator or audience; the title "The Corpse Exhibition" also appeals to the notion of aesthetics and thanatological voyeurism in relation to its subject matter: the bodies of the dead. Though not mentioned in the story, Blasim's title evokes its real-world counterpart: the plastinated cadavers created by Gunther von Hagen in his controversial, but massively popular touring exhibition "Body Worlds," which features the preserved bodies of actual humans, ostensibly to demystify human anatomy. Blasim's story has no such scientific value; instead, it is a commentary on the role of art, a professional work ethic, and empathy. In this story, the dead—victims to Iraq's violence—are not viewed in any sympathetic or empathetic way that would elicit feelings of concern or identification with others. Blasim's story utilizes a distancing technique that limits that possibility. Set during the Iraq Civil War, in the interregnum produced after the US invasion, "The Corpse Exhibition" describes a group of killers, who murder civilians solely for the purpose of displaying their bodies as temporary artwork in public spaces, such as in streets or in front of public buildings. These killers are able to murder people *because* of the chaos of the war and there appears to be no didactic or disciplinary purpose in these displays.[16] The story is told in first-person perspective by a prospective killer, who appears to be there for a job interview. This narrator, who is silent through the entire story, is an unnamed interlocutor, who is listening to the monologue of a professional killer explaining the details of the job. The killer is detached in his professionalism even as he takes pride in good work being done. It turns out the "work" he describes is the murder of civilians and the display of their bodies in the city. The language of administrative management suffuses the killer's discourse. As he outlines his profession to the interlocutor, he describes the formal bureaucratic process involved in murder:

> After studying the client's file you must submit a brief note on how you propose to kill your first client and how you will display his body in the city. But that doesn't mean that what you propose in your note will be approved. One of our specialists will review the proposed method and either approve it or propose a different method. This system applies to professionals in all phases of their work [...] All your questions, proposals, and written submissions will be documented in your personal file.
>
> (3)

The killer adds an incentive to his interlocutor, reminding him that if his work is good and his imagination "fresh, fierce, and striking" that "senior positions ... await you in the hierarchy of the institution" (5). If empathy exists here, it is *negative empathy* aligned with the perspective of the speaker—the killer—who monopolizes the story with a lengthy explanation of his work. To return briefly to the concept of negative empathy, which is attributed to German philosopher Theodor Lipps, Stefano Ercolino has suggested that we understand it as a form of empathy "associated with unpleasurable feelings" as well as "the peculiar feeling of *permanent shock* caused by reading" a jarring narrative, like Jonathan Littell's *The Kindly Ones* (2010), a novel about a ruthless SS officer and the focus of Ercolino's essay (2018: 247, 254, original emphasis). Similarly, in Blasim's story, the killer cultivates negative feelings, horror, and astonishment as he extols the "creativity" of his art (2014: 7). Throughout, his bureaucratic discourse abstracts the suffering of his Iraqi victims, dehumanizing them, presenting them as aesthetic objects, rather than individualized humans (to be empathized with). Murder is euphemized as work and people's bodies are transfigured into art. Some of the victims include innocent lives, most notably a breastfeeding baby, whose corpse is displayed, alongside its mother's in the middle of a busy Baghdad street (6). As an aside, the figures of the mother and child are, of course, a powerful symbol of care, vulnerability, and futurity, so there is also a salient irony in the killer's praise of the "genius" display of mother and child who look "alive" in death (6). The killer's goal is to produce what he calls an "extraordinary work of art" (6). The description of the abjection of humans, their bodily dismemberment and display is understood either administratively (in shades of Eichmann) or as serving an artistic expression. In the choreographing of murder and the display of anonymized bodies, the killer finds "*the justice* of discovering the insignificance and equivocal essence of the world" (7, emphasis added). The details of *lived* human lives are rendered irrelevant. Unlike other historical atrocities, such as those perpetrated under National Socialism, where genocide was invested with symbolic significance as "the guarantee for the future of the Third Reich" (Fritzsche 2016: 125),[17] the exhibitions of dead bodies in Iraq are displayed in order to signify an absence of meaning and an absence of humanist feelings. We are privy to the killer's perspective and it provides an incommensurate gulf; it recoils from the ideals of human rights and communicates the absence of a future.

It is important too to note that the killer rejects the kind of political or ethno-religious motivation that has been diagnosed by scholars about the war in Iraq. The killer scorns the massacres caused by terrorists, assassins, nihilists, "fanatical Islamic groups," or government agencies, which have certain aims (2014: 4). Instead, he views Iraq's interregnum as "one of the century's rare opportunities" for artists of murder, and he warns that once the "situation stabilizes" the killers will have to leave. To understand the killer's objective means to dispense with any sociopolitical or anthropological understandings of the war (i.e., the escalation of competing groups in the power vacuum caused by the George W. Bush administration). Instead, the killer's viewpoint extolls the chaos only because it enables his idiosyncratic atrocities: these are exceptional but they are also oddly institutional and bureaucratic. As the killer explains, creating a corpse exhibition (for there are many in this story) offers a way for the artists of death to "shine like a precious jewel amid the wreckage of this country" (5). In other words, the killer is extolling the potential opportunities to burnish a career *because* of a chaotic war. It is impossible to identify with the killer's goals of gruesome artistry; empathy for his victims is elusive, since the people he describes are abstracted. Their deaths are rationalized and redeemed to achieve the killer's artistic objectives. He cares mostly for how the work is carried out, how it is presented, and how his colleagues and superiors regard it, far more so than the public's response to the displays. The killer is focused on the technique and the skills needed to create art, even as that art represents an unimaginable atrocity to the reader. The corpse exhibitions function as "pitiless art," to use the words of philosopher, Paul Virilo, that reflects back to the world "excess heaped upon excess, desensitization to the shock of images and the meaninglessness of words" (2006: 36). In other words, the corpse exhibition shatters notions of justice as well as human decency, including the idea that humans have feelings toward others' suffering. The corpse exhibition is a spectacle of terror that also reflects back a world lacking in empathy.

In fact, in Blasim's story, empathy represents a sickness, rather than a desirable form of affective and ethical engagement. The killer relates a story about a recent hire called "the Nail" who fails to carry out a proposed murder of a small child. If you'll recall from my introduction of the story, the artist-killers must submit a proposal, detailing each plan for a murder and "display" to their seniors in the organization. The Nail undertakes this task, but then, according to the killer, becomes "infected with banal humanitarian feelings ... [and] like any sick man had started to question the benefit of killing others" (2014: 8). He plans to fake the murder but is apprehended by the organization's mortician, "a great artist" who kills the Nail for his intransigence (9). This murder is horrific, involving the mortician flaying the Nail "with great skill" and hanging his skin "like a flag of victory" outside the Ministry of Justice (10). Perhaps the Nail's feelings of regret and empathy for his victims emerge from his proximity with the death of others as well as a selfish fear of being held accountable in the afterlife; whatever the reason, those feelings are dismissed as trite sentiments. The story ends with the narrator (who is so far, the addressee, but *also* the first person narrator who communicates the Killer's words but has not yet spoken from his perspective) also harboring feelings of empathetic unsettlement for the victims. These emotions are not disclosed directly, but rather, are interpreted by the killer, who reads the "insipid look" in the narrator's eyes and his "shaking" body as a cue to "thrust the knife in [his] stomach" (10). The story ends here with the death of the narrator *because* of his "humanitarian feelings" and so posits the risks of empathetic identification (8). The fact that earlier in the story, the skin of the Nail is displayed "in front of the gate of the Ministry of Justice" (10) can be read as a critique of emotional *feelings* toward others' suffering. In this scenario, fellow feeling does not constitute anything like justice; indeed, it represents a complete failure of justice.

Having established the failure and risks of empathy in the first story of his collection, Blasim turns to how empathy itself is produced and mediated in various ways. In his story "The Song of the Goats," Blasim describes a storytelling competition for "Memory Radio" a new documentary radio station that puts out a call for "the best stories" recorded and "narrated by the people involved" (139). A crush of people shows up at the broadcaster's studio to tell their stories. Their stories relay experiences of trauma and terror in Iraq; but, after they are narrated to the packed hall, the stories are "ridiculed" by the crowd of listeners (141). A battle of competing victimization ensues, with individuals calling attention to their personal stories of trauma which, they claim are "stranger, crueler, and more crazy" than the story being told earlier, in an apparent bid to narrate the most unique story of horror (141). Each storyteller attempts to connect with the listener in ways that would elicit the strongest affective response. As one woman exclaims in reaction to the storyteller: "That's a story? If I told my story to a rock, it would break its heart" (141). The *effect* of the story on the listener is more important for the storyteller, than the actual story itself. The emotional feelings of the listener are of central importance here, suggesting the storyteller's calculations into how traumatic stories are narrated and circulated for an audience as affective capital. Radio Memory, after all, is one of the mediums through which people's experiences of the war are disseminated internationally, though many people participate in the hope of winning the broadcaster's "valuable prizes" (139). This story, in other words, implicates Blasim as a writer, who spins his story of victimhood for personal gain, a point noted by *New York Times* book reviewer, David Kipen, who writes, "Is Mr Blasim suggesting the complicity of writers like himself, who transmute the deaths of their countrymen into literary fiction for self-congratulatory Western readers tough enough to take it?" (2014: paragraph 9). But Blasim's story also implicitly gestures toward the complicity of those readers, or rather, those listeners tuning into Radio Memory. His story recognizes the market demand for authentic stories of suffering. Within this consumer demand, empathy plays an ambiguous role. Even if listeners vicariously imagine themselves in the place of such victims, this desire may well represent gratification or enjoyment, rather than any ethical objective to reach understanding with the other, or embark on some form of moral action.

Blasim's attention to the dissemination of grievances and pain cannot be extricated from his emphasis on form, which can be traced in the "exhibition" of the first story (though the end-result is markedly different), or in the "photocopier churning out copies" of people's trauma in the story "A Thousand and One Knives." This account of the different forms through which empathy is amplified or diminished provides a view of what Steven E. Aschheim calls "the political economy of empathy" where the affective energies of empathy are "politically structured, channeled ... directed, encouraged or blocked" (2016: 22). Aschheim's concept of an economy of empathy is useful as it reminds us to think about structure, (imagined) geographies, culture, power, and politics: his theory highlights the dynamics of empathy across different contexts as well as the ways in which empathy is "apportioned, allocated, controlled, confined, resisted, or allowed to ... overcome differences" (22). In Blasim's stories, differences are not overcome. Instead, the stories suggest an ironic perspective on how empathy is produced and the many ways in which it fails in the face of ongoing violence in certain places. Perhaps for this reason, Blasim does not disclose Memory Radio's winning story and so refuses to satiate the reader's curiosity.

In his stories, Blasim challenges readers to consider what they are seeking as they read about Iraq's war. Many of his stories unsettle the reader's desire to empathize or even sympathize with the war's victims, its beneficiaries, or its opportunists. Yet, the stories all call attention to the *form* through which suffering and violence are transmitted sometimes generically—as I have detailed through the art exhibition, the photocopies, and the radio. This attention to form allows Blasim to address how grievances and pain are mediated for and consumed by others: in this he brings into view an economy of uneven empathies and feelings. This serves as a caution to readers to be more critical of easily felt sentiments that do not necessarily correspond to any political or social justice. In his stories, Blasim suggests that human rights—the rights of others to have rights, to paraphrase Hannah Arendt—should not have anything to do with *feeling* or with a reader's particular and arbitrary *attachments*. Blasim's stories refuse to create affective connections to the individual, nor do his stories allow his readers to see the unique *humanity* of the individual, and identify with that pain. Instead, his stories generate baffling and unsettling feelings through his representation of the excesses of war, the saturation of suffering, the amplification and marketing of trauma to an audience, as well as the impossibility of ever knowing "the real" story of Iraq. Suffering, in Blasim's stories, is interlinked to indifference through its mediation, its framework of representations. In this move, Blasim highlights his readers' dilemma: to enjoy the book or to ignore its troubling message reinforces its acceptance of suffering and human rights violations. Here, Blasim makes his own role as ironic raconteur all too visible and so displaces responsibility from himself onto the reader.

Notes

1   Among these attempts, the narrative form dominates, whether through nonfictional genres of testimony, eye-witness accounts, journalism, and life-writing or through fictional genres of short stories, poetry, and novels.

2   Luckhurst identifies that most representations of the Iraq War are found in the "aesthetic disciplines"—photography, video, and new media artwork by American and Iraqi artists—which he diagnoses as a response to the war's virtual dimensions, and especially the digital circulation of photos, cataloguing American abuse in the Abu Ghraib prison (2012: 715). In contrast, Luckhurst argues that most US literary representations of the war are implicit or indirect, which he sees as an outcome of the deep divisiveness felt by Americans about the war, its "disastrous" failure of any post-invasion strategies (2012: 722), as well as the mixed role of US soldiers, seen as both perpetrators of violence against civilians and victims of a "merciless military-industrial complex" (2012: 721).

3   It's important to note that some of *The Corpse Exhibition* is made up of selections of Blasim's published writings, taken from two earlier collections of writings. In this sense, despite Penguin's assertions that this is about the Iraq War, some of the stories address earlier periods in Iraq, including the 1991 Gulf War as well as the regime of terror under Saddam Hussein.

4   A 2006 article in *The Lancet* claims that the war caused 654,965 deaths, around 2·5 percent of the population (see Burnham et al. 2006). See the IBC database to calculate data of deaths recorded in Iraq: https://www.iraqbodycount.org/database/

5   Other translated authors from Iraq include the stories from sixteen Iraqi writers compiled and translated by Shakir Mustafa, a professor of Arabic at Northeastern University, in his anthology, *Contemporary Iraqi Fiction* (2008). Ahmed Saadawi's novel, *Frankenstein in Baghdad* about the Iraq War was translated as recently as 2018, but had won the 2014 International Prize for Arabic Fiction.

6   Blasim won the Independent foreign fiction prize in 2014 (Flood 2014).

7   From the cameras guiding smart bombs, to embedded journalists, to films reflecting the effects on the American psyche like *The Hurt Locker* (2008), *The Green Zone* (2010), *Boys of Abu Ghraib* (2014), *American Sniper* (2014), *Shock and Awe* (2017), the vast majority of representations of the Iraq War are by Western observers.

8   The first quotation here is attributed to Penguin Books and is used on its website for Blasim's *The Corpse Exhibition* as well as on the cover of the 2014 text. See: https://www.penguinrandomhouse.ca/books/313242/the-corpse-exhibition-by-hassan-blasim/9780143123262

9   For Coplan (2011), this takes place through the perspective-taking of another.

10   For example, see Thomas Schramme's essay "Empathy and Altruism" (2017).

11   For E. Ann Kaplan (2011), empty empathy creates a feeling of identification with the Other, but it is structured through the affect of hopelessness or passivity and so results in paralysis. In contrast, Megan Boler's notion of passive empathy relates to the assimilation of another's difference, through the voyeuristic and pleasurable activity of reading or viewing the Other, safely from a distance ([1997] 2006: 260). Neither of these empathies lead to any consequential or positive social action.

12   To be clear, this podcast mostly deals with Syria, rather than Iraq, but similar questions remain about how Western demand for stories about the Middle East shapes certain Orientalist versions and fabulations about it.

13   Peter Heath's suggestion about the structure of romance in the *Arabian Nights* is useful here since Blasim's story also mimics the developmental narrative of the romance, which moves from security through a series of trials and back to a state of security: "It is important to note that for protagonists these steps do not represent linear movements but rather developmental progressions within moral and psychological matrices, movements from innocence to experience, ignorance to knowledge, naivete to maturity" (1987: 10–11).

14   Additionally, Blasim seems to question the reader's ability to comprehend or differentiate such pain, when a nation's suffering is so extensive.

15   Blasim's collection of stories has been assembled from two earlier collections of writings, and so may not reflect a particular order.

16   As with Blasim's other stories, we can also read the displays as a symbol of a country in crisis, without necessarily overdetermining the meaning of the story in any way.

17   Peter Fritzsche explains, the genocide of the Jews was visually recorded and photographed in order to show "authoritative documentation of the hard realities of a titanic military struggle in which enemy civilians posed existential dangers" (124). These documentations signified a celebration of an "epic historical moment, which gave meaning to the brutality of the massacres" (2016: 124).

References

Aschheim, S. E. (2016), "The (Ambiguous) Political Economy of Empathy," in A. Assman and I. Detmers (eds), *Empathy and Its Limits*, 21–37, New York: Palgrave MacMillan.

Baraban, E. V., S. Jaeger, and A. Muller (eds) (2012), *Fighting Words and Images: Representing War across the Disciplines*, Toronto: University of Toronto Press.

Blasim, H. (2014), *The Corpse Exhibition and Other Stories of Iraq*, trans. J. Wright, New York: Penguin.

Bloom, P. (2016), *Against Empathy: The Case for Rational Compassion*, New York: HarperCollins.

Boler, M. ([1997] 2006), "The Risks of Empathy: Interrogating Multiculturalism's Gaze," *Cultural Studies*, 11 (2): 253–73.

Breithaupt, F. (2016), "Empathy for Empathy's Sake: Aesthetics and Everyday Empathic Sadism," in A. Assmann and I. Detmers (eds), *Empathy and Its Limits*, 151–65, New York: Palgrave MacMillan.

Burnham, G., R. Lafta, S. Doocy, and L. Roberts (2006), "Mortality after the 2003 Invasion of Iraq: A Cross-sectional Cluster Sample Survey," *The Lancet*, 36 (9545): 1421–8. Available online: https://www.thelancet.com/journals/lancet/article/PIIS0140-6736%2806%2969491-9/fulltext

Chouliaraki, L. (2010), "Journalism and the Visual Politics of War and Conflict," in S. Allan (ed), *The Routledge Companion to News and Journalism*, 520–32, New York: Routledge.

Chouliaraki, L. (2012), "The Aestheticization of Suffering on Television," in E. V. Baraban et al. (eds), *Fighting Words and Images: Representing War across the Disciplines*, 110–31, Toronto: University of Toronto Press.

Coplan, A. (2011), "Understanding Empathy: Its Features and Effects," in A. Coplan and P. Goldie (eds), *Empathy: Philosophical and Psychological Perspectives*, 3–18, Oxford: Oxford University Press.

Craps, S. (2016), "On Not Closing the Loop: Empathy, Ethics, and Transcultural Witnessing," in J. G. Singh and D. D. Kim (eds), *The Postcolonial World*, 53–67, New York: Routledge.

Davies, E. (1994) "The Museum and the Politics of Social Control in Iraq," in J. R. Gillis (ed), *Commemorations: The Politics of Memory and National Identity*, 90–104, Princeton: Princeton University Press.

Debord, G. ([1967] 2021), *The Society of the Spectacle*, trans. R. Adams, Cambridge, MA: Unredacted Word.

Eisensee, T. and D. Strömberg (2007), "News Droughts, News Floods, and U.S. Disaster Relief," *The Quarterly Journal of Economics*, 122 (2): 693–728.

Encarnación, O. G. (2005), "The Follies of Democratic Imperialism," *World Policy Journal*, Spring: 47–60.

Ercolino, S. (2018), "Negative Empathy: History, Theory, Criticism," *Orbis Litterarum*, 73: 243–62.

Fifer, E. (2017), "Dead Reckoning: The Darkening Landscape of Contemporary World Literature," *World Literature Today*, March: 14 paragraphs. Available online: https://www.worldliteraturetoday.org/2017/march/dead-reckoning-darkening-landscape-contemporary-world-literature-elizabeth-fifer

Flood, A. (2014), "Exiled Iraqi Is First Arab Winner of UK's Top Prize for Foreign Fiction," *The Guardian*, May 22: 13 paragraphs. Available online: https://www. theguardian.com/books/2014/may/22/exiled-iraq-first-arab-winner-uk-foreign-fiction-prize

Frank, A. W. (2016), "Knowing Other People's Stories: Empathy, Illness, and Identity," *Concentric: Literary and Cultural Studies*, 42 (2): 151–65.

Fritzsche, P. (2016), "Management of Empathy in the Third Reich," in A. Assmann and I. Detmers (eds), *Empathy and Its Limits*, 115–27, New York: Palgrave MacMillan.

Grace, D. (2004), *The Woman in the Muslin Mask: Veiling and Identity in Postcolonial Literature*, London: Pluto Press.

Heath, P. (1987), "Romance as Genre in 'The Thousand and One Nights': Part I," *Journal of Arabic Literature*, 18: 1–21.

Kaplan, A. E. (2011), "Empathy and Trauma Culture: Imaging Catastrophe," in A. Coplan and P. Goldie (eds), *Empathy: Philosophical and Psychological Perspectives*, 255–76, Oxford: Oxford University Press.

Keen, S. (2007), *Empathy and the Novel*, Oxford: Oxford University Press.

Kellner, D. (2010), "Media Spectacle, Presidential Politics, and the Transformation of Journalism," in S. Allan (ed), *The Routledge Companion to News and Journalism*, 116–26, New York: Routledge.

Khader, S. J. (2018), "Victims' Stories and the Postcolonial Politics of Empathy," *Metaphilosophy* 49 (1–2): 13–26.

Kim, S. J. and M. M. Hammond (eds) (2014), *Rethinking Empathy through Literature*, New York: Routledge.

Kipen, D. (2014), "An Iraq Blasted Open, Sketched from the Inside," *The New York Times*, January 28: 14 paragraphs. Available online: https://www.nytimes.com/2014/01/29/books/the-corpse-exhibition-stories-about-a-war-torn-life.html

Latifa, and S. Hachemi (2001), *My Forbidden Face: Growing Up under the Taliban: A Young Woman's Story*, trans. L. Coverdale, New York: Hyperion.

Luckhurst, R. (2012), "In War Times: Fictionalizing Iraq," *Contemporary Literature*, 53 (4): 713–37.

Maughan, P. (2013), "Iraqi Author Hassan Blasim: 'We Need to Express the Disaster of Our Lives'," *New Statesman*, February 15. Available online: https://www.newstatesman.com/2013/02/iraqi-author-hassan-blasim-we-need-express-disaster-our-lives

McLoughlin, K. (2011), *Authoring War: The Literary Representation of War from the Iliad to Iraq*, Cambridge: Cambridge University Press.

Moeller, S. D. (1999), *Compassion Fatigue: How the Media Sell Disease, Famine, War, and Death*, New York: Routledge.

Mustafa, S. (ed) (2008), *Contemporary Iraqi Fiction: An Anthology*, trans. S. Mustafa, Syracuse, NY: Syracuse University Press.

Nussbaum, M. C. (1997), *Cultivating Humanity: A Classical Defense of Reform in Liberal Education*, Cambridge, MA: Harvard University Press.

Powers, K. (2012), *The Yellow Birds*, New York: Little, Brown and Company.

Prinz, J. (2011), "Against Empathy," *Southern Journal of Philosophy*, 49: 214–33.

Rodenbeck, M. (2014), "Iraq: The Outlaw State," *The New York Review*, September 25. Available online: https://www.nybooks.com/articles/2014/09/25/iraq-outlaw-state/

Rorty, R. (2002), "Human Rights, Rationality, and Sentimentality," in B. Savić (ed), *The Politics of Human Rights*, 67–83, London: Verso.

Schramme, T. (2017), "Empathy and Altruism," in H. L. Maibom (ed), *The Routledge Handbook of Philosophy of Empathy*, 203–14, London: Taylor and Francis.

Said, E. W. ([1978] 1994), *Orientalism*, New York: Random House.

Tumber, H. and J. Palmer (2004), *Media at War: The Iraq Crisis*, London: Sage.

Whitlock, G. (2006), *Soft Weapons: Autobiography in Transit*, Chicago: University of Chicago Press.

Williams, R. ([1961] 2001), *The Long Revolution*, Peterborough, ON: Broadview.

Vaughan, B. K. and N. Henrichon (2006), *Pride of Baghdad*, New York: Vertigo.

Virrilio, P. (2006), *Art and Fear*, trans. J. Rose, London: Continuum.

Zoya, J. F. and R. Cristofari (2002), *Zoya's Story: An Afghan Woman's Struggle for Freedom*, New York: HarperCollins.

6

Rachel Cusk's Empathy Work

Alissa G. Karl

One of the final scenes of *Kudos,* the third novel in Rachel Cusk's *Outline* trilogy, finds the narrator in a wine bar with a group of divorced women who are professional acquaintances. The narrator listens to and recounts their stories of separation and their subsequent lives, and one of the women tells the group about her five-year-old daughter saying to a visitor: "Mama's always talking about her work ... but in fact it isn't work—what she calls work is what other people would call a hobby" (2018: 222). The little girl's remark, and the context in which it is made, marks a fitting conclusion to Cusk's novelistic trilogy in a number of ways. First, its topical focus on parenting after divorce exemplifies the episodic narration of all three novels, in which the narrator listens to the often highly personal accounts of others. The child also raises the question of what counts as "work"; here, she questions the status of her mother's profession as translator, but her remark might be applied to all that readers have encountered in the three novels thus far. This is because Cusk's narrator is largely occupied with *listening to others* throughout all three books. Is this work? Some might argue that it isn't: a recently passed pay equity law in New Zealand, for instance, incited controversy when it attempted to codify "listening" as a type of skilled work because, detractors claimed, "anyone can listen" (Sussman 2020). I will contend here, however, that the listening with which Cusk's trilogy is preoccupied and around which it is structured is elaborated as empathy work that is particular to our contemporary labor regimes, and this empathy work is commodified—and, hence, waged—as it takes the form of the novel.

For some time now, scholars and commentators have posited the novel as a genre that is especially good at cultivating empathetic frames of mind.

The story goes, and as the introduction to this volume has elaborated, that such empathy contributes to everything from the development of bourgeois individualism to the strengthening of democratic societies. A few years ago, a study bolstered convictions about the novel's ability to generate emotions beneficial to liberal social arrangements when its authors affirmed that "literary fiction ... uniquely engages the psychological processes needed to gain access to characters' subjective experiences. ... Readers of literary fiction must draw on more flexible interpretive resources to infer the feelings and thoughts of characters" (Kidd and Costano 2013). In short, this study held that literary fiction—namely, the novel—primes us to experience empathy.

The empathetic subject, however, is not ahistorical or politically neutral, and this chapter examines how the notion of empathy presumes forms of subjectivity and character that can (and should) be interrogated and historicized. The novel can also help us do this kind of work: if, as Sarah Brouillette notes, "[l]iterary scholars have shown how indispensable formations of the subject as 'origin of expression' have been to the history of capitalist cultural markets and to the formation of private rights to intellectual property," then we might also think of that originary subject in terms of other features of capitalist history—namely, labor (2014: 49). What if we consider the novel not as a form that trains or generates empathy, but as a product that is the outcome of creative, empathetic, and other affective forms of labor? And what if we do this in the context of contemporary labor regimes of de-industrialized capitalism, in which both affective labor and creative labor are prominent sources of surplus value? Rachel Cusk's recent *Outline* trilogy of novels (2014–18) helps us press these questions. Cusk's novels turn our attention from empathy as a state of mind that we want to cultivate or practice, and toward the labor regimes in which empathy is implicated. I'll demonstrate how Cusk's novels reference the novel genre's legacy as a vehicle for empathetic training, but in fact fully immerse those functions within contemporary regimes of affective and creative labor.

Cusk's extended treatment of empathy work can be located within a late resurgence of labor as an analytical category. In *Wages against Artwork*, Leigh Claire La Berge observes that the 1970s mark a point at which "institutionalized labor and critical theories of labor began to wane at the same time" (2019: 20). And as La Berge points out, it doesn't seem to be a coincidence that while labor receded both as a political force and as a category of analysis in the last decades of the twentieth century, during that same time we have also experienced the real subsumption of labor to capital, under which formal labor has expanded to all areas of life. When almost any activity has the potential to generate surplus value, almost any activity can be labor. Yet an increasing share of that labor is what La Berge calls "decommodified," in that it generates surplus value for *someone*—just not pay for the person who did the work. In short, it seems to be the case that we are working ever more, without fully being paid for our efforts, and critical attention has only recently turned to this condition.

Yet feminist accounts of labor—especially Marxist ones—have tended to these questions for decades. For instance, the Wages for Housework feminists of the 1970s demanded that we account for the social reproduction undertaken in manual and affective domestic work: from child rearing, feeding, and homemaking to, in Silvia Federici's words, "smiling [and] fucking" (1975). These feminists claimed that all such labors of social reproduction are foundational to formally waged labor because they reproduce the workers and society from which capitalism extracts value. No workers, no accumulation. As such, Nicole Cox and Silvia Federici assert that "[women] have never belonged to ourselves, we have always belonged to capital every moment of our lives" (1975: 12). Although they did not use the term "affective labor," these feminists insisted that affective work associated with social reproduction generates value that capital cannot do without.

Wages for Housework's attention to affective work decades ago are useful in constructing an account of empathy as labor today precisely because of their consistent refrain that affective, domestic labors are embedded within, but often invisible in the value formulation of, commodities. It is appropriate to start with their foundational insights to understand empathy as work—and empathy as *labor*—under the more general rubric of a reinvigorated attention to labor as a critical category. Here I follow Fredrich Engels's basic distinction of work (as an activity that creates a use-value) from labor (as that which generates exchange value).[1] As I elaborate in this essay, Cusk's *Outline* trilogy offers a contemporary account of empathy as labor; Cusk's works, I claim, update the insistence of many 1970s feminists that affective and empathetic labor are a part of capitalist accumulation for our de-industrialized times, and they do this in a few key ways. First, *as novels*, these texts address the ways in which individual affect, subjectivity, and creativity are marshalled as commodified, exchangeable capacities, in the generation of other such exchange values, and in the service of a broader economics of privatization. Furthermore, at the level of their narrative form and, again, by virtue of their status *as novels*, the works in Cusk's trilogy overlap and co-locate affective and creative labors in ways that reckon with those labors' multiple status as long-unpaid labors of social reproduction, and as newly commodified expectations placed upon workers in an de-industrialized economy.

Affective Labor and De-industrialization

In Cusk's *Outline* trilogy, affective labor—primarily in the form of what I call "empathy work"—ranges across waged and unwaged, formal and informal designations. Indeed, this makes the distinction between what is "labor" and what is "work" somewhat tricky; in addition, affective labor also merges with creative labor in significant ways. Cusk's trilogy de-links empathy work from its presumed sites of production, and entwines it with the creative labor of making artworks. While critics and theorists have not placed accounts of affective and creative labor into conversation to any significant extent, Cusk's texts prompt us to think more carefully about the potential overlap of affective and creative labor by presenting them as the very same activity.[2] In listening to and relaying the monologues of others and then presenting an account of that listening *as* a series of novels, Cusk's trilogy offers empathetic work (the care work of listening and tending to others) as a creative product, and a creative product that is constituted by a documentation of empathetic listening; as such, both empathetic listening and its creative shape as a novel are emphasized as *products* of labor. But in this revelation, Cusk's novels also exhibit a canny, professional, even entrepreneurial mastery that exposes just how those products are made.

Of course, from a number of current perspectives, nearly all activities might be considered "labor" under the conditions of so-called real subsumption, and it is worth taking a moment to address such conditions as well as the contexts of de-industrialization and how affective labor is positioned within them. In the Marxist account, real subsumption is the capitalist's extraction of value from labor by alterations in the means of production themselves (as distinct from formal subsumption, in which surplus value is extracted from the worker by virtue of simply lengthening the working day).[3] Accounts of labor over the past few decades have addressed the ways in which capital has expanded to so many areas of life that labor doesn't just happen at the formal worksite, but nearly everywhere. Capital has developed the ability to extract value from communicative, affective, intellectual, creative, and relational characteristics—not just of workers in their role as such, but of the population as a whole. An oft-cited formulation from Mario Tronti has it that "[t]he social character of production has been extended to the point that the entire society now functions as a mode of production" (La Berge 2019: 23). If we believe that we inhabit such a condition or something approaching it, we see substantial ramifications for how we can even imagine labor as such. As La Berge puts it, "capital might turn anything (an email, a fantasy, a nap) into a site where surplus value is generated" (2019: 24).

The increasingly capacious scene of exchange value generation that La Berge describes is properly contextualized within the era of de-industrialized capital that those of us in high-GDP countries have inhabited for the past few decades; indeed, one of the arguments of this chapter is that empathy today must be framed more precisely within the labor regimes of de-industrialized capital. As I use the term here, de-industrialization names capital's substitution of finance for industrial production as its main engine of value extraction since the 1970s, and the concomitant transformations in labor markets and conditions that resulted from that change. Specifically, "industrial" labor (that is, the labor of making physical things) has shifted markedly to lower-GDP, so-called "developing" economies, while highly developed capitalist economies have substituted service labor of all kinds in its place and registered a marked decline in the power of organized labor as a result.

Commentators on de-industrialized labor reckon with a few consistent phenomena: the aforementioned real subsumption of ever more activities to capitalist value extraction and the indistinction of labor and non-labor that follows from it; the tendency to extract value from knowledge, communicative, emotional, creative, and relational forms of labor (or to these kinds of features when attached to other labor—see the Trader Joe's grocery worker who cheerfully inquires about your favorite snacks upon checkout!), and the appropriation of countercultural and feminist critiques of labor into mainstream labor regimes themselves whereby, as Brouillette puts it, "the artists' vaunted resistance to routine work has helped transform the total organization of elite labor" (2014: 44). Sianne Ngai and Jasper Bernes, for instance, have elaborated the ways in which artistic and cultural productions register our ambivalent responses to the de-industrialized labor scene; at the levels of form, genre, and for Ngai, affect, artworks play out the ramifications of labor under capitalism, both contesting and continuing its mandates.

We cannot make sense of Cusk's experiments with empathetic and creative labor outside of the conditions of de-industrialization, and indeed they most potently signify within this historical economic context. Cusk's works test what Luc Boltanski and Eve Chiapello call the "representations and justifications" of labor under capitalism now, re-mixing and reconfiguring them in order to "present capital as an acceptable and even desirable order of things."[4] Cusk's texts can certainly be said to inhabit the scene of real subsumption as they superimpose empathetic and creative modalities in the service of generating commodities (novels). However, I would suggest that these novels intervene in key presumptions about contemporary capital's regimes of value extraction by way of the interaction of empathetic and creative work in the texts. If one of the features of labor under real subsumption includes what Brouillette describes as a kind of fetishization of creativity—one that is trained upon an "authentic expressive self [who] participate[s] in market activity" (2014: 13)—then Cusk's dual focus on empathetic and creative labors indicates that the self who would purportedly perform both *may be a product* of that very labor. That is, not only do Cusk's novels resist the conflation of women and their affective and creative work (which the Wages for Housework feminists also insisted), but they also insist that these are labors that generate distinctive products–even in the form of subjectivity itself. Empathetic labor under de-industrialized capitalism is a commodity to be sure, and Cusk also subjects that product to women's entrepreneurial mastery. Where Wages for Housework spoke to a late-industrial context in which women's affective labor was unwaged but also instrumentalized by capital, Cusk develops a hard-nosed view of the sly means that women might need to undertake to get paid.

Cusk's novels of empathy work must, then, be situated in a context in which almost anything can be labor and in which the generation of surplus value is a wide-ranging affair. Within this frame, Cusk's novels should also be positioned as just that—*as novels*—for the ways in which they reconfigure the aesthetic norms of the genre for present labor conditions. Annie McClanahan has recently asked this very question about how contemporary novels attend formally to the kinds of work that we do now. As McClanahan and others note, Marx relies upon the characterological tropes of the nineteenth-century realist novel to examine the social and economic changes visited upon workers, such that "the aesthetic correlative of the regulated wage contract ... [may have been] the realist novel, with its commitment to representing protagonists who could remain consistent while they developed and matured and who could be free in their individual particularity but protected as constituents of a collective social class" (2019). McClanahan inquires, however, into how recent renovations in narrative character might correlate with changing conditions of work, and how shifting characterological norms might redefine our relationship to labor. Cusk's *Outline* trilogy takes up these very questions as her novels evacuate the notion of "strong character" to suggest that such "character" does not precede work, to contest the idea of "labor as calling," and to focus on the *terms* of affective and creative labor. The form and conventions of the novel—a genre largely centered around character—are the ground upon which Cusk undertakes a characterological experiment: she demonstrates that character and self follow from labor, rather than preceding it. Later in this essay I will elaborate more fully how Cusk's work with character is part of her account of empathy work as creative and also distinctly professionalized production. I'll begin my discussion of how the *Outline* trilogy intervenes in our into thinking about labor, the novel, and empathy with an analysis of the texts as accounts of extended listening.

"Will you just listen?"

Outline, *Transit*, and *Kudos* are comprised of a series of episodic conversations that the narrator, who is a novelist, has with friends, strangers, and professional acquaintances. Actually, these "conversations" are usually lengthy monologues and stories that these people share, to which the narrator listens, and that she recounts. Here I'll discuss the ways in which the trilogy's scenario of extended listening is also an account of the status and function of affective and creative labor. Despite the first-person narration throughout, readers have limited direct access to the narrator's interiority or to information about her as a character. Her thoughts are largely exposed through and as her narration of others; we learn through those interactions that she is (in the first novel, quite recently) divorced and has two sons. Indeed, the narrator is hardly even named in the novels; she is named precisely once in each. Commentators on these three novels have liberally conflated Faye's character with Rachel Cusk herself, often terming them "autofiction." They do this, perhaps, because prior to the publication of the *Outline* trilogy, Cusk published two widely circulated memoirs, *A Life's Work* (2001) and *Aftermath* (2012) in which she recounted her experiences of early motherhood and divorce, respectively. Because Faye is divorced and is a novelist like Cusk, these commentators hold the works to be autofictional. Assessing the novels as examples of autofiction is not necessarily antithetical to the reading that I am pursuing, though doing so does risk obscuring a view of them as products of labor.

All three novels are structured by encounters that I see as empathy work–in some cases, double shifts of it, as the characters with whom the narrator interacts subject her to intensive listening, often to very personal and intimate matters. Each of the three novels opens with an extended encounter with a man (two of them strangers who sit next to Faye on airplanes; the third a former lover encountered on the street in London), and proceeds through a dozen or so episodic monologues apiece. Faye listens to strangers, friends, acquaintances, other writers, journalists (she indeed manages to interview those who would interview her), tour guides, her hairdresser, the contractors working on her flat, and a series of women who, notably, talk at length about their divorces.

But these novels don't just *thematize* empathy work (although they certainly do that). Because the narrator is working throughout all of the novels as an author, the trilogy involves readers in the empathy work that the narrator undertakes and emphasizes it as formal labor. Faye travels to teach workshops, promote her books, give readings and interviews, and attend literary conferences. If her literary profession is exposed in the novels as an industry of talking and listening, for much of these novels Faye is *at work* under arrangements that Boltanski and Chiapello emphasize as those of late, de-industrialized capitalism in which changes in the structure of compensation–from the "full-time salaried *cadre* ... to the periodic contributor" paid through honoraria, royalties, and the like—are accompanied by the "[e]rasure of the separation between private life and professional life" (2018: 155). As such, while one can read all of Faye's life in these novels as a form of work, the texts likewise stress the economic arrangements behind much of the empathetic listening in which she engages.

In *Affect and American Literature in the Age of Neoliberalism*, Rachel Greenwald Smith recognizes how prioritizing "access" to individual emotion has become a key contemporary literary feature. For Smith, "the belief that literature is at its most meaningful when it represents and transmits the

emotional specificity of personal experience" coincides with the priorities
of the so-called neoliberal era (2015: 1). By this account, fiction of recent
decades is marked by an alignment between subjects and the works they
encounter, privileging a "personalization of aesthetic experience" and
affording emotion "political significance" only when it is attached to
individuals (2015: 20, 17). The basic narrative premise and structure of
the *Outline* trilogy might *seem* to evoke this kind of individual affective
access, but at the same time those novels emphasize that such access is a
product of labor. It is clear, for instance, that in the first novel, *Outline*, Faye
has traveled to Athens to teach a creative writing course because she needs
the money. While the narration does not confirm this outright, we infer it
through Faye's phone calls with a banker with whom she is trying to arrange
a mortgage (and for which she is declined for the amount that she wants).
The two other writers teaching on the course also expressly mention the lure
of pay for these kinds of teaching gigs, and how it often wins out over the
time they need to complete their own writing. In this way, not just for Faye,
but for the other writers and by extension for *these* novels—Cusk's novels,
that is—writing is labor.

Empathetic listening is the primary vehicle for affective access in
the trilogy, and such listening is presented as a work product in that the
monologues of others constitute the narrative of the novel. In addition, most
acts of listening take place decidedly at work, or on work sites. *Outline*
occurs entirely on a work trip, but Faye's listening is more than incidental to
this. In one episode, Faye is in the classroom with her students on the first
day of her writing workshop. She asks each student to share something that
they noticed on the way to class that day. The students take turns sharing
their observations, which often veer into personal matters. Faye listens,
allowing each to speak at length without interruption. Then:

> My phone rang on the table in front of me. It was my younger son's
> number. I picked it up and said that I would call him back later.
> "I'm lost," he said. "I don't know where I am."
> Holding the phone to my chest I told the group that there was a minor
> emergency and that we would take a short break.
>
> (2014: 150)

In this moment, Faye's affective labors for her children and for her students
overlap. The scene enacts simultaneous modes of affective access: the
listening for which Faye's students are paying, the access via phone, at any
time, that Faye's son receives from her and the affective access that readers
receive from the novel. Such a consistent thematic line plays off a chord
of expectations about such access—namely, that women provide it, usually
unpaid, and that novels legitimately offer it as creative products. The detail
in which Faye "hold[s] the phone to [her] chest" pulls on these multiple
threads: Faye is caught between the demands of unpaid and paid affective

work, and the open phone line pressed to her chest registers the immanence of constant care work obligations that so many women workers in service and caring jobs confront.

Yet, with the open line pressed to her chest and the class dismissed for a short break, we also see a narrator, a parent, and a worker both managing these various requirements and holding them at bay. Faye and Cusk suspend the demand for affective access, pausing to delay the delivery of empathetic goods. The scene's momentary withholding allows for a rumination upon the terms and conditions under which that affective access might be granted. When Faye does deliver some of the goods to her son, she does so by asking him to describe his surroundings to her, which is essentially the same assignment she had just given to her students. Whether inadvertent or strategic, Faye's efficiency at parenting and teaching reveals that affective access is a resource to be carefully managed. For while it would seem from the basic narrative premise and structure of the *Outline* trilogy that Cusk is trading in this kind of individual affective access, these novels also reject that kind of access, too. Most consistently, the narrator's intent listening does expose "emotional" and "personal" content. Yet the novels quite emphatically refuse any kind of reciprocal access to the narrator. As such, I'd argue that they expose this kind of "individual access" for what it is—a literary figure, a construction, a work product. Furthermore, the novels supplant "affective access" by distinctly commodifying affect: Faye is an empathetic listener who is also always working for pay, and the novels themselves are commodified representations of affective authenticity. As such, the *Outline* trilogy's focus on extended listening insists upon the economic arrangements behind affective and empathetic authenticity—all of this in the context of the rise of service work and its attendant requirements for empathetic and affective labor in highly industrialized sites of production (like Cusk's UK).

In Cusk's trilogy, we are invited to examine empathy work as such— as work—from a number of angles. One of the prominent ways in which this occurs is through the novels' play with "work" and "home" settings. As I mentioned a moment ago, the three novels see the narrator largely— though not entirely—outside of the home. In *Outline*, the first novel, the narrator travels to Athens to teach a creative writing course. In the third novel, *Kudos*, the narrator is again on the road, at a literary conference abroad. In the middle novel, *Transit*, the narrator does travel to a literary festival in her home country of the UK, though the novel also sees her move into a run-down flat that she has purchased (again, we're led to believe that it's what she can afford, post-divorce) that requires heavy renovation. The home becomes a site of actual construction labor and she meets frequently with her builders during the novel. The home is also in disarray, requiring extra personal work with neighbors (who complain about construction noise) and her children, who must be shuttled to their father's home and also cared for remotely. The trilogy as a whole, then, takes place in worksites and yet scrambles domestic and professional scenes, locating empathy work between and among them. If *Transit's* home renovation is a literalization of Cusk's abiding interest in, as one reviewer aptly put it, "lay[ing] bare the scaffolding of bourgeois family life" (Sehgal 2017) then that scaffolding and the empathy work of which it is in part comprised has moved into the realm of professional labor. When, for instance, Faye sits in her crumbling flat which is about to be demolished to the studs, she observes an "idyllic" cosmopolitan family out the window, across the back garden fence (2017: 49–50). Faye's positioning inside her darkened worksite of a flat of course emphasizes that the *home* that is domesticity's outcome is definitively a site of *labor*. At the same time, the demolition of the home is one way of remarking that the affective work typically done at home is not a "natural" fit in the domestic space.

In all of their settings, the novels are founded upon acts of listening that characterize domestic and caring labor—typically home-based work. Given that the novels are structured around intensive listening, Cusk's settings signify precisely because of their *un*homeliness. In her book *Extreme Domesticity*, Susan Fraiman sets out to "sever domesticity from the usual right-wing pieties and the usual left derision"; in so doing, she examines what happens when domesticity is decoupled from both sentimentality, and from normative versions of marriage (2017: 3). Fraiman's project helps us to see the stakes of Cusk's removal of empathy work that is associated with the home from the site of the home itself. The narrator does empathy work as part of her professional errands at the same time that she performs long-distance care work in her calls with her sons from abroad. In all of their "working away" settings, the novels locate empathy work decidedly *outside* of the home or other domestic scenes. In a similar way, the narrator's divorce repositions the empathy work she undertakes, much like that work is not performed in a tidy home, it is severed from normative marital arrangements. The narrator "listens" to many men—prominently, two men who sit next to her on airplanes, an ex-boyfriend, and a couple of male novelists—but none of them are her partner. Fraiman argues that paying a new kind of attention to divorce has the potential to "liberate" domesticity from "protocols of service to others," and she traces a tradition of women writers and entrepreneurs across the nineteenth and twentieth centuries who "distanc[e] themselves from marriage and [trade] on their domestic knowledge to ends more self-promoting than self-sacrificing" (2017: 98). In Cusk's trilogy, divorce functions as a device that shifts empathy work decidedly into the public: Faye's empathy work is not confined to the home, and is available to all—strangers, but also her children and friends, and in the service of her professional life. Faye's divorce is one of the factors that shake empathy work loose into other sites—namely, the labor market. This is not to say that in deploying empathy work out in the markets and in her profession, the narrator unproblematically recaptures "herself" from formerly stultifying marital arrangements. In fact, the overwhelming effect of the intensive bouts of listening in the trilogy is the effacement of the narrator herself—a feature that enacts Cusk's key characterological experiment.

Character Work

Where the trilogy presents empathetic listening as work, these acts of listening also signify within the conventions of the novel genre and its history as a vehicle for empathetic feeling. Shameem Black points out how various modern and contemporary authors have dislodged "the utopian alignment among art, empathy and human ethical development they inherited from the Romantics," and yet that association nonetheless persists as a literary presumption (2009: 788). Beyond the literary scene specifically, a prioritization of personal development and individual interiority in creative, professional, and consumerist contexts has solidified at least since the 1980s. Crucially, as Brouillette argues (2014: 13) and as I'd contend Cusk demonstrates, the primacy of these attributes is part of broader labor market conditions. Faye's deliberate obscurity as narrator and the effacement of her character (at the same time that she is clearly the one doing all the work), registers within the domains of both the novel genre and of creative and care work. That is, if the novel's conventions are subtended by labor conditions, then Cusk's experiment with character is not just an intervention into the features of the novel genre (although it is that); her work with character necessarily interrogates the expectations around these forms of labor.

An abiding pattern across the trilogy, for instance, is the combination of Faye's unreciprocated empathetic listening and her characterological vagueness. By the end of three novels we still know little about Faye, and in many instances it is clear that those to whom she listens do not listen to her in turn. For example, during the conversation the narrator has with her first airplane neighbor in *Outline*, they discuss the neighbors' children and his divorce. Here, Faye gives a rare personal rumination, on her own young sons' relationship with one another, that becomes quite thoughtful and even lyrical. Upon concluding her reflections to her neighbor, Faye says: "My neighbor was silent for a while. Presently he said that in his case his children had been his mainstay, through all the ups and downs of his marital career" (2014: 83). The neighbor does not take up the thread that the narrator has unwound. Instead, he shifts the conversational focus to how he feels about his own children. He's either not listening to her, or he doesn't care about what she's just said—or both.

At the end of the third novel, *Kudos*, the narrator's son says to her on the phone, "Faye … will you just listen?" before telling her his own story in detail (2018: 227). The son has been involved in a minor accident, but his demand still strikes any reader as deeply ironic given that listening is all that Faye has been doing for three novels. But while it might seem unfortunate that the narrator does all of this unreciprocated empathy work (only to have her son fail to recognize that she's been doing it at all!), the persistent effacement of the narrator throughout the trilogy effectively severs all of this listening and empathy work from anything resembling Faye's own subjective content. So while one reviewer says that it is unclear whether or not Faye's "silence" is empowering (Mitchell 2018), I don't agree that this is the most pertinent question to ask about Faye's relative obscurity to the reader. What we "know" most about the narrator is through a kind of negative image of the others' stories to which she listens. At a time when we are all entreated to "find ourselves" in our paid labor, *Faye is not her empathy*; she is not her work. This is one of the trilogy's most provocative insights about empathy work. And where the artistic critique of wage labor has become a feature of the labor regime as we are entreated to find personal purpose in our jobs (and meant to blame ourselves when we don't), Cusk undercuts this appropriation by positing empathy work as the skilled labor of an entrepreneurial woman.

The novels depict listening as labor of a particular kind. They don't "recover" largely female work from overlooked obscurity; rather, they allow readers to closely observe the listening by which the novels are constituted. In one key moment, Faye in fact lets us in on it: while listening to her first airplane neighbor talk about his marriage she remarks: "I remained dissatisfied by the story of his second marriage. It had lacked objectivity, it relied too heavily on extremes, and the moral properties it ascribed to those extremes were often incorrect." She continues that she "did not believe certain key facts" (2014: 29). The narrator is listening like a novelist, through the prism of writerly craft; she is engaged in skilled labor. Faye's listening here recalls Fraiman's claims about American homemaking guru Martha Stewart, who Fraiman says evidences an "obstinately *literal* investment in domestic practices: their step-by-step concreteness, their attention to the craft and sweat expended on small acts of manual labor" (2017: 115). Stewart, of course, is both divorced and a millionaire media mogul; her meticulous domestic work is thus in the service of a highly public financial enterprise that is dislodged from the normative bourgeois family. In much the same way, Cusk emphasizes that Faye's listening is highly analytical; its scrupulousness seems to foreclose the possibility that it could be selfless.

In fact, though this moment takes place very near the beginning of the first novel, it actually preempts and frames Faye's son's exhortation that she "just listen" at the end of the third. Because the narrator has of course been listening throughout and has been doing so not just critically, cannily, and professionally; her skilled and deliberate empathy work has been building this series of novels all along. By extension, then, Faye's character in the novels is a product of that work, not a personage that precedes it.

McClanahan's point that Marx's correlation of nineteenth-century wage labor with realist character might be revised for contemporary conditions rings true here. Cusk is renovating novelistic character under today's conditions of de-industrialized labor in which character does not prefigure the work, but emerges from it. So when one reviewer complains that in *Outline* and *Transit* "[r]arely is a character's voice allowed to stand out for too long before being consumed by Faye's stolid placidity, thus blurring the separation between narrator, character and author" (Jensen 2017), they have indeed hit upon the very impact of Cusk's characterological experiment. Character, narrator, and, by extension, authorship are products of the work, not its preconditions. In fact, we might read the trilogy's insistence that character is product as a version of a central demand of the Wages for Housework feminists of the 1970s: the denaturalization of domestic work. If character is made through work and not an essence that precedes it, then anyone might do any work and domestic and affective labors are not more suited to women. The insistence upon character as product supports this older demand that domestic and affective work be waged—a matter on which Cusk elaborates by showing us how very shrewd women can be as they undertake waged affective work.

We Are Not Our Work

The *Outline* trilogy's distinctive affective ambivalence can be read, then, in light of Cusk's positioning of Faye (and even of herself) as a product of her affective and creative labors. In all three novels, intimate matters are conveyed through Faye's distanced, business-like tone, a "cool and controlled" (Sehgal 2017) posture that suggests the paid therapist who, like the novelist, is a skilled professional who works without getting worked up. With her notion of the "zany," Ngai elaborates a prominent cultural mode through which she claims the "'putting to work' of affect and subjectivity for the generation of surplus value" is apparent.[5] While Cusk's affective ambivalence is not "zany" in the way that Ngai characterizes it, the trilogy's conveyance of sensitive content in highly controlled tone operates in a conversant fashion; with this combination, Cusk exposes the condition under which intimate life is work.

Cusk's affective ambivalence emphasizes a key point that Ngai makes about how "feminine conventions [of] caring labor in the reproductive sphere have entered the 'mechanics' of productive work" (2012: 208). Cusk's professional tone reveals care as labor and contributes to the project of exposing "the labor of social reproduction … [for] what it really is"—the creation of value that does not always appear as such (Ngai 2012: 209). And Cusk's novels have indeed created value: the books in the trilogy are bestsellers, *New York Times* Books of the Year, and the whole nine yards. Cusk has unquestionably extracted value from empathy work by turning it into a creative commodity.

The overlap of affective and creative labors in the *Outline* trilogy occurs in a number of forms—from Faye's parenting and teaching to the novel's creative packaging of affective content—and as such intervenes in critical questions about contemporary labor. As Brouillete has shown, creativity has become a key source of revenue particularly since the 1990s (2014: 20–30). We might say that Cusk follows suit with affective labor; the exposure of empathy *as labor* via the creative commodity allows Cusk to wage affective efforts. Cusk's exposure of the novel as a commodity made of the frequently unwaged stuff of affective labor is, then, a crucial intervention. As La Berge points out, the question is not "Is said object a commodity or not" but rather "How and when do humans as laborers sell their labor power in the form of the commodity?" (2019: 16). Cusk has opened up this very inquiry for readers; by emphasizing the *sale* of affective labor, she references the primary designation of some work as waged and some as not under the development of monetary systems and capital[6] and confronts that very dichotomy of waged and unwaged. But Cusk doesn't just expose and redress the devaluation of empathy work (although she does do that). Her workaday settings and businesslike demeanor offer an important slant on what empathy work "does" in the first place: here, it makes products. The novels' episodic formats present empathy work as a series of tasks, performed one after the other. Readers can be forgiven for losing interest in the specific content of the dilemma that each character shares; Cusk's construction of the novel through successive monologues effectively levels each story in relation to all the others. When a reviewer claims, then, that *Transit* begins to feel too contracted, "neat" and "pithy" (Jensen 2017), we must recognize that this is exactly the effect of Cusk's novels' exposure of their own status as work products. Perhaps we learn from Cusk that empathy work ought to be waged like other labor. Or perhaps we see how Cusk has assigned a wage to empathy work herself.

Notes

1   On the distinction between the terms "labor" and "work," I follow Friedrich Engels's footnote in Marx's *Capital*: "Labor which creates use-values and is qualitatively determined is called 'work' as opposed to 'labor'; labor which creates value and is only measured quantitatively is called 'labor' as opposed to 'work'" (1990: 138). Engels calls those activities that end up generating exchange (or quantitative) values "labor," and other endeavors that generate use-values "work." Here I attempt to stick to this distinction, but it should be noted that part of what is at stake, not just in Cusk's novels but in our

contemporary moment, is the degree to which activities are implicated in regimes of exchange, and when and how we might determine that they are.

2 For a brief discussion of the gap that remains between theories of affective and of creative labor, see La Berge (2019: 16).

3 For a thorough account of formal vs. real subsumption, see the Endnotes Collective (2010).

4 Boltanski and Chiapello write: "If, contrary to prognoses regularly heralding its collapse, capitalism has not only survived, but ceaselessly expanded its empire, it is because it could rely on a number of share representations—capable of guiding action—and justifications, which present it as an acceptable and even desirable order of things" (2018: 10).

5 Ngai, *Our Aesthetic Categories*, 188.

6 Here I refer to Sylvia Federici's discussion of this historical process (2004: 75–6).

References

Bernes, J. (2017), *The Work of Art in the Age of Deindustrialization*, Stanford: Stanford University Press.

Black, S. (2009), "Ishiguro's Inhuman Aesthetics," *Modern Fiction Studies* 55 (4): 785–807.

Boltanski, L. and E. Chiapello. ([2005] 2018), *The New Spirit of Capitalism*, trans. Gregory Elliott, London: Verso.

Brouillette, S. (2014), *Literature and the Creative Economy*, Stanford: Stanford University Press.

Castano, E. and D. Kidd. (2013), "Reading Literary Fiction Improves Theory of Mind," *Science* 342 (6156): 377–80.

Cox, N. and S. Federici. (1975), *Counter-Planning from the Kitchen: Wages for Housework, A Perspective on Capital and the Left*, Brooklyn: New York Wages for Housework Committee.

Cusk, R. (2014), *Outline*, New York: Farrar, Straus and Giroux.

Cusk, R. (2017), *Transit*, New York: Farrar, Straus and Giroux.

Cusk, R. (2018), *Kudos*, New York: Farrar, Straus and Giroux.

Endnotes Collective (2010), "The History of Subsumption," *Endnotes* 2. Available online: https://endnotes.org.uk/issues/2/en/endnotes-the-history-of-subsumption (accessed July 28, 2020).

Federici, S. (1975), "Wages against Housework," Power of Women Collective and Falling Wall Press.

Federici, S. (2004), *Caliban and the Witch: Women, the Body, and Primitive Accumulation*, Brooklyn: Autonomedia.

Fraiman, S. (2017), *Extreme Domesticity: A View from the Margins*, New York: Columbia University Press.

Greenwald Smith, R. (2015), *Affect and American Literature in the Age of Neoliberalism*, New York: Cambridge University Press.

Jensen, M. (2017), "'The Only Form in All the Arts': On Rachel Cusk's Autobiographical Fiction," *The Los Angeles Review of Books*, April 3, 2017. Available online: https://lareviewofbooks.org/article/form-arts-rachel-cusks-autobiographical-fiction (accessed September 19, 2021).

La Berge, L. (2019), *Wages against Artwork: Decommodified Labor and the Claims of Socially Engaged Art*, Durham: Duke University Press.

Marx, K. ([1867] 1990), *Capital*, vol. 1, *A Critique of Political Economy*, trans. Ben Fowkes, NY: Penguin Classics.

McClanahan, A. (2019), "Introduction: The Spirit of Capital in an Age of Deindustrialization," *Post 45* 1: Deindustrialization and the New Cultures of Work. Available online: http://post45.org/2019/01/introduction-the-spirit-of-capital-in-an-age-of-deindustrialization (accessed October 2, 2020).

Mitchell, J. (2018), "To Endure the Void: On Rachel Cusk's 'Outline' Trilogy," *Los Angeles Review of Books*, August 13, 2018. Available online: https://lareviewofbooks.org/article/endure-void-rachel-cusks-outline-trilogy (accessed October 20, 2020).

Ngai, S. (2012), *Our Aesthetic Categories: Zany, Cute, Interesting*, Cambridge: Harvard University Press.

Sehgal, P. (2017), "Home Is Where the Art Is: Rachel Cusk Finds Inspiration in Domestic Crisis," *Bookforum*, February/March 2017. Available online: https://www.bookforum.com/print/2305/rachel-cusk-finds-inspiration-in-domestic-crisis-17185 (accessed October 20, 2020).

Sussman, A. (2020), "'Women's Work' Can No Longer Be Taken for Granted," *The New York Times*, November 13, 2020. Available online: https://www.nytimes.com/2020/11/13/opinion/sunday/women-pay-gender-gap.html (accessed November 14, 2020).

7

Affective Possibilities beyond Empathy

Kathryn Cai

This chapter examines Ocean Vuong's novel *On Earth We're Briefly Gorgeous* (2019) to explore how we might broaden the spectrum of feelings that become recognizable in relation to social structures and thereby exceed frameworks of empathy that depend on identification and recognizability. In this chapter, I turn to theorizations of affects and their indeterminacy to broaden the possible feelings and states we might recognize as possible within particular acts and situations. This attention to affects allows us to move beyond an understanding of empathy as a mode of relation predicated on sameness and full comprehension of another's experience.

Along these lines, the relationship between empathy and literature has been heavily debated. Critiques of empathy in fields like the health humanities broadly dispute the potential for personal responses to others' experiences to produce actions that might enact expanded forms of ethics and responsibility. These critics call for a greater attention to social structure, rather than empathy per se (Boler 1997; Garden 2007; Metzl and Hansen 2014), while critiques of empathy in anthropology articulate how it can operate in highly culturally specific modes (Hollan and Throop 2008). Similarly, literary scholar Amy Shuman examines empathy as a way of understanding how individual stories acquire meanings that transcend their personal content. Shuman argues that the possibility of empathetic responses to stories, such that someone can feel things they have never experienced, requires an ethics of responsibility that entails examining the structures of power that shape the experiences of both reader and teller (2005: 8). I argue that this attention to social structures, such as race and class, and power dynamics necessarily also entails an interrogation and expansion of the emotions that we can even recognize and relate to particular experiences. In this regard, an attention to affects allows us to move beyond behaviors and experiences that we can easily identify and name through our own frameworks. Instead, affects allow us to attune to the nebulous, not-yet-coherent senses of something that might deviate from coercive, static, and often culturally specific expectations for displays of feeling that can be easily seen and categorized.

Theorists of affect such as Kathleen Stewart, Jane Bennett, and Sara Ahmed consider affect as the body's capacities to both affect and be affected by other bodies in its worldly surroundings, and they stress the indeterminacy of any affect. While these scholars point to affect's imbrication in the social and economic conditions of the world, they also suggest that affect presents the potential to navigate these conditions in unexpected ways. In *Ordinary Affects,* for instance, Kathleen Stewart writes that affects are "[r]ooted not in fixed conditions of possibility but in the actual lines of potential that a *something* coming together calls to mind and sets in motion" (2007: 1). According to Stewart, ordinary affects are active and social forces that are constantly in flux in the world around us and are central to relating to this world. They constitute a "scene of immanent force, rather than [...] dead effects imposed on an innocent world" (2007: 1). Ordinary affects are

> things that happen. They happen in impulses, sensations, expectations, daydreams, encounters, and habits of relating, in strategies and their failures, in forms of persuasion, contagion, and compulsion, in modes of attention, attachment, and agency, and in publics and social worlds of all kinds that catch people up in something that feels like *something.*
>
> (Stewart 2007: 1)

Affect is an active "*something*" that one can sense in all these different modes of living but that eludes clear definition and is not rooted in intellectual or cognitive categorization and comprehension. As such, affects also participate in shaping the world as something that individuals perceive and to which they react, however unconsciously or fleetingly. As Lauren Berlant articulates in relation to the present, affects can hold the potential to make broader life conditions felt and visceral: they "register[] the conditions of life that move across persons and worlds, play out in lived time, and energize attachments" (2011: 16). Affects thus allow us to perceive the movements of world historical conditions, and in doing so, they give form to these changing conditions (2011: 16). Within the ordinary everyday, they also suggest ways of navigating the structures that shape a life: in Berlant, shifting attachments that enable one to continue living on in the world (2011: 15) and in Stewart, "a shifting assemblage of practices and practical knowledges, a scene of both liveness and exhaustion, a dream of escape or of the simple life" (2007: 2). These capacities of affect for sensing the movements of the world and giving them expressible form as they relate to embodied experiences take shape in Vuong's novel as opportunities for acknowledging the full complexity of another's experience, even when it is beyond our known contexts and easy identification.

Vuong's *On Earth We're Briefly Gorgeous* examines the violent legacies of the American war in Vietnam and migration to the United States. In Vuong's novel, these legacies are not straightforwardly passed down through generations but reverberate within everyday gestures that contain complex, often inseparable overlaps between violence and care. Vuong's novel is a coming-of-age story written from the perspective of the narrator, known to us only through his family's pet name for him, Little Dog, and addressed explicitly to his mother, Ma, who cannot read.

Throughout the novel, Little Dog grapples with his relationship with his mother and the complexity of her experiences and trauma as it manifests in their domestic life, often violently. Ma, whose given name in Vietnamese is Rose, has immigrated to the United States as a refugee in the wake of war and works grueling hours in a nail salon every day. Her past is deeply shaped by wartime trauma but also by her own experiences of domestic violence. Her life during Little Dog's childhood is also marked by the steady wear of her hours at the nail salon, which take a heavy physical toll, and the constant grind of poverty and alienation she experiences as someone who does not speak English in America. These collective traumas often emerge in domestic violence toward Little Dog, which eventually ends when he gets older and tells her to stop. The novel, however, invites us to take in these details and engage a greater recognition of Ma that does not seek to categorize or pass judgment. In other words, it asks us to engage in a form of recognition for the complexity of a person's experience that is related to empathy but that takes shape without categorization or full cognitive comprehension of these experiences. In doing so, the novel explores how the literary can evoke affects that make visceral and articulable embodied experiences connected with broader world conditions that may not yet have common expression in this work's context, giving it form and genre; according to Berlant, how the "aesthetic or formal rendition of affective experience provides evidence of historical processes" (2011: 16) and makes experience apprehensible, if not in easily categorizable terms.

To do so, the novel puts forth a broadened conception of language beyond its indicative and descriptive functions. Vuong has previously written poetry, and in *On Earth We're Briefly Gorgeous*, Vuong's first novel, he juxtaposes scenes and gestures that illuminate one another, much like in poetry. This juxtaposition occurs without clearly narrating the connections between scenes. Similarly, the novel also does not progress with a linear timeline. The juxtaposition of unexpected scenes that jump through time allows layers of significance to emerge between them. This significance often takes affective form, as something we can sense but not easily name or categorize. In the juxtaposition of scenes, multiple affects also coexist and bleed into one another without resolving into a single clear meaning that can be easily categorized. Limited utterances and gestures in the novel thus take on more meanings and significance through juxtaposition with others than can be gleaned on their own.

Throughout the novel, Little Dog also explores his own emerging queer sexuality, and the novel articulates how Little Dog's and his mother's experiences are fundamentally intertwined. In their affective complexity and indeterminacy, the utterances and gestures throughout the novel also become opportunities to extend recognition to another, both within the world of the novel and in the novel's engagement with its readers. In the novel, the giving and receiving of this fundamental recognition is a world-altering act, in that it creates the space for both Ma and Little Dog to find a way to continue existing in a world that does not acknowledge their experiences and does not welcome them. In doing so, the novel asks its readers to extend the same recognition to Ma and Little Dog, even beyond full comprehension of their experiences. Perhaps even more radically, beyond simply seeing the trauma and limitations that war, poverty, and foreignness impose, it also asks us to recognize the generative possibilities for creating a life that emerge from such seemingly stunted origins.

The novel explicitly extends this project of making a place for themselves across Little Dog's queerness and Ma's history with war, and again, affect plays a crucial role. In *Cruising Utopia*, José Muñoz articulates queerness's world-transforming and utopian potential. Muñoz considers queerness as a "structuring and educated mode of desiring that allows us to see and feel beyond the quagmire of the present" (2019: 1). For Muñoz, "[q]ueerness is that thing that lets us feel that this world is not enough, that indeed something is missing" (2019: 1). Queerness is an embodied and performative act that "is not simply a being but a doing for and toward the future. Queerness is essentially about the rejection of a here and now and an insistence on potentiality or concrete possibility for another world" (Muñoz 2019: 1). Muñoz draws on philosopher Ernst Bloch to articulate the concept of "concrete utopias," which are rooted in the "historically situated struggles" and "hopes of a collective, an emergent group, or even the solitary oddball who is the one who dreams for many" (2019: 3). Concrete utopias are the "realm of educated hope" that are "marked by an enduring indeterminacy" in both affect and methodology (Bloch in Muñoz 2019: 3). As Muñoz articulates, the "[h]ope along with its other, fear, are affective structures that can be described as anticipatory" (2019: 3).

Affects thus disclose and participate in shaping the world. Indeed, the close relationship Muñoz identifies between affect and queerness in reaching for a different world also intersects with the refugee and immigrant project of building new lives and worlds. Scholarship on affect in Asian American Studies has often identified the family as a site of inculcation into the demands of capitalism (Lee 2013: 6; Ninh 2014: 47). More recently, however, scholars in Afro-Asian studies have turned to affect as a way to access "tacit, minor, or ephemeral affective relations" (Reddy and Sudhakar 2018). These scholars, like Muñoz, recognize affect as an excess and presence that can be felt in the aesthetic (Muñoz 2019: 3). Building on this scholarship on affect, I want to examine how literature can point to the diffuse, difficult-to-capture, and sometimes ephemeral, but still significant, movements of affect in everyday life. These affects can point to desires for different worlds that emerge from the conditions of the present and offer other possibilities to recognize and be moved by others that do not rely on identification. And indeed, as *On Earth We're Briefly Gorgeous* shows, these affects also participate in remaking the world to include bodies like them. This remaking does not happen in a dramatic overthrow and a wholesale transformation of the present but in small, everyday moments imbued with affective resonances that ask for and receive recognition between individuals, including the readers of the novel. The capacity of language, broadly conceived to include embodied gestures and acts, to function as a bridge between individuals plays a central role in allowing both Ma and Little Dog to remake the world into a place that can accommodate them and even present possibilities for the future. The recognition that they ask for and offer one another, and that they also ask for from the novel's readers, also asks us to begin exercising the attunement for imagining a more capacious world ourselves.

The Limits and Possibilities of Language

To begin considering the novel's emphasis on affect, I want to consider how the novel explicitly explores the limits of written and spoken language's ability to articulate feeling directly. Vuong interrogates the assumptions about language's primacy that are embedded within the very language we use. The novel turns to juxtaposition, which allows embodied gestures and acts to evoke the diverse, sometimes contradictory affects that arise within and between scenes. In doing so, Vuong challenges our own capacities to describe these affects with the spoken and written language we have. The novel invites us instead to sit with and sense affects in all their inarticulable complexity rather than seek to name and categorize them, allowing them to emerge as fundamental requests for recognition to which both the individuals within the novel and we as readers can respond.

In exploring the limits of language, the novel portrays scenes of everyday moments in which spoken and written language cannot be summoned. Little Dog's home life is a mix of mutual tenderness and domestic violence.

In the first moment the narrator recalls this violence early in the novel, Little Dog writes that the "first time you hit me, I must have been four. A hand, a flash, a reckoning. My mouth a blaze of touch" (Vuong 2019: 5). In this short description, touch is primary. Most fundamentally, after Ma hits him, Little Dog's mouth is simply "a blaze of touch" that transcends the capacity of language to describe the experience or the range of this touch's possible emotional or physical effects.

This moment of violence is followed by others that are interspersed with Ma attempting to aesthetically and imaginatively conjure new scenes in the world. Little Dog narrates Ma asking him to teach her to read and then growing frustrated and embarrassed. She pushes the book away and says, "I can *see*—it's gotten me this far, hasn't it?" (Vuong 2019: 5). In another moment in this sequence, Ma has taken up coloring and describes what it feels like to color in a scene to Little Dog. Ma asks Little Dog, "Have you ever made a scene [...] and then put yourself inside it?" (Vuong 2019: 6). In the narrative, Little Dog asks, "How could I tell you that what you were describing was writing? How could I say that we, after all, are so close, the shadows of our hands, on two different pages, merging?" (Vuong 2019: 6). Although these moments depict Ma's limits with language, they also begin to suggest a more expansive conception of what language is. Little Dog begins to imaginatively merge their hands, his writing and hers coloring. A visual scene, then, carries the same significance as writing, which also affirms Ma's defiant declaration of her ability to see. From its opening pages, the novel thus imagines how other forms of communicating are equal and akin to written and spoken language, as well as how written and spoken language and these other forms augment one another to bring together a range of diverse, even seemingly contradictory, affects. For instance, Vuong juxtaposes the scenes of reading and coloring with another memory in which Ma throws a "box of Legos" at Little Dog's head, the "hardwood dotted with blood" (Vuong 2019: 6). Ma quickly apologizes, then brings Little Dog to McDonald's, where she watches him eat and tells him that he needs to "get bigger and stronger" (Vuong 2019: 6), a combined gesture and statement that conveys tenderness, love, and atonement even in the wake of an assault that would seem to suggest the opposite.

Alongside this exploration of language's expansiveness, Ma's inability to read or speak English is also not straightforwardly celebrated, and the novel viscerally depicts its painful consequences in the world. In a different section of the novel, Ma excitedly comes home from work and wants to go to the store to buy oxtail for a nourishing soup in winter. However, when they arrive, she is unable to tell the men behind the meat counter what she wants in English. Although Ma is so fair skinned, with auburn hair, that she is often mistaken for being a white American, Ma's lack of English quickly dispels this misconception. As Little Dog remarks, "[o]ne does not 'pass' in

America, it seems, without English" (Vuong 2019: 52). Language, then, is a crucial signifier of race and belonging, and Ma's lack of English immediately and irrevocably marks her as other. At the store, Ma resorts to miming a cow, a performance that aligns her not just with an animal but also the pieces of meat for sale—perhaps the ultimate speechless inhuman object. The men behind the counter laugh, sometimes even kindly, and Ma, humiliated, gives up and "[grabs] a loaf of Wonder Bread and a jar of mayonnaise instead" (Vuong 2019: 31).

Vuong's novel, however, again subtly undermines the primacy of spoken and written language as a privileged and valorized form of communication. Earlier in this section, Little Dog meditates on Ma's limitations with language, not just English but also Vietnamese. He remarks that "[w]hen it comes to words, you possess fewer than the coins you saved from your nail salon tips in the milk gallon under the kitchen cabinet" (Vuong 2019: 29). Ma would often "gesture to a bird, a flower, or a pair of lace curtains from Walmart and say only that it's beautiful—whatever it was" in Vietnamese: "Đẹp quá" (Vuong 2019: 29). She once saw a hummingbird and asked Little Dog what it is called, only to forget immediately. However, Little Dog returns home one day to see a hummingbird feeder in their yard. She had bought the feeder by recognizing the bird on the box: "a bird you could not name but could nonetheless recognize" (Vuong 2019: 29). Little Dog's anecdote of the hummingbird portrays Ma's limits while also validating her assertion of her ability to see and her complex appreciation for beauty even when she cannot name its subject. The moment of language's failure in the grocery store is thus fleshed out with wider complexity and significance when juxtaposed with Ma's recognition and appreciation of the hummingbird. In the grocery store, while they are waiting in the checkout line, Ma sees a tray of mood rings and again sadly whispers "Đẹp quá" (Vuong 2019: 31–2). She buys one for each of them, herself, Little Dog, and his grandmother, and they go home and admire them together. Bookending the scene at the meat counter, the meanings of "Đẹp quá" are fleshed out by these intersecting contexts to include a small attempt at consolation amidst the painful humiliation of everyday life in America. The complex affects that emerge as these different scenes come together suggest Little Dog's understanding of his mother without the need for her to explicitly articulate her feelings. It also allows and asks us as readers to see and feel for Ma as a complex individual, beyond what her language can say.

Going further, at this moment in the narrative, Little Dog reflects that the spoken language they both have is a living record of Ma's experience with traumatic rupture. As a child of five, she watched as her school exploded and burned from an American napalm attack. Little Dog reflects that "[o]ur mother tongue, then, is no mother at all—but an orphan" (Vuong 2019: 31). Vuong's construction of this language is one that contains a primal rupture, a movement from "mother" to "orphan" that recognizes the mother's fundamental loss. Mother's antithesis here is not a woman who has lost a child but a woman who is herself parentless. Little Dog's formulation shatters an otherwise easy construction and concept of a mother tongue. The language that Ma has is actually "no mother at all," unable to engender the natural, unthinking relationship and continuity that we expect of a native language. Instead, this language is itself an "orphan," lost and unable to find its origins. It is arrested in a time of trauma, "a time capsule, a mark of where [Ma's] education ended, ashed" (Vuong 2019: 32). With this knowledge, "Đẹp quá" comes to take on even more signification. Addressing Ma, Little Dog muses that "to speak in our mother tongue is to speak only partially in Vietnamese, but entirely in war" (Vuong 2019: 32). Ma's words always contain the trauma and rupture of violence. They are not only a reflection of the limits to language that violence imposes, however. We know at this point that Ma's limited vocabulary also has the capacity to gesture to a wide range of referents through its embodied interplay with gestures and lived contexts. In doing so, these words and gestures demonstrate how meaning flexibly emerges from the lived intersections between language and embodied experience. Ma's words are a reflection of resilience as well as language's limits and destruction.

Vuong's exploration of the limits and possibilities of language resonates with anthropologist Veena Das's formulation of language that possesses the possibility for intersubjective recognition in the wake of world-shattering violence. Das's work has focused on the aftermath of the Partition of India, which was marked by the "large-scale abduction and rape of women" (Das 1996: 67). Das draws on Wittgenstein and Stanley Cavell to examine "transactions between language and body" in order to "ask how one should inhabit such a world that has been made strange through the desolating experience of violence and loss" (Das 1996: 68). In these transactions, the strangeness of this world, "revealed by death, by its non-inhabitability, can be transformed into a world in which one can dwell again, in full awareness of a life that has to be lived in loss" (Das 1996: 69). Language and its intersubjective potential are thus fundamental to a transformation of the world into a place that is once again habitable.

Das begins by reading a scene in Wittgenstein's *The Blue and Brown Books* about the capacity for personal pain to be located in another body. For Das, the statement that Wittgenstein includes— "I am in pain"—becomes a way to move out of private suffering into sharedness and recognition, without, necessarily, "understanding" (Das 1996: 70). As such, pain is not an "inexpressible something that destroys communication or marks an exit from one's existence in language." Instead, pain "makes a claim asking for acknowledgment, which can be given or denied. In either case, it is not a referential statement that is simply pointing to an inner object" (Das 1996: 70). Language becomes the "bodying forth of words" that exceed their literal referents and gesture to a greater meaning that asks to be recognized, even if this language consistently fails to fully articulate them and bridge the divide between a self and other (Das 1996: 70). The meaning that asks to be recognized thus extends beyond things that can be articulated and can be clearly and straightforwardly understood. Instead, this meaning can also be understood to be affective: a sense of something in another to which we also give attention.

In her analysis, Das returns to a short story that she had previously analyzed that is set during the Partition, "Khol Do," by Sadat Hassan Manto. In it, Manto depicts a young woman, Sakina, who is separated from her elderly father while they are on a journey. The father seeks help from a group of young men, who find Sakina, reassure her, and convince her to get into a jeep with them. An indeterminate amount of time and unspecified events pass, but when the daughter is finally reunited with the father, she is being carried into a medical clinic on a stretcher. She appears to be a "near dead body," but the father recognizes her and follows the stretcher as it is being carried into the doctor's examination room. The doctor, reacting to the heat in the room, points to the window and says "khol do" ("open it"), and Sakina's "hands move towards the tape of the *salwar* (trouser) and fumble to unloosen (lit. open) it." The father joyously shouts, "my daughter is alive—my daughter is alive" (Das 1996: 76).

Das writes that she previously understood Sakina to be "condemned to a living death" in which the "normality of language has been destroyed, as Sakina can hear words conveying only the 'other' command," while her father cannot even "comprehend the non-world into which she has been plunged, for he mistakes the movement in the body as a sign of life whereas in truth it is the sign of her living death" (Das 1996: 76–7). Revisiting it years later, however, Das writes that "[o]n deeper meditation, there is one last movement that I did not then comprehend":

> In giving the shout of joy and saying "my daughter is alive," the father does not speak here in personalized voices of tradition. In the societal context of this period, when ideas of purity and honor densely populated the literary narratives, as well as family and political narratives, so that fathers willed their daughters to die for family honor rather than live with bodies that had been violated by other men, *this father wills his daughter to live even as parts of her body can do nothing else but proclaim her brutal violation.*
>
> (Das 1996: 77)

For Das, the father's declaration that "my daughter is alive" is akin to Wittgenstein's declaration "I am in pain": "Although it has the formal appearance of an indicative statement, it is to beseech the daughter to find a way to live in the speech of the father [...] This sentence is the beginning of a relationship, not its end" (Das 1996: 77–8). Das thus articulates how "transactions between language and body" can extend an existential invitation beyond what is explicitly declared and work to transform the world into a place that is perhaps once again habitable.

In Vuong's novel, "Đẹp quá" is also fundamentally a transaction between language and body, a verbal expression of something within Ma that manifests in the world as an assertion of her complex personhood. It also embodies the possible limits of recognition that Das identifies in its lack of referent, simple construction, and abbreviated phrasing. As a request for recognition, it is easily missed and difficult to refer to directly. Vuong, however, makes "Đẹp quá" central in the scenes he portrays. The novel's exploration of ordinary language reflects Das's recognition of the interpersonal and everyday as the site of world-altering potential. In the novel, this potential takes shape through the affective resonances that emerge in greater complexity between scenes and gestures, thereby providing ever more robust recognition that can encompass and allow violence, trauma, tenderness, and love to coexist without resolving into a single clear concept. The space for these multiple, sometimes conflicting senses extends beyond a sense of empathy as a possibility that can only emerge through clear cognitive understanding and relation. Instead, attunement to the many, sometimes changing and contradictory, affects that emerge within and between experiences allows for a different kind of recognition that moves beyond similarity and full comprehension.

The Monstrosity/Hybridity of Embodiment

In the novel, this recognition also offers Little Dog a way to continue extending its world-altering potential into the future. Although Ma is a mother whose own experience is continually shaped by the limits created by war and violence, she nevertheless has a legacy for Little Dog. While she cannot pass onto Little Dog what she herself does not possess in the form of a language unmarked by trauma, the way of being in the world that she has made for herself in the wake of violence shapes Little Dog through an intertwined and fundamentally embodied language. Vuong's novel calls into question assumptions that are embedded into the very constructions and images of the everyday language that we often take for granted. In doing so, the novel suggests that other meanings can "body[] forth" and participate in remaking the world on the scale of the ordinary and everyday. In this way, the novel experiments with the possibilities of producing a kind of futurity that is not simply a replication of the past in its traumatic limits.

Little Dog and Ma share an embodied language from the time of his conception, what Little Dog understands as the primal language of the embodied connection and "blood utterances" between mother and fetus.

For Little Dog, "the placenta is a kind of language—perhaps our first one, our true mother tongue" in the "nutrients, hormones, and waste [that] are passed between mother and fetus." Although the placenta is a "disposable organ" (Vuong 2019: 137), the bond it creates fundamentally reshapes each body. As Little Dog articulates in the very beginning of the novel, "I am writing to you from inside a body that used to be yours. Which is to say, I am writing as a son" (Vuong 2019: 10), from a body that is already hybrid from its beginnings.

Here the novel again asserts a "mother tongue" that diverges dramatically from the "mother tongue" we assume in that easy linguistic construction but which is no less—and indeed perhaps more—primal. From these embodied beginnings, that also contain within them the shattering rupture of violence, the novel imagines how a different kind of future might be forged that intertwines both Ma's and Little Dog's existential struggle. Their connecting thread is what the novel explicitly posits and explores as the "monstrosity" that characterizes both queerness and motherhood, and in particular, a motherhood that emerges from the trauma of war and refugeeship. In the novel, this link between their shared monstrosity as an imagination of alternative ways of being emerges from Ma's seemingly non sequitur declaration one day that "I'm not a monster. I'm a mother" (Vuong 2019: 13). Out loud in the narrative, Little Dog affirms that she is indeed not a monster, but

> [w]hat I really wanted to say was that a monster is not such a terrible thing to be. From the Latin root *monstrum*, a divine messenger of catastrophe, then adapted by the Old French to mean an animal of hybrid origins: centaur, griffin, satyr. To be a monster is to be a hybrid signal, a lighthouse: both shelter and warning at once.
>
> (Vuong 2019: 13)

In this explication, a monster is a multifaceted creature, both of "hybrid origins" and a "hybrid signal," a harbinger. In contrast to its seeming simplicity in colloquial language, its complex meanings are already embedded within its Western roots, Latin and Old French, and speak to the hybridity of cultures and bodies meeting and merging in sometimes tense and unexpected ways that is also foundational to early Western civilizations. Purity, then, is fundamentally an illusion, which the monster explicitly and discomfitingly signals. As a "hybrid signal" and a "lighthouse" that are both "shelter and warning at once," the monster is both tied to the foundations of this world and also a scene of its disruption and the harbinger of something else. The monster must live its otherness within a world that does not wish to accept it and fears it but also depends on it to signal what is to come.

Like the novel's treatment of literacy discussed above, this imagination of monstrosity is not straightforwardly valorized or liberating. Little Dog goes on to say that "parents suffering from PTSD are more likely to hit their children." Monstrosity thus encompasses violence but also the kind of care that might emerge from a history of violence: "Perhaps there is a monstrous origin to it, after all. Perhaps to lay hands on your child is to prepare him for war. To say possessing a heartbeat is never as simple as the heart's task of saying *yes yes* to the body" (Vuong 2019: 13). In this moment, Little Dog muses on the particular insight of a parent who has lived through war: that living is never simply a biological act that one can assume will continue without disruption. The moments in which Ma hits Little Dog are yet again expanded to evoke the inarticulable impulse and challenge of passing this embodied understanding on to him, though these motivations are also not fully knowable to us or even to Ma herself. They "perhaps" mark a hand hitting a child and imbue it with care, hovering in a liminal space of multiple contradictory and coexisting affects and histories that shape a gesture.

Little Dog's meditation on Ma's monstrosity is followed by a memory that connects them further. He remembers buying a dress with Ma at Goodwill, where she asks him whether the dress is fireproof. Although he is too young to be able to read, he answers that it is. Days later, he puts on this dress to ride his bike outside while Ma is at work, not knowing that "at recess the next day, the kids would call me *freak, fairy, fag*" (Vuong 2019: 14). Little Dog remarks that "I would learn, much later, that those words were also iterations of *monster*" (Vuong 2019: 14). The monstrosity of queerness and the monstrosity of Ma's motherhood are thus irrevocably intertwined, both in the eyes of the world and through the embodied traffic that has shaped each of them since Little Dog was in the womb.

Ma and Little Dog are both of "hybrid origins" and "hybrid signals." Their monstrosity's liminal place in the world evokes Muñoz's understanding of queerness as something "that allows us to see and feel beyond the quagmire of the present" and as "that thing that lets us feel that this world is not enough, that indeed something is missing" (Muñoz 2019: 1). Such affective resonances ask for recognition throughout the novel despite Little Dog's and Ma's lack of place in the world, and indeed, they point to "something [that] is missing": a world in which they might live and thrive despite their otherness. The novel also imagines a way toward this world. As Muñoz argues, queerness is an embodied and performative act that "is not simply a being but a doing for and toward the future. Queerness is essentially about the rejection of a here and now and an insistence on potentiality or concrete possibility for another world" (Muñoz 2019: 1). Little Dog explicitly articulates this embodiment toward a different world; later, as a college student, he imagines, "[s]taring into the mirror, I replicate myself into a future where I might not exist" (Vuong 2019: 139).

In the novel, the monstrous possibilities of queerness cannot be disentangled from Ma's monstrosity, which has fundamentally shaped Little Dog. As Little Dog writes, "[y]ou're a mother, Ma. You're also a monster.

But so am I—which is why I can't turn away from you" (Vuong 2019: 14). And their bond is reciprocated by Ma, albeit nonverbally and with unclear motivations. When as a teenager he finally tells his mother that he is queer, she laments, "when did this all start? I gave birth to a healthy, normal boy" (Vuong 2019: 131). But after their conversation, they also go home together, a gesture that Little Dog interprets with greater significance as a form of unsaid acceptance. Telescoping forward in time from Ma's disbelief during their conversation, Little Dog imagines the scene that will take place later at home, when seeing a blade of grass caught in Little Dog's hair, Ma will "reach over, brush it off, and shake your head as you take in the son you decided to keep" (Vuong 2019: 140). They thus extend recognition to and make a place for one another, laying the foundations for their monstrous persistence in a wider world that does not welcome them.

Indeed, Ma's embodiment and orientation to the world shape even Little Dog's foundational exploration of his sexuality. As a teenager, he meets a boy, Trevor, who becomes his friend and lover. For Little Dog, Trevor presents another visceral way of pursuing a place in the world. His desire for Trevor reflects Muñoz's articulation of queerness as actively remaking the world, "not simply a being but a doing for and toward the future" (2019: 1). He describes Trevor as "a boy breaking out and into himself at once" and reflects that "[t]hat's what I wanted—not merely the body, desirable as it was, but its will to grow into the very world that rejects its hunger" (Vuong 2019: 110). In fact, Trevor and Ma share the same defiance, which emerges from experiences of violence. Upon meeting Little Dog, Trevor, whose father is physically abusive, declares that "I fucking hate my dad" (Vuong 2019: 97). This moment sparks Little Dog's fascination:

> Up until then I didn't think a white boy could hate anything about his life. I wanted to know him through and through, by that very hate. Because that's what you give anyone who sees you, I thought. You can take their hatred head-on, and you cross it, like a bridge, to face them, to enter them. (Vuong 2019: 97)

The beginning of Little Dog's sexual exploration is therefore not rooted in tenderness but in his impulse toward a shared negativity—hatred—that he immediately recognizes from Ma. Indeed, Little Dog also learns from Ma that this negativity contains, illogically, a generative possibility that can lead to different futures than what seems possible at this moment. This moment illustrates Ma and Little Dog's shared transformation of conditions not conducive to their survival or thriving into something that contains possibilities for exploration, growth, and defiant futurity, a kind of transformative alchemy that Little Dog has learned first and foremost from Ma. Rather than pass judgment on these modes of living, which we may not ourselves experience or comprehend, the novel asks us to move beyond empathy predicated on sameness and to feel, attend to, and be moved by affective resonances and the pictures of different kinds of life that emerge from them. Indeed, Little Dog's and Ma's monstrosity is something we all share, as children who are similarly conceived and born through sharing another's body. While this shared condition does not posit sameness between these bodies, the generative potential of monstrosity to recognize hybrid, perhaps threatening origins and to reach for a different world is a project in which we can all participate.

Throughout the moments it illuminates, the novel thus issues a broader request for recognition that is not predicated on full cognitive understanding of another and imagines how this request, answered, might begin to build a different world. The novel itself, ostensibly written by Little Dog, is a piece of writing that emerges from the traumatic disruption that has fundamentally shaped Ma's life. While it recognizes the generative possibilities that emerge from the language, expansively imagined, that Ma possesses, it also explicitly asserts that "destruction is not necessary for art" (Vuong 2019: 179). Instead, it asks, explicitly and in the affective complexities it allows to radiate forth between words and embodied moments, "why can't the language for creativity be the language of regeneration" (Vuong 2019: 179)? In its totality, the novel asserts the belief that regeneration can, against all logic, emerge from trauma and violence. It reaches for a different language that is not only a reflection of violence but one that "bod[ies] forth" to create a more expansive world.

References

Berlant, L. (2011), *Cruel Optimism*, Durham: Duke University Press.

Boler, M. (1997), "The Risks of Empathy: Interrogating Multiculturalism's Gaze," *Cultural Studies*, 11 (2): 253–73.

Das, V. (1996), "Language and Body: Transactions in the Construction of Pain," *Daedalus*, 125 (1): 67–91.

Garden, R. (2007), "The Problem of Empathy: Medicine and the Humanities," *New Literary History*, 38 (3): 551–67.

Hollan, D. and C. J. Throop. (2008), "Whatever Happened to Empathy?" *Ethos: Journal for the Society of Psychological Anthropology*, 36 (4): 385–401.

Lee, Yoon Sun. (2013), *Modern Minority: Asian American Literature and Everyday Life*, New York: Oxford University Press.

Metzl, J. and H. Hansen. (2014), "Structural Competency: Theorizing a New Medical Engagement with Stigma and Inequality," *Social Science and Medicine*, 103: 103–26.

Muñoz, J. E. (2019), *Cruising Utopia, 10th Anniversary Edition: The Then and There of Queer Futurity*, New York: New York University Press.

Ninh, e. K. (2014), "Affect/Family/Filiality," in R. C. Lee (ed), *The Routledge Companion to Asian American and Pacific Islander Literature*, 46–55, New York: Routledge.

Reddy, V. and A. Sudhakar. (2018), "Introduction: Feminist and Queer Afro-Asian Formations," in V. Reddy and A. Sudhakar (eds), *The Scholar and Feminist Online*, 14 (3).

Shuman, A. (2005), *Other People's Stories: Entitlement Claims and the Critique of Empathy*, Urbana and Chicago: University of Illinois Press.

Stewart, K. (2007), *Ordinary Affects*, Durham: Duke University Press.

Vuong, O. (2019), *On Earth We're Briefly Gorgeous*, New York: Penguin Press.

8

Affective Misplacement and the Image City

Tate Shaw

In a letter to Rochester, New York Police Department Chief La'Ron Singletary, in reference to the body worn camera videos documenting the March 23, 2020, "mental hygiene arrest" of Daniel Prude, Rochester Mayor Lovely Warren says she is "concerned that these body worn camera videos are not just viewed through the lens of the badge, but through the eyes of the people we serve" (Smith 2020: 2). Prude, a Black man, died of complications from asphyxia resulting from the arresting officers' use of a "spit sock" hood and the forceful application of a knee to his back, pressing his naked torso into the snow-flurried pavement. In a memo to Warren, Rochester Deputy Mayor James Smith quotes the mayor's letter back to her using The Lens of the Badge as a section heading. Smith expands the metaphor to address how the arresting officers saw Prude, the view of the medical response technicians who were uncaring toward him, the municipal attorneys' myopia when processing information requests "in terms of data to be redacted or included rather than as a human life lost" (2020: 2) and the optics of a Rochester Police Department (RPD) lieutenant calling the county medical examiner prior to Prude's autopsy to prime them with the narrative that his death was the result of a drug overdose and resisting arrest, as opposed to the official homicide ruling eventually established.

But citizens' eyes are subject to lenses, too. I live in Rochester. Technically, I have a Rochester address, but my home is in a neighboring suburb. Rochester demographics are about fifty-fifty Black and other people of color to white people like me. A small city of about 200,000, it seems smaller due to racial and economic segregation. People whose vocation is to work with images make up a fraction of the community. For instance, I am part of the image-making community as the director of a nonprofit photographic, book, and media artist space and I personally know one of those whose job it is to process body worn camera videos for the RPD, including that of Prude's arrest. I tried watching the entire video, which was publicly released by a lawyer representing Prude's family, but only made it through about a minute before my central nervous system alarmed me to x-out the screen. It was Prude's nakedness in the cold night, his quick, alert compliance to get face down on the ground, that had me quit. It seemed inhumane enough that those charged with serving and protecting had not offered Prude, naked and unstable, a blanket or coat. Smith observed that "the simple concepts of human decency and dignity appeared to be woefully lacking or non-existent" (2020: 3).

Daniel Prude's treatment by RPD and the subsequent uprising that followed in Rochester—also known as The Image City for its corporate ties to Kodak, Xerox, and Bausch and Lomb—have formed a culmination that follows nearly two decades of my work in the image-making community in Rochester. In the past several of those years, I have been reconsidering empathy in relation to photographic images and the affective accountability of photographers and photobook producers to their subjects.[1] This entails how empathy is created by photographic images and photo-bookworks of art interdependent with the social and cultural systems in which they are made and operate, how empathetic narrative is reified as capitalistic objects like images and books, how reifying empathy as photographic production misplaces the resulting affect, as well as the prospect of empathetically responsible photographic production. Forming key and distinctive examples are two archive photobook projects made as documents of or in connection to The Image City. Both are projects I have been involved with and supported through the institution I direct in Rochester, Visual Studies Workshop (VSW). One is a photo archive project and book by historically significant photographers from the Magnum Photos agency that attempted to artfully document Rochester in 2012 when Kodak announced bankruptcy. More recently in 2020–1, VSW supported the exhibition and newspaper publication of a photo archive project by a native son, Joshua Rashaad McFadden. These bipolar projects show on the one end the capitalist reification of abstract affective response of empathy as definite, concrete form, that images conditioned by capitalistic values and imperial histories protect empathy as a subject through the objects of its production, and that photo empaths attuned to produce *the best* or *most* empathy are privileged over the subjected humans who created the sharing of affect in the first place. On the other end, there is the potential for more long-term caregiving between photo empaths and their subjects through an empathetic documentation and archiving practice.

Empathy Creation in Images and Systemic Interdependence

To consider how empathy is created from photographic images and yet systemically interdependent, let us return to the Prude arrest video. There is an argument for viewing it in its entirety which claims that doing so has the potential to increase my compassion if I train myself to feel with the person suffering. Increasing my compassion is prosocial, meaning I would be more likely to help or intervene in a situation when witnessing another's suffering (Singer and Klimecki 2014: 875). The affective influence of emotion released by the imagery may help me better understand the suffering through my own spontaneous, vicarious sharing in the affect; in other words, it may help me to empathize. But because Prude is Black and I am white, I might be more likely to view him as part of an outgroup and less likely to help because empathetic response is more frequently disrupted with outgroup members (Cikara, Bruneau, and Saxe 2017: 150).

When I'm present to other people, or what I'm reading, or watching, my empathy levels are high to very high. Yet I would not remain present to the Prude arrest video. I fall more on the empathetic distress side of the spectrum so am more likely to freeze in the face of suffering (Singer and Klemecki 2020: 876). Furthermore, I don't believe that my personal viewing of the images could ever bear out enough empathy in me to challenge the systemic or individual racism involved. One recent study I read "clearly demonstrate[s] that anti-Black stereotypes and/or White racial identity may also 'suppress' the impact of empathetic feelings of those who observe or become aware of instances when White police officers use excessive force against Black Americans" (Johnson, Lecci, and Antonia 2020: 64). Through media integration my affective response has long been primed to see the stereotypical view of Black people in terms of criminality, justifiably harmed, or reasonably reacted against in supposed self-defense. I am unwilling to voluntarily view more such images from the thick distance of a laptop or a phone, with my personal socio-cultural identity characteristics. I have, for my forty-five years, been primed enough in these directions such that internally contesting my own reactive, individually racist thoughts and actions toward Black people will be a lifelong process as it is.

Pictures are fictions and interrogating whether we believe what we see or see what we believe is central to their interpretation. Empathy in the beginning formed out of aesthetics, in translation from *Einfühlung*, feeling into things—like art objects or books of images. Now many cognitive psychological and neurological studies of empathy use still and time-based images as part of their evidence-gathering methods. If the spontaneous, vicarious sharing of affect is activated by witnessing the emotional state of another, and if we can study these turns through the use of photographic images, then an implied framework hinges on recognizing what is outside ourselves and mirroring the recognition inside us, or upon the understanding of what is inside us that primes our interpretation of an external image. It is this inside-outside pivot that is perhaps essential to understanding both empathy and, in more metaphorical terms, photo-bookworks of art.

When images circulate of systemically racist actions like that of Prude's treatment, they are necessarily confrontational but we must allow them entry to our psyche in order for them to have us feel with others. In January 2021 another body-worn camera video was under public scrutiny in Rochester and beyond. RPD officers handcuffed and pepper-sprayed a nine-year-old Black girl in order to command control over her arrest. As usual, there was a public call by the mayor and other officials for more empathy and compassion including from the RPD chief. And as expected the president of the union representing the RPD stated "Those officers and those scenes, they broke no policy[.] There's nothing that anyone can say they did that's inappropriate" (Hong 2021). On the one hand, the images may be viewed with and create empathy, independent of their system of creation, and the suffering seen as unjustifiable, even by the chief of the RPD. The generative empathetic response to the video and subsequent call to more empathy may indeed help more people to feel with others. Yet on the other hand, no matter the level of affective and cognitive confidence we have in our feelings of what we believe to be another's emotions, there is the hegemonic potential to see in the documents what its agents define as acceptable. This incident reveals, then, the interdependence of empathetic documents and their systemic frameworks, but also the problem of failing to acknowledge that interdependence. By calling for more empathy are we only attempting to cultivate more individual *growth*? And if so are we then oblivious to the capitalist function of that cultivation and its systemic domination of even feelings themselves?

Empathetic Narrative as Capitalistic Object

A personal-systemic example will perhaps make both the interdependence and capitalist reification process clear. An artist who had previously been in residence at VSW lives on Pennsylvania Avenue near the Rochester Public Market. On a Saturday night in September 2020, at the height of public protests in response to the video of Prude's arrest, an invite-only party took place at a neighboring house on Pennsylvania Ave. It mixed with another party, an altercation turned violent, and sixteen people were shot, two fatally: Jaquayla Young and Jarvis Alexander, both of whom are Black. The artist connected me with Alexander's family so that VSW's production space might donate prints of pictures of the young man for memorial services. When I spoke on the phone with Alexander's aunt, I felt genuine sadness and compassion for the family and their sudden, inconceivable loss. She texted me several images. Staff and assistants made 200 hand-size prints and two dozen mounted posters of young Jarvis flexing in his high school football uniform, wearing a green headband that framed his smooth, attractive face in a ring of black curls, as a child in a Superman muscle-costume posturing for the photographer, grinning wryly in the foreground of a selfie, his younger cousin behind him flashing a broader smile. I met the cousin when delivering the prints. As I handed them over to this skinny boy of about sixteen, we briefly locked eyes then simultaneously looked down at the pile of images. A wave of emotion reached me, channeled through the conduit of prints. It transformed the entire hallway corridor, and quickly propelled him back to his apartment, and me to my car. Up to that point, what I had felt for Alexander's family had been sympathy. My feelings turned into empathy when I vicariously shared in the boy's affective reaction to his cousin's image. Despite our transformative interchange and the sharing of affect, we do not have equal share in our community. If I ever encounter him again, we will most likely not recognize one another. But I have the register of sensation and connection to think and write about him now. Whether I participated in doing some good for the family or not, it is the case that the capitalist reification process transforms Alexander's demise and his family's pain in ways that are beneficial to me as a critic and academic and yet are incompatible, incomparable, and virtually impossible to advantage by families of dead, young Black men like Alexander, as if they would care to exploit his death.

The ethics of my anecdotal inclusion of Alexander's memorial images are absolutely questionable but I do so to involve your criticality of the potential for affective misplacement, the reification process (Lukacs 1967), and of me as a more privileged writer. I can use the complexity and empathy imparted by images of a young Black man who was shot and killed as my own creative and intellectual product. What mystifies is the ease with which this reification occurs and yet the systemic complicity of its function is profound and has been part of photography and its larger industry, including its critics, from the beginning. Ariella Aïsha Azoulay describes this in *Potential History: Unlearning Imperialism*:

> Let's recall. From the inception of photography, it was assumed—and violently obtained—that the people photographed were to provide the resources and the free (or cheap) labor for the large-scale photographic enterprise that from the very beginning was based on capitalistic logic. While it is obvious that there is no photograph without photographed persons, the structure of primitive accumulation was already naturalized in the beginning of the nineteenth century, when photography took shape, that the expropriation of the photographed persons from rights in the photos could be institutionalized as the order of things. Through imperial enterprises of visual surveys of all sorts in invaded and colonized

places, of profiling and surveillance, and of the ideology and practices of documentary and news, primitive accumulation imposed structures of capital on the photographic commons. This was rarely discussed, as if not to taint the artistic, educational, and informational ethos and values. Photographers, who were also charged with alleviating the violence of extraction, were offered some benefit from the imperial domination of photographic markets, single authorship of their photographs, that is, some privileges and symbolic capital in exchange for which they were expected to act as middle-persons extracting the object of their craft from others. Accorded the right to deprive other participants of their share in the photographs and in the world that they shared and to conceal the exploitative meaning of the photographic encounter, photographers mostly did not enrich themselves; this was reserved for bigger imperial sharks such as collectors, corporations, industrialists, archives, or museums.

(2019: 282)

Photo-bookworks, particularly those with the express desire to document people, their cares, and suffering, are part of this systemic imperial structure. These empathetic narrative works perhaps intended to do some good in terms of making the lives of less-seen people visible. Several 1930s and 1940s post-Depression books coming directly out of the New Deal Farm Security Administration (FSA) were pure empathy drivers. *You Have Seen Their Faces* by photographer Margaret Bourke-White and popular novelist Erskine Caldwell is a deeply sentimental portrayal of people in the rural South criticized for Caldwell's stereotypical, eugenicist statements made to appear as first-person accounts alongside Bourke-White's propagandistic photography (Holdman 2014: 41). Much more factually conscientious is *An American Exodus: A Record of Human Erosion* by Dorothea Lange and her sociologist husband Paul Schuster Taylor, which puts the reader inside the western migration from the Oklahoma Dust Bowl. *Let Us Now Praise Famous Men* by writer James Agee and photographer Walker Evans followed earlier FSA work and was contemptuously inspired by *You Have Seen Their Faces* (Holdman 2014: 42). In her history of empathy, Suzanne Lanzoni recognizes *The Family of Man*, curator Edward Steichen's sentimental effort to universalize humanity after decades of world war through an exhibition and book with the Museum of Modern Art in 1955. That same year *The Sweet Flypaper of Life* by Roy DeCarava brought us inside 134th Street in Harlem and included Langston Hughes's sentimental narrative of day-to-day life there as delivered by his character Sister Mary Bradley.

This empathetic, art-meets-documentary strategy was foundational for photo-bookworks. The internationally renowned documentary photography cooperative Magnum Photos formed in 1947 around the time much of the above came into print. Magnum continues today and is famed for an approach that is part aesthetics, part journalistic reportage. Though the photographers have their own autonomous projects and practices, they are often editorially commissioned for stories. In the early 2010s, a group within Magnum undertook a series of road trip documentary pieces called Postcards from America. Fashioned after the aforementioned FSA projects, the Magnum photographers traveled with writers, producers, and videographers in an RV, seeking to document stories without the usual editorial constraints (Schmeltzer 2012).

From the outside, Postcards from America appeared as Magnum photographers *feeling* their way to focal points of American conflict, like the US/Mexico border and Florida at the time of a presidential election. When any world event occurs these days we tend to feel it, bodily. In a conversation with Erin Manning titled "Affective Attunement in the Field of Catastrophe," philosopher Brian Massumi notes:

> The complexity of the interlocking systems we live in, on the social, cultural, economic and natural levels, is now felt in all its complexity, because we're reaching certain tipping points, for example in relation to climate change and refugee flows. There is a sense that we're in a far-from-equilibrium situation where each of the systems we have depended upon for stability is perpetually on the verge of tipping over into crisis, with the danger that there will be a sort of cascade of effects through adjoining systems, like a domino effect. It's a very unstable, quasi-chaotic situation. And there's no vantage point from which to understand it from the outside. We're immersed in it. We're absorbed in the imminence of catastrophe, always braced for it—which means it has become immanent to our field of life. That imminence-immanence is a mode of contact, of direct affective proximity, even if it occurs 'at a distance' through the action of the media or, more to the point, within an increasingly integrated media ecology.
>
> (2015: 113–14)

Magnum's Postcards from America seemed created to express such *imminence-immanence* and for bearing witnesses to an impending pandemonium. Our affective contact with these situations is through the types of images such an autonomous yet highly effective group of image-makers as Magnum can create, as well as where they create them.

Reifying Empathy as Photographs and Their Production

If documenting places and people in off-kilter societal, cultural, and economic conditions comes out of a tradition of imperialist visual surveys, and if Magnum's Postcards from America was attuned to delivering artful reports from states of instability, then with hindsight we in Rochester should have seen the tragedy in Magnum contacting us in early 2012 about a project in the making called House of Pictures—to be housed, as it were, at VSW and by the other photography institutions of the city.

> Rochester, that ultimate company town, struck us as itself a house of pictures. The place that housed Kodak, the place where photography grew up, ate breakfast, slept at night … And when Kodak declared bankruptcy a few weeks before our arrival, we wondered about the differences between a house of pictures and a house of cards.
> … How different, we asked on the road to Rochester, is the photographer's labor from the engineer's, from the stirrer's, from the weaver's?
> How, we mused, do we remember the place that manufactured our own memories?
>
> (Goldberg et al., 2013: 426)

At a closing event for House of Pictures, in a half-darkened theater a projected diptych paired two images: one of a mansion behind a hedgerow and beside it at equal scale, a dilapidated, two-family home with cracked fiber asbestos siding, a scarred roof, and plywood in place of windows. The mansion, connected by corridors to where we sat, is George Eastman House, symbol of status, culture, and altruism in Rochester. The rundown house is familiar to anyone who has driven around this town. It was one of thousands of foreclosures in the city that year with a median home value of about $35,000; around 75 percent of the foreclosures were located in majority Black and brown neighborhoods with an average family income of $25,000 (Center for Community Progress 2013). Nightly in this very theater, films from one of the world's most prominent film collections are screened as part of the moving image exhibition and lecture programs of the museum. The museum, connected to the house, is named for and formerly the dwelling of George Eastman, founder of Eastman Kodak Company.

A few hundred of us from the Rochester area were in the theater to see what the ten members of Magnum had made to artfully document our town. They had only been in Rochester for two weeks but months before arriving they delivered lists of what they wished to photograph in order for producers to start compiling locations and gaining access to architecture, factories, eateries, high schools, city government offices, funerals, strip clubs, places to wander the streets, various community and club events, and ride-alongs with police. They set up situations to photograph and asked people to unclothe themselves, hold up guns, signs, and plates of food. They convened in a mansion across East Avenue from the Eastman House, where their egos locked horns over locations, styles of picture making, and manners of working. They were hoisted several stories to photograph from bucket trucks and went underground in Rochester's now-abandoned subway tunnels. They set up a photo booth to make free portraits at the Rochester Public Market on a Saturday morning in late April where crowds of over 20,000 from seemingly all-possible backgrounds mix and buy produce, breakfast sandwiches, fresh roasted coffee, flowers, and whole fishes.

Along the back of the Public Market on Pennsylvania Avenue, the street where Jarvis Alexander was fatally shot, the photographers had coveted "a blue house, peaked roof, crammed up against the fence" (Goldberg et al., 2013: 426). Months before arriving, a Magnum representative had directed the local producer to get them a house in which they would create an installation of their pictures to be viewed at the end of the project.

> We wanted to create an experience that existed outside of formalized institutions and that engaged with a resident community. The country was still in the aftermath of the housing crisis, and the concept of a house, of ownership and residency and identity, was at the forefront of everyone's minds. We figured it would be relatively easy to buy a house in Rochester, maybe a foreclosed one, to bring up some of the printers, and to spend two weeks filling the house with pictures. Maybe we would sell the house at the end. Maybe we would give it to a community group. Maybe we would abandon it and leave the pictures to fend for themselves.
>
> (Goldberg et al., 2013: 427)

When you internet search "empathy and photography" a Magnum Photos site documenting a conference and part of their Theory & Practice archives is first in line. It describes empathy as "both an objective and a tool in documentary photography" (Magnum Photos 2020). Which is why obtaining a possibly foreclosed house in which to work and present your local engagement makes sense. Being situated within the house's walls, within a *real* neighborhood, engaging with the neighbors and the street, could provoke the spontaneous sharing of affect, vicariously, in a part-evidentiary, part-phenomenological exercise. It could obtain the objective and be the vehicle of emotional connection for both the photographer and photography viewer. Hence when the local producer, a colleague of mine at VSW, couldn't get a house, some of the photographers drove around town to look for one, and found the Blue House. They approached those dwelling in it but the tenants had concerns about their landlord and the installation. Though it fell through, the Blue House was to be one of the project's symbolic houses of pictures. The others were the eleven-bedroom mansion where the photographers communed together, shuffling and discussing their daily proof prints on an editing table, a well-documented overnight homeless shelter and food pantry caring for thousands of Rochester citizens each month called House of Mercy, the large room of photo prints they presented at VSW at the end of the event, and of course, George Eastman House International Museum of Photography and Film (Goldberg et al., 2013: 426).

Each of the ten photographers had the lofty, preconceived task of making 100 good pictures to contribute to an archive box of 1000 prints. It was made in a limited edition of five copies, one of which was presold, sight unseen, for $20,000 to George Eastman House.[2] In part the archive boxes would fund the entire enterprise of producing, traveling, housing, feeding, and printing pictures for these ten photographers working at this level of integrity in the photographic field. Other local institutions, including VSW, contributed perhaps another $150,000 worth of in-kind assistance and support for the venture. The irony that the price tag of a prepurchased box of a thousand images digitally printed on paper was just under the median annual income of a family living in a neighborhood where they wished to paste-up the pictures in a possibly foreclosed house was lost on no one. Not least of all the photographers, who made it so flatly obvious with the pairing of houses there on the museum screen at the closing event. Or perhaps it *was* lost on everyone involved, certainly myself included.

Those producing, displaying, and publishing works of art have generally understood for a generation what those who are empirically studying empathetic response to figurative art have begun to document as distinguishable contextual frames that prime that empathetic response:

> first, the *pictorial context* of the image, i.e., the relationship of the emotionally salient aspects (affective affordances) to the pictorial field or structure as a whole, second, the *spatial and experiential context* of the presentation of the image, and third, the *cultural-social context* of the actual experiential situation, in which the viewer's personal dispositions interact with cultural factors and form expectations.
>
> (Kesner and Horáček 2017: 4)

Regardless of the pictorial context of the House of Pictures images, the idea that the spatial and experiential context was for Magnum to wallpaper one of the city's thousands of foreclosed or low-income rental homes seems utterly careless to me now, especially since the cultural-social context of the project sets a majority white audience upon a majority Black neighborhood in order to see the photos. To repeat the aforementioned Deputy Mayor Smith, "the simple concepts of human decency and dignity appeared to be woefully lacking or non-existent" (2020: 3). We as (white) producers and audience were so concerned with the potential for empathetic transference that we sought to exploit a Black neighborhood in a city that is one of the five worst places to live when African American.

There is an early twentieth-century advertisement for camera flash sheets that stated: "Kodak knows no dark days."[3] But the photographers with Magnum were only in Rochester because the formerly blue chip Eastman

Kodak Company had faced gloom on the horizon for a decade. In the previous nine years, Kodak had closed thirteen manufacturing plants and shed 47,000 jobs, many from the Rochester suburbs. The month I moved to the city in 2003, 3,000 people were laid off and Kodak's dividend was slashed by 70 percent. The Postcards from America book that came from the House of Pictures project is called *Rochester 585 716*, the phone area codes of the region. A thick archive of a thousand images was designed in the fashion of a phone book. It is the people's version of the photographers' archive box and the message was clear: Rochester had gone the way of the telephone book. The photography industry that once held epic potential for shared connection and was a wayfinder to myriad service economies was outmoded. As a container metaphor it clearly spoke to the analog era, the time when Kodak was relevant and their market share dominant. Kodak gets grief for sitting on its 1975 invention of the digital camera for decades, and for foregoing what would have been at least a half-century of revolutionary digital image product development. But the picture is both more complicated and simple than that (Shih 2016). The lifespan of the film industry's corporate patriarch had peaked, grown gray, and was dying and this had a lot of its photographer progeny reflecting on the death of the Great Yellow Father.[4]

At the time of Magnum's Rochester visit in 2012, seemingly everyone working in photography had for the past few years been making sad-beautiful pictures of decay and decline. Sites of tragedy beckoned. Photographers descended on postindustrial cities to make what has since been termed Ruins Photography or, more critically, Ruin Porn (Woodward 2013). Detroit, the largest US city to file for Chapter 9 bankruptcy protection, was a favored destination for this type of work. In February of 2012, a large but slim photo-bookwork was published out of Italy, bound in brown paper with a plain sticker affixed to its hardcover, labeling it *Found Photos in Detroit*. It is a massive coffee table book metaphorically meant to be read as a banal archive folder. In its introduction the Italian photographers, Arianna Arcara and Luca Santese, note, "[W]e found these photos on the streets of Detroit. We took them and started to sift between the thousands of Polaroids, letters, prints of photographic evidence, police documents, mugshots and family albums" (2012: preface). Of its eighty pages and 167 photographs, roughly half are images of people, all but one of them of only Black people. The other half of the images are virtually all of homes, some in states of wreckage, or domestic interiors including several documents of bloody violence. Because the photos were literally taken from the streets and therefore subject to the environment, the emulsions are cracked, wavy, aged, and discolored from weathered moldering that brought unexpected patinas of sometimes bright color and abstract forms to bear on the picture planes. These surfaces are highly exploited in the last fifth of the book, where, as its end draws near, the bright hues and water damaged inflections overtake the entire double-page openings in ecstatic bleeds to the edges. On the publishing blog of Alec Soth, the Magnum photographer who first spotted the Blue House in Rochester, writer Vince Leo reviews *Found Photos in Detroit*, and ruminates on the theme of abandonment. "The only thing we know for sure about these photographs," he states, "is the most important thing to know: they have all been abandoned" (2012). The photographers also note in the publishing credits at the end that they found the photos "abandoned in the streets of Detroit" (2012: postscript). To Leo, "the message is clear: It is Black culture, their houses, their rule of law, their very selves that have been abandoned. Like homeless ghosts, the social reality of these photographs haunts Detroit and America, signifying a despair so deep that abandonment is the only method left to represent their loss" (2012).

What Leo identifies as a system that has abandoned Black people with the ruin and abandonment of photographs themselves is how the photographers, photobook publisher, and the photobook critic transfer their own understanding of the difficulties that they imagine those "unmoored from the ties" of these photographs face. In other words, it's how the photographers empathize: damaged and discarded photos of people equal the psychic and physical pain of the damaged, discarded souls figured therein. The comments on Leo's review reveal how deeply the photographers are convinced that photographs as a medium connect viewers to the photograph's subjects. Soth acknowledges that "photographs of people use people. It makes us uncomfortable. But it is also what makes the medium so potent"; Soth continues: "this friction between aesthetics and real life/lives gives the book a disquieting energy that makes it come alive" (Leo 2012). Another commentator imagined a narrative wherein the people depicted or their amateur photographers were either foreclosed upon or evicted and had to unexpectedly move and leave their cherished possessions. Arcara and Santese commented themselves, describing how, when they stumbled upon their first Polaroid for the archive lying in the street, "as photographers, we felt powerless in front of this material by far stronger than any image we could shoot" (Leo 2012).

Deeming these pictures abandoned may be a generous view of their ontology and perhaps a cautious word choice to evade questions of authorship. Because as paradoxical as it seems, documentary photography requires authorship as much as art through the embeddedness, the access, the intimate disclosures revealed by its authors. A different view of the found objects is fully acknowledged in scare quotes by the photographers describing the pictures in relation to the economic and housing crisis symbolized by Detroit echoing the juncture Magnum found itself in for House of Pictures: they are the "aftermath" (Leo 2012). It is a perhaps more apt descriptor of the photos and the people and homes forming their subject. Just like the foreclosed Rochester house desired by the Magnum photographers, these leavings were the remnants of a slow, systematic destructive event taking place in postindustrial US cities. Aftermath is a record of the period of time following a disaster. Calling the found photos abandoned assets, they were left alone and uncared for. Abandonment hints at blame for those who left their belongings for someone else to come along and look after them. As noted above, the Magnum group was all too comfortable abandoning their proposed creation for the pictures to "fend for themselves." The Detroit found pictures' literally damaged surfaces had a romantic patina (what one photo friend calls "the art sauce"[5]) that aestheticizes and strangely justifies, perhaps inadvertently, the psychic and physical harm of those treated worst within the American regime. But Arcara and Santese and the Magnum photographers did what many people would justify doing. They documented destroyed worlds in order to caretake the aftermath's continued existence through the formation of an archive. Azoulay recognizes this as a longstanding move:

> The role of institutions such as archives and museums in the 'preservation' of the past is the effect of a vast enterprise of destruction conducted at the expense of and as a substitute for destroyed worlds. Fueled and justified by the pursuit of the new, what is destroyed is produced as past and elaborate procedures of salvage and preservation are devoted to extract and study cherished samples of proof of bygone times and their own progress. The "past" consists of discrete objects, documents, and relics detached from what were or could have been the sustainable worlds of which they were part, and whose destruction is often justified for the sake of their rescue. If what they preserve is extracted from living worlds, and if living worlds are producing objects whose destination is the museum and archive, their study cannot be confined to what is in them but should include what role they play in this enterprise of world destruction ...
> (Azoulay 2019: 19–20)

Assembling documents of these individual lives and objects in the flat, seemingly nonhierarchical space of the archive book or box turns any opportunity for the private sharing of affect into the constantly surveilled and usable registers of the public and the state, as if it were possible to separate them out in the first place. Allan Sekula writes that "Every portrait implicitly [takes] its place within a social and moral hierarchy. The private moment of sentimental individuation, the look at the frozen gaze-of-the-loved-one, are shadowed by two other more public looks: a look up, at one's 'betters,' and a look down, at one's 'inferiors'" (Sekula 1986, 10). Arcara and Santese's methodology enacts this public vertical scale by literally *looking down* at the ground of the public domain for images "abandoned," presumably by and of Black people.

Similarly, Azoulay's notion of "regime-made disasters" asks us to be attentive to a differential body politic, under which the "forms of being governed by that regime—as citizens, as noncitizens, or as flawed citizens—are different" (Azoulay 2012: 30). A regime-made disaster, according to Azoulay, is one that is "generated and reproduced" by regimes founded in such differential rule (Azoulay 2012: 32). Such regime-based disasters don't happen all at once and may not be recognized as such by citizens other than their victims, or they may be viewed as a necessary or uncontrollable circumstances. Over-policing, redlining, subprime mortgages all fit the bill of regime-made disasters in a capitalist system. In these disasters, though, Azoulay points out that not only are some groups protected by their privileges, but those who are "deprived of [such] protective fabrics" have their "victimhood ... preserved through visualizations that associate them with the position and figure of the victim in the long term in what I call 'archival acceptability'" (2012: 32).

> Archival acceptability is the form violence takes as it is generated through imperial shutters. It entices people to act differently than they would have acted if the crimes did not benefit from a plausible acceptability. The violence of the archival acceptability is powerful because it lures people to commit acts that in other circumstances would appear lucidly as the crimes of appropriation, looting, dispossession, deportation, and ethnic cleansing.
>
> (2019: 204)

Azoulay affirms that photographers and photography viewers, with our integrated media viewing from a distance, are, however virtually, among the protected and privileged, still set apart from those experiencing the disaster. No matter how deeply felt our *affective proximity*, it remains contiguous as opposed to interior. Though we may be governed by the same democratic regime, our gaze is shaped by a differentiation that is structurally imposed. Images documenting the aftermath of regime-made disasters can be seen as another objective and tool of the regime effectively perpetuating the differential treatment of those involved.

If we understand a photograph or photo-bookwork to be more than its intention or the viewer who identifies with it, if we understand that an image is part of a regime, however democratic, then no matter the level of empathy imparted, the images remain subject to that regime's hegemonic interpretation. At the end of Sekula's above-referenced essay, which contributed a social history of police images to documentary photography, he suggests Walker Evans's "1938 *American Photographs* can be read as attempts to counterpose the 'poetic' structure of the sequence to the archive" (1986: 58). Evans became a new kind of photographic empath, one who induced the sharing of affect between images in their order and disjuncture from one another in sequence. Individual images, more prized by collectors, museums, and archives can't singly gloss the sweeping work. By structuring the work as a book-length photographic sequence, its ontology leans literary. Yet making the work more individually authored does not make it any more independent from the American regime. Or for a more recent example consider the highly authored work of Gregory Halpern, a Magnum photographer based in Rochester, who has been widely recognized for his darkly romantic photo-poetic bookworks, including his 2016 award-winning title on California, *Zzyzx*. Halpern's work descends from Evans and often includes empathetic portraits of people he encounters in public, a good portion of whom are people of color whom we understand, from the beautiful-suffering of their weathered and affective appearance, to be socially marginalized in some way. When I asked him publicly about the power of such portraits to *other* those recorded, he stated plainly that he viewed the portraits he made as representative of himself, more metaphor for his thoughts and feelings, than a sign of another or a group.[6] Yet if we view the work as more than its authorship, one can imagine the dominant US political regime of late 2016 interpreting the empathy imparted in *Zzyzx* pages differently than how Halpern accounts for it. Perhaps they could be used as touchstones reflexive of fear and anxiety over addicts in California's border-crossing streets and sanctuary cities, living out in the crumbling public infrastructure, never mind that the regime's differential treatment by way of longstanding structural policy had denied public services or destabilized the systems that exiled the people there in the first place.

When assuming Azoulay's position that a photograph is part of a regime, "one comprehends the limited nature of common categories such as 'compassion', 'pity', 'empathy', 'rage', 'concern', 'empowerment', and 'victimization', which in fact describe only a single axis of relations between the photographer and the photographed while erasing all other relationships that were inscribed in the photograph" (2012: 39). And as Sekula points out, perhaps those following the course set by Evans may "fail to recognize the degree to which they share Evans' social fatalism, his sense of the immutability of the existing social order" (1986: 58). Such *immutability* to me is most prevalent in the prominent photo-bookworks, rewarded for their single authorship, that frequently assume an intimacy with and access to a *place* as the framework of their design. Despite the sensitivity of their image-making approach, it is far less empathetic to categorize anonymous citizens under place names, which is what happens with these bookworks. We can file Halpern's *Zzyzx* under "California," his *Omaha Sketchbook* under "Nebraska"; Soth's *Sleeping by the Mississippi* or *Niagara* under "Mississippi River" and "Niagara Falls"; *Found Photos in Detroit* under "Detroit"; Evans' *American Photographs*, Robert Frank's *The Americans*, Stephen Shore's *American Surfaces*, Zoe Strauss's *America*, Halpern's book *A*, and so many others under "America"; and of course *Rochester 585 716* under "Rochester." This place-based strategy effectively continues the colonialist project of documenting people and land while calling dibs on regions and exploiting them economically. We champion Frank et al. as the photo empaths of their eras, particularly when they identify with the most vulnerable citizens of the times. They did the hard work of empathizing, either in the photographing or the editing and sequencing of the images, and they are rewarded for it with notoriety, sometimes financially, and with further opportunity and access. Such empathy imparted through photographic practice increases its own cultural value through its documents, and encourages others to hit the road,[7] claim regions and people as their own, and visually maintain those othered by the regime in their relegated places. In this way, to continually justify one's empathy is also to justify and maintain one's privilege.

Empathy and Accountability in Photo Archive-Bookworks

In archival studies, Michelle Caswell and Marika Cifor argue that archivists have *affective responsibilities*. "From the approach of a feminist ethics of care, archivists are seen as caregivers, bound to records creators, subjects, users, and communities through a web of mutual affective responsibility" (2016: 24). Though I single out Magnum Photos, without a doubt there are several Magnum photographers who practice affective responsibility in photo archive and bookwork projects. Zoe Strauss's life's work with the *Under I-95* project in Philadelphia and her *Homesteading* project for the 2013 Carnegie International, Pittsburgh share the work with the people and community they record. Carolyn Drake and Olivia Arthur both appear to approach the communities they document from a feminist ethics of care. Susan Meiselas's *Encounters with the Dani* and *Kurdistan: In the Shadow of History* historically accounts for the exploitation of the people and places depicted. It is not surprising that Meiselas focused the majority of her time as part of House of Pictures on in-depth work with one factory, Hickey Freeman, a suit manufacturer and tailoring company that employs workers descended from dozens of countries.

The feminist ethics of care approach also describes Joshua Rashaad McFadden's bookworks and growing archive of portraits of Black men. McFadden, himself a Black man who grew up in Rochester with grandparents who worked for Kodak, a mom who gave him a camera at seven, and a dad who, concerned with his education, moved him to the Rochester suburbs for high school, was twenty-two years old and in college at an HBCU when he learned of seventeen-year-old Trayvon Martin's unconscionable murder. It was February 2012, the same month the planning for House of Pictures was in full swing. McFadden singles out Martin's murder as the catalyst for the project that became his first photo-bookwork, *Come to Selfhood*. "I just could not understand it, that is, until I realized that, with Travyon Martin, it was this idea of the black hoodie, what he was wearing. The fact that he had brown skin and wore a black hoodie made him 'highly intimidating and suspicious' to George Zimmermann," Martin's killer (2016: 4).

When that happened I began to think about, again, image and perception, and how my peers and I carry ourselves, how we look and what we want to wear. Then it began to hit home as I thought about how me and my family are not exempt from tragedies like this, how there is no immunity for us. I kept thinking, That's me! That's one of my little brothers, that's my older brother.

I also thought about how our fathers have gone through the same situations.

Why are we not able to simply just be? We are not criminals, yet we are treated as such.

(2016: 4)

One answer to McFadden's heartfelt question may be in the history of photography as a populist medium where, in the nineteenth-century United States, the growing ease and gratification of making and appearing in a photograph was thought to have other potentially useful aims. Sekula notes the portrait photographer Marcus Aurelius Root's arguments for the utilitarian and moral aims of photographs.

Not only was photography to serve as a means of cultural enlightenment for the working classes, but family photographs sustained sentimental ties in a nation of migrants. This 'primal household affection' served a socially cohesive function, Root argued—articulating nineteenth-century familialism that would survive and become an essential logical feature of American mass culture. Furthermore, widely distributed portraits of the great would subject everyday experience to a parade of moral exemplars. Root's concern for respectability and order led him to applaud the adoption of photography by the police, arguing that convicted offenders would "not find it easy to resume their criminal careers when their faces and general aspects are familiar to so many, especially to the keen-sighted detective police".

(1986: 8–9)

Sekula identifies the origins of the classification of types and systems of appearances that ultimately signify brown skin and black hoodie as criminal. Using images as targets is a form of Azoulay's notion of archival acceptability; the violence of imperial uses of images empowers Zimmerman to police his neighborhood and commit extrajudicial violence. It is how a jury justifies the killer's legal acquittal for murdering Martin. It is how the RPD union president sees nothing inappropriate in a nine-year old girl's arrest requiring six police cars and ending with the girl being pepper-sprayed. And yet in the sense of Root's moral exemplars, the target of photography also becomes the aim of Frederick Douglass, one of Rochester's historically iconic and admired figures, who purposefully made himself the most photographed man of the nineteenth century in order to change visual perceptions of Black men, to have them appear in the highest stature. A similar aim is what led McFadden to create another kind of archive, one that makes public visibility of Black men both empathetic and oppositional.

For *Come to Selfhood*, McFadden made formal portraits of Black men, including himself, and paired them across the gutter with a family photo of their father or father figure. Bound in between the two images, printed on soft, laid paper that is smaller in size than the pages, are handwritten answers to one of McFadden's questions of the men:

- How did role-models play a role in your development as a black (man of color) male?
- Describe the ideal figure (person of character) that represents black male masculinity.
- What are some common perceptions of men of color in America? Then, explain how these perceptions had an impact on you.
- How have experiences shaped who you are as an individual?
- How does a man of color, black man, etc. develop a positive identity within a dominant culture that doesn't fully support people of color?
- Who are black men when they aren't victims of oppression?
- Do you identify as a black man, why or why not?
- Describe who is in the photograph (2016: gatefold).

The stillness and strength of each man photographed against a black background, the brightness of their eyes, the differences in their posture and features, the likenesses with their fathers, some of whom are in military uniforms, or lounge on couches, wear graduation gowns, or pose at discos, prompt the viewer's empathetic feeling for each of them individually. Yet you cannot be in their skin or stand in their shoes because you can't comprehend, if you're a white person in the United States, going through everyday life perceiving and feeling what Cameron Goins writes to be common perceptions of men of color in America:

—we're violent
—we're ignorant
—we're criminals
—we're loud
—we're aggressive
—we sell drugs
—we trap

These perceptions impact me every day because as a black male I am automatically stereotyped because of my skin as opposed to my character. I am constantly judged due to the media's perception (McFadden 2016: 24–5).

The term stereotype comes from printing: a metal printing plate cast from a mold in another material like plaster or papier-mâché. It's the ubiquity and repetition of what is made from a mold cast that make it nearly impossible to challenge it with empathy. There is no human depth of feeling, vicarious sharing of affect, or swapping of self-knowledge one can muster to match the industrialized, repetitive impact of millions of images.

As a white man reading McFadden's book for the first time, I noted a flash of recognition that the family photo of Cameron's father, Keith Goins, shows him to be young—maybe nineteen years old—around Cameron's age. In *Camera Lucida* Roland Barthes wrote about recognizing his recently deceased mother in an image of her as a child, calling the recognition "a sentiment as certain as remembrance" (Barthes 1981: 70). Instead of supposing that Cameron Goins selected this specific image of his father because he had such a recognition, what immediately crossed my mind is that Keith Goins died young. He was probably shot and killed, I thought. In place of rationality, sentimentality, or any induction of empathy or sensitivity to the everyday family photos of fathers in *Come to Selfhood*, my image reference-bank of the hundreds if not thousands of family, school, sports, and institutional photos of Black men ranging in age from fifteen to twenty who had been killed or were being sought by police had long primed who I might see pictured in this photo-bookwork. I got caught denying Black interiority, a challenge posed by scholar and educator Michelle S. Hite (2015). My story of these men is not written by McFadden or those in his archive. A regime-based disaster narrative about them was inscribed in me long ago. As a white reader, *Come to Selfhood* is necessarily confrontational with my individual racism assumed by years of living in a differential system. For Lyle Ashton Harris, a Black artist from the generation before McFadden, it is "a resistant gesture, a dismantling of an embedded history and narrative of Black Masculinity which writes Black men as without fathers, without history, without softness. Simultaneously, it is a constructive act: a building of a visual history and archive of Black intimacy" (McFadden 2016: 7).

It helps that McFadden, his father, grandfather, and brothers are included in his archive. As he does with all of those he has photographed, he uses their names, and collects their handwritten reflections on perception and emotion. McFadden's is an inside-out project, which is perhaps the opposite of how we are often publicly called to more empathy, from the outside-in— to step from the outside into another person's shoes or skin. The outside-in approach maintains in- and outgroup distinctions whereas the inside-out method assumes a form of internal wholeness being revealed. In exhibitions McFadden requests that viewers reflect upon Blackness and masculinity in writing, making his viewing community, the users of his archive, accountable and binding them to him and those he photographs. In many of the notes I've seen and read, gallery viewers write supportive comments to the men in the portraits themselves, sharing their perceptions, lifting them up. Others write themselves into the archive, sharing their own perceptions and experiences living as Black men and women.

Like many, McFadden felt the affective reverberations of George Floyd's murder by police but like a documentary photographer, he got in his car and drove to Minneapolis to be there first hand and record the aftermath. He also went to Louisville, documenting protests of Breonna Taylor's killing by police, and to Atlanta, following the fatal police shooting of Rayshard Brooks, and to protests in Washington DC, New York City, and back to the protests following the public release of Daniel Prude's arrest in his hometown of Rochester, where a year prior he had returned to live and teach. He sent the images out to the rest of us via Instagram, the *New York Times*, *The Atlantic*, CNN, and other media outlets. But the pictures don't seem disconnected from his art and photo archive-bookwork practice. There is a sense of caregiving in the work, that he feels responsibility toward those he photographs. He speaks of building "an archive that will articulate the many identities of Black people" (McFadden 2021), for instance the recent inclusion of some portraits of Black men who are also police officers. These images feel participatory, like a world with the potential to be shared.

For his effort, McFadden is earning work from editors and attention from followers. Curators and publishers are taking notice. VSW exhibited his work and helped him publish a newspaper called *Evidence* that references Frederick Douglass's *North Star* and *Frederick Douglass Paper*, nineteenth-century newspapers published out of Rochester (McFadden 2020). McFadden gives thousands of the *Evidence* papers, documenting the named men and their comments in his archive, away to anyone and everyone for free. On the newspaper and bonded to their plastic sidewalk distribution boxes is the Nina Simone lyric, "I wish I knew how it would feel to be FREE."

McFadden's *Evidence* was recently included in a group exhibition with the highly recognized photography publisher Aperture in New York City; at the same time he had prints in a group show on the theme of gathering clouds at George Eastman Museum. The museum has him slated for an early retrospective solo show in 2021. He has and will continue to earn numerous justly deserved rewards and recognition for his hard work of empathizing with people, places, events, and the times. What is worth questioning, however, is whether those currently supporting him, including my own personal and institutional efforts, are once again reifying empathetic documents? Are we using Joshua Rashaad's life's work to maintain some cultural and visibility market share, at a time when audiences appear more openly interested in confronting the US Black experience? Or will we be accountable to share in the caretaking of his life's work? If so, for how long?

In summary I'll end with a final Rochester image. Each year, after five or six straight months of winter and over a hundred inches of snow that brightens an atmosphere of starkly gray skies, there is the mud season. Revealed when the snow melts are thousands of images—fragments of junk mail, free advertisements, cigarette packs, candy wrappers, dropped scratch-offs and NY State Powerball printouts—formerly obscured and stuck in the mud like paper fossils, flattened and soggy, inks faded or bleeding into one another. In the aftermath that is 2021 the mud season may indeed reveal more "Black Lives Matter" or "Justice for Daniel Prude" related papers scattered around town than the usual post-snow litter. Because we now find ourselves in a kind of mud season of the soul where, after the layers of white wash melt away, images of the wrongly discarded reveal themselves and require taking up. Our Image City moniker may come from the town's celebrated, picture-making past but the moving images of differential treatment toward such regime cast-offs as Daniel Prude and a nine-year-old Black girl in crisis more prominently reveal such experiences to also be identifiable with Rochester. House of Pictures and others have tried to get us feeling with the disenfranchised in our city but because of the reification of empathy, what the project did was have us look at it and its makers. In so doing the photographers get romanticized as empaths, they and their patrons benefit from the affective misplacement that visualizes a perpetual and inescapable victimhood for its subjects, and the surface image of the city as *the* place of and for photography gets further burnished. Whereas Joshua Rashaad McFadden's work shows a photographic practice capable of avoiding empathetic reification. Its subjects and viewers share in the creation and caretaking of their own visualization while simultaneously contending with a hegemonic image of Black men that attempts to predefine them. McFadden's practice stirs the question of how a more broadly shared visualization of the city might appear.

Notes

1   I wish to acknowledge the ideas and resources shared with me by artist and colleague Hernease Davis that greatly informed my thinking about empathy as a subject of and produced by photography.

2   I know the purchase price from working closely with the producer on the project, Rick McKee Hock, who was a VSW staff colleague at the time. https://www.eastman.org/eastman-house-acquire-important-photographs-rochester-10-magnum-photographers (accessed April 21, 2021).

3   https://library.duke.edu/rubenstein/scriptorium/eaa/kodak/K02/K0255-150dpi.html (accessed April 21, 2021).

4   Kodak was once called the Great Yellow Father for its paternalistic hiring practices, or alternatively Daddy Kodak, https://www.nytimes.com/1997/11/16/nyregion/deferring-great-yellow-father-kodak-workers -say-layoffs-may-be-necessary.html

5 This is attributable to Dan Larkin or Keith Johnson, both friends and photographers in and out of Rochester. I can't remember who I first heard it from.

6 This public conversation took place at a book launch event on November 4, 2016 at VSW.

7 Thanks to artist and educator Rachel-Fein Smolinski, who in a conversation with me questioned the teaching of Robert Frank's *The Americans* because it made so many of her young, white, male students desire to make work in a similar style.

References

Arcarra, A. and L. Santese. (2012), *Found Photos in Detroit*, Milan: Cesura Publish.

Azoulay, A. (2012), "Regime-Made Disaster: On the Possibility of Nongovernmental Viewing," in Y. McKee and M. McLagan (eds), *The Visual Cultures of Nongovernmental Politics*, New York: Zone Books. Available Online: http://cargocollective.com/AriellaAzoulay/Regime-made-Disaster

Azoulay, A. (2019), *Potential History: Unlearning Imperialism*, London: Verso Books.

Barthes, R. (1981), *Camera Lucida: Reflections on Photography*, trans, Richard Howard. New York: Hill and Wang.

Center for Community Progress (2013), "Analysis of Bulk Lien Sale City of Rochester," Available Online: https://www.communityprogress.net/analysis-of-bulk-tax-lien-sale—city-of-rochester-pages-401.php (accessed April 21, 2021).

Cikara, M., E. Bruneau and R. Saxe (2017), "Us and Them: Intergroup Failures of Empathy," *Current Directions in Psychological Science: A Journal of the American Psychological Society*, 20 (3): 149–53.

Goldberg, J., C. Klatell and D. Wylie. (2013), *Rochester 585 716*, New York: Aperture.

Hite, M. (2015), "On the Edge of a Bank: Contemplating Other Models by Which to Live," *The Journal of Contemplative Inquiry*, 2, Available Online: https://journal.contemplativeinquiry.org/index.php/joci/article/view/21.

Holtman, J. (2014), "'White Trash' in Literary History: The Social Interventions of Erskine Caldwell and James Agee," *American Studies*, 53 (2): 31–48.

Hong, N. (2021), "Rochester Officers Suspended after Pepper-Spraying of 9-Year Old Girl," *New York Times*, January 31, 2021, Available Online: https://www.nytimes.com/2021/01/31/nyregion/rochester-police-pepper-spray-child.html.

Johnson, J., L. Lecci and A. Antonia (2020), "How Caring is 'Nullified': Strong Racial Identity Eliminates White Participant Empathy Effects When Police Shoot an Unarmed Black Male," *Psychology of Violence*, 10 (1): 58–67.

Kesner, L. and J. Horáček. (2017), "EmpathyRelated Responses to Depicted People in Art Works," *Frontiers in Psychology*, 8 (2): 1–16.

Leo, V. (2012), "Found Photos in Detroit Reviewed by Vince Leo," *Little Brown Mushroom* Blog, Available Online: https://littlebrownmushroom.wordpress. com/2012/07/11/found-photos-in-detroit-reviewed-by-vince-leo/ (accessed April 21, 2021).

Lukacs, G. (1967), "Reification and the Consciousness of the Proletariat," in *History and Class Consciousness*, London: The Merlin Press. Available Online: https://www.marxists.org/archive/lukacs/works/history/hcc05.htm (accessed April 21, 2021).

Magnum Photos (2020), "Theory and Practice: Empathy and Photography," Available Online: https://www.magnumphotos.com/theory-and-practice/ empathy-photography/ (accessed April 21, 2021).

Massumi, B. and E. Manning. (2015), "Affective Attunement in the Field of Catastrophe" Interview by Jonas Fritsch and Bodil Marie Stavning Thomsen," in *Politics of Affect*, 112–46, Cambridge: Polity Press.

McFadden, J. (2016), *Come to Selfhood*, Siena: Ceiba Editions.

McFadden, J. (2020), *Evidence Volume 1*, Rochester: Visual Studies Workshop Press.

McFadden, J. (2021), "Building an Archive," *Communication Arts,* Available Online: https://www.commarts.com/columns/mcfadden (accessed April 21, 2021).

Schmeltzer, P. (2012), "Postcards from America," *Sightlines*, Walker Art Center, Available Online: http://walkerart.org/magazine/postcards-from-america (accessed April 21, 2021).

Sekula, A. (1986), "The Body and the Archive," *October*, 39 (Winter): 3–64.

Shih, W. (2016), "The Real Lessons from Kodak's Decline," *MIT Sloan Management Review*, Available Online: https://sloanreview.mit.edu/article/the-real-lessons-from-kodaks-decline/ (accessed April 21, 2021).

Singer, T. and O. Klimecki. (2014), "Empathy and Compassion," *Current Biology*, 24: R875 R878.

Smith, J. (2020), "Managerial Review of the Death of Daniel Prude," *City of Rochester Interdepartmental Correspondence*, Available Online: https://www. cityofrochester.gov/WorkArea/DownloadAsset.aspx?id=21474845191 (accessed April 21, 2021).

Woodward, R. (2013), "Disaster Photography: When Is Documentary Exploitation," *ARTNews*, Available Online: https://www.artnews.com/art-news/ news/the-debate-over-ruin-porn-2170/ (accessed April 21, 2021).

INDEX

www.ingramcontent.com/pod-product-compliance
Lightning Source LLC
Chambersburg PA
CBHW050512280326
41932CB00014B/2297